To Steve,
    A dynamic & unusually
gifted young physician who was always
a formidable intellectual challenge.
It was a pleasure & privilege to
have had you on the ID Service this
past summer.

                    Dennis Maki MD
                    Dec 1974

A
Way of Life

and selected writings of

Sir William Osler

12 July 1849 to 29 December 1919

(formerly titled Selected Writings of
Sir William Osler)

With an Introduction by
G. L. Keynes, M. D., F. R. C. S.

Dover Publications, Inc., New York

This Dover edition, first published in 1958, is an
unabridged and unaltered republication of the work
originally published in 1951 under the title *Selected
Writings of Sir William Osler*. It is published
through special arrangement with Oxford University Press, publishers of the original edition.

International Standard Book Number: 0-486-20488-X
Library of Congress Catalog Card Number: 58-12614

Manufactured in the United States of America
Dover Publications, Inc.
180 Varick Street
New York, N.Y. 10014

THIS BOOK IS EDITED AS
A CENTENARY TRIBUTE TO
OUR PATRON SAINT
BY A COMMITTEE OF THE
OSLER CLUB OF LONDON
WITH THE HELP OF
W. W. FRANCIS

✴

W. R. BETT · W. J. BISHOP
A. W. FRANKLIN · J. F. FULTON
R. H. HILL · G. L. KEYNES
M. J. LINNETT · A. M. MUIRHEAD

EDITOR'S NOTE

THESE essays have been chosen by a Committee, with remarkable accord, to give the medical student a taste of Osler. He will meet here not Osler the pathologist, not Osler the clinical professor, but Osler the essayist and historian. Yet in Osler these interests were not truant from true medicine itself, for he believed that history and the knowledge of men were as much part of medicine as the latest technical devices and the knowledge of science.

When Osler first wrote his Text-book, in the sphere of treatment the age of reason had hardly started, though the age of faith had passed. The advances of these fifty years have eaten largely into the idea of man healing man, and now committees cure diseases. Yet the ordinary man with his ordinary medical ills seeks first a fellow human for advice and comfort as well as drugs. And so Osler the physician telling of his interests in the history of medicine and medical men, of his ideas about the doctor's vocation, and of his love of books has still a part to play in the training of doctors for the practice of the art.

The editor thanks the Osler Club for entrusting to him the pleasant task of editing and for the occasion to rediscover how good an essayist Osler is. On behalf of the Club he thanks the Osler executors and literary trustees for their help and their blessing on the enterprise, and the Oxford University Press for all that they have done.

Above all the editor thanks Dr. Francis for reading the proofs so eruditely, so skilfully, and so expeditiously.

September 1950   ALFRED WHITE FRANKLIN

ACKNOWLEDGEMENTS

are made to the following for permission to reprint the material specified:

AMERICAN MEDICAL ASSOCIATION JOURNAL ('William Beaumont'). BODLEY'S LIBRARIAN, OXFORD ('Illustrations of the Bookworm'). BRITISH MEDICAL JOURNAL ('The Old Humanities and the New Science'; 'Sir Thomas Browne'; 'The Growth of Truth'). CANADIAN MEDICAL ASSOCIATION JOURNAL ('Gui Patin'; 'The Young Laennec'; 'Teaching and Thinking'). CONSTABLE & CO., LONDON ('A Way of Life'). JOHNS HOPKINS PRESS and THE EDITORS OF THE BULLETIN OF THE JOHNS HOPKINS HOSPITAL ('Michael Servetus'). NEW ENGLAND JOURNAL OF MEDICINE ('Books and Men'). NEW YORK MEDICAL JOURNAL ('Letters to My House Physicians'). OXFORD BIBLIOGRAPHICAL SOCIETY ('Robert Burton'). YALE REVIEW (Parts I and II of 'Robert Burton', copyright Yale University Press). THE OSLER TRUSTEES for the remaining articles.

CONTENTS

ILLUSTRATIONS

INTRODUCTION

WILLIAM OSLER was born in Canada at Bond Head, near Lake Simcoe, on 12 July 1849. The passing of his centenary has seemed to be a fitting time at which to remind the English-speaking world of the significance of the life and writings of this great man by publishing a new selection of his essays. It is indeed to the English-speaking world, and not only to its doctors, that his message is addressed, for Osler was as great a humanist as he was a doctor. The sweep of his mind and interests embraced every phase of human activity, and his example of how to live can inspire the lives of many others besides the younger members of his own profession.

Osler, though the son of a parson, was not a good little boy; his sinfulness took the form of amusing mischief, not always quite harmless, but certainly not such as would consign him to everlasting flames. This trait of not being quite a good boy remained with him throughout life, and doubtless had a share in forming his character, so that solemnity, pomposity, and lack of human kindliness and understanding were never seen in his dealings with other people or in his writings. He even allowed his *alter ego* to acquire a shadowy personality endowed with the name Egerton Y. Davis, who is the source of many stories, both true and apocryphal, concerning his better half. None of Davis's writings have been admitted to the present collection. Nevertheless, there was always the whimsical humour and the skill as a raconteur that helped to make for Osler the aura that so delighted everyone who came within its range.

Osler had not, it seems, imagined himself as a doctor when he was young. He was instead destined for the church, and in order to train for this went to Toronto University. He lived with a doctor, James Bovell, whose personality and library influenced him profoundly, so that after a year's work he decided to give up theological for medical studies—whereas Dr. Bovell did the opposite, becoming minister of an English church in the West Indies. Osler completed his clinical studies in Montreal, graduating at McGill University in 1872, and then travelled to Ireland and Scotland, finally settling down to work for more than a year in the Physiological Laboratory at University College, London. A few months in Berlin and Vienna helped to widen his experience and after a few more months in London he returned to Canada in the early part of 1874. The broad foundation of his medical career had thus been laid, and in August 1874 he entered on his first appointment as lecturer in McGill University.

Osler was now only 25 years old, yet his feet were already well set on the road to academic and professional advancement. His personality was irresistibly attractive and his intellect was clearly outstanding. During the next ten years at Montreal he did much original work in pathology and biology and his reputation as a clinician grew fast, so that in June 1884 he was invited to accept the Chair of Clinical Medicine in the University of Pennsylvania. The decision to leave Montreal for Philadelphia was hard to make. He was in Leipzig at the time, and he related in after years that he made his choice by the spin of a four-mark piece—though history suggests that Egerton Y. Davis may have had a hand in it. The five years spent in Philadelphia were fruitful, enabling Osler to reach his full stature as clinician, teacher, and writer. His advent was described as 'a breath of fresh air let into a stifling room', for his approach to teaching was unconventional in its insistence on the importance of work at the bedside rather than in the lecture-room. At the same time his mastery of the subject was clear to all, and the easy charm of his personality smoothed his path in all individual relations. In a short time Osler had established his position as a stimulating teacher who could soundly base an inductive method of diagnosis on factual evidence. He could inspire young men with clinical enthusiasm, while directing their attention to the literature and history of their studies. A further advance was inevitable and on 1 May 1889 he gave his famous valedictory address

entitled *Aequanimitas* to his students in Philadelphia. The call
had come to the post of Physician-in-Chief at the new Johns
Hopkins Hospital, Baltimore, where there would be a new
medical school to organize and fresh clinical worlds to conquer.

The next sixteen years spent at Baltimore saw the consolida-
tion of Osler's career and the full flowering of all his interests.
The greater part of the year 1891 was devoted to the writing of
his greatest work, *The Principles and Practice of Medicine*, in which,
as Bodley's Librarian said many years later, he 'succeeded in
making a scientific treatise literature'. A medical classic had
come into the world, but not without effort. Osler's energy
throughout the years at Baltimore was prodigious, his knowledge being built up laboriously at the bedside, in the laboratory, and in the post-mortem room, while he could still find
time for an immense literary output and the cultivation of
innumerable friendships. He had the advantage of the closest
association with other remarkable men such as Halsted, Welch,
Kelly, and Harvey Cushing, and the stimulus of the admiration
and devotion of his students.

The publication of his text-book not only ensured him immortality as a medical writer, but also precipitated one of the
major events of his life—his marriage. Dr. Malloch relates that
his future wife, the widow of Dr. Samuel Gross of Philadelphia,
refused to have him until the book was finished. Finally he
threw a copy of the book into her lap with the remark: 'There,
take the darn thing: now what are you going to do with the man?'
They were married, unknown to his friends, on 7 May 1892,
and never did any man choose a wife who could better fill the
role of partner in a life utterly devoted to the cure and comradeship of fellow beings. It has been said that Grace Revere Osler
was an even more remarkable woman than William Osler was
a man, though she was always content to subordinate her life to
his. Their only son, Revere, was born in December 1895 and
was killed in Flanders in August 1917, a tragedy which broke
his father's heart.

The years at Baltimore were the fullest period of Osler's life, and by 1904 his practice as consulting physician had grown so large that the pressure of affairs had become more than he could bear. He had reached the age of 55, and had determined to retire at 60. When, therefore, he received an invitation to occupy the chair of Regius Professor of Medicine at Oxford he accepted without much hesitation—fortified by his wife's celebrated telegram: 'Do not procrastinate accept at once.' The leave-taking at Baltimore was prolonged and difficult, and was complicated by a storm in the American press over his whimsical references in his Valedictory Address to Anthony Trollope's scheme of 'a peaceful departure by chloroform' at the age of 60. At last it was all over, and Osler took up residence in Norham Gardens, Oxford, in May 1905. Life in Oxford was soon to be almost as full as before, and, as consulting practice again began to grow, was not as restful as Osler had expected. A quiet enjoyment, however, pervaded all his activities—the almshouses at Ewelme, of which he was Master, the proximity of the Bodleian, the collegiate life in Christ Church, together provided an academic background which gave him intense satisfaction. His house in Norham Gardens soon became known as 'The Open Arms', a sufficient indication of the hospitality enjoyed by his innumerable friends. A baronetcy was conferred on Osler in 1911, which he accepted partly because of the pleasure he knew it would give his old associates in Canada.

When war broke out in August 1914 Osler had reached the age of 65, but he soon became drawn into the vortex. Repeated attacks of broncho-pneumonia undermined his health, which was further affected by his son's death in 1917. In 1919 Osler reached his seventieth birthday, which was celebrated with overwhelming enthusiasm in all English-speaking countries, but he was by then physically a broken man, and just before the year was out he died—on 29 December—painlessly, though after a distressing illness.

The foregoing sketch of the main events in Osler's career is all that is necessary as a brief reminder to readers of this new selection from his writings. The full story of his life may be read in the two long volumes of Harvey Cushing, his friend and former colleague at Baltimore, himself one of the greatest surgeons that the American continent has yet produced. Twenty thousand copies of this book were printed between 1925 and 1936, a fact which testifies to the extraordinary hold exercised by Osler's personality over those who knew him or had heard of him during his life. But the generation that knew Osler is quickly passing, and with it must pass the memory of his living presence. His text-book of Medicine, although it can remain a pattern of style in medical writing, like every other text-book, cannot, with the advances of the Art and Science, be for long an active influence. Osler's memory cannot, indeed, be better served than by a reading, or a re-reading, of his addresses and essays. The bulk of the available material is so great that it has not been easy to decide what should be included, but the attempt has been made to represent many sides of Osler's personality. One of these—his concern for the minds of the younger members of his profession—is shown in the form of *Letters to my House Physicians*, which have not found a place in any former collection.

Books were the familiar background of Osler's life, and he freely acknowledged himself a bibliomaniac. Sir Thomas Browne's *Religio Medici* was his first love and his last, and his favourite edition lay on his bier in the chapel of Christ Church Cathedral on the night of the New Year 1920. Details of his career as a lover of books will be found in his unfinished introduction to *Bibliotheca Osleriana*, the catalogue of his medical-historical library, compiled by his nephew, Dr. W. W. Francis, in accordance with Osler's plan, and published ten years after the collector's death. The books are housed at McGill University by Osler's bequest, but the cataloguing was done during Lady Osler's lifetime in the library at Norham Gardens. The introduction, reprinted here, is a chapter in the autobiography, and the testament, of a man who believed in the paramount importance of books in the lives of young and old—but particularly of the young. Osler never spared himself in the service and instruction of the young, and his best epitaph is found in the words of Sir Arthur MacNalty quoted by Harvey Cushing at the conclusion of his biography:

'He advanced the science of medicine, he enriched literature and the humanities; yet individually he had a greater power. He became the friend of all he met—he knew the workings of the human heart metaphorically as well as physically. He joyed with the joys and wept with the sorrows of the humblest of those who were proud to be his pupils. He stooped to lift them up to the place of his royal friendship, and the magic touchstone of his generous personality helped many a desponder in the rugged paths of life. He achieved many honours and many dignities, but the proudest of all was his unwritten title, "The Young Man's Friend".'

G. L. KEYNES

July 1950

POSTHUMOUS ACTIVITY IN THE CONSULTING ROOM, 13 NORHAM GARDENS

Dr. Francis and Mr. Hill at work on the Catalogue

I

CREATORS, TRANSMUTERS, AND TRANSMITTERS

AS ILLUSTRATED BY SHAKESPEARE, BACON AND BURTON

AT the command of Prospero, the authors of the one and a half millions of books and manuscripts that rest in and beneath these historic buildings would arrange themselves in three groups—creators, transmuters, and transmitters. The first would not crowd the benches of this school; for the second it would be easy to find accommodation in the city; while the third would swarm black over Port Meadow and 'the soft, low-lying Cumnor hills'. So restricted is the intellectual capital of the race that it goes easily on the seven-foot shelf of President Eliot's (of Harvard) library. The vast majority of all books are dead, and not one in ten thousand has survived its author. Like the race of leaves the race of books is. The Bodleian is a huge mausoleum. Books follow a law of nature. Thousands of germs are needed for the transmission of an individual of any species. In the case of the salmon only one in a thousand is fertilized and of these not one in a thousand reaches maturity. So it is with books—a thousand or more are needed to secure the transmission of a single one of our very limited stock of ideas. Were all the eggs of all the salmon to reach maturity the sea could not contain this one species, while the world itself could not contain the books that would be written did even one in a thousand transmit a fertile idea. It is enough, as someone has said, if 'every book supplies its time with a good word'.

Remarks made at the opening of the Bodley Shakespeare Exhibition, 24 April 1916.

In the days when Sir Thomas Bodley concluded to set up his staff at the Library door at Oxford, there lived in this country the last of the great transmitters, Robert Burton; the first of modern transmuters, Francis Bacon; and the greatest of the world's creators, William Shakespeare.

Emerson's remark that 'every book is a quotation' is true in a special sense of the encyclopaedias and dictionaries that fust unused on our shelves. From the huge tomes into which, at the behest of St. Louis, Vincent of Beauvais in the thirteenth century boiled down all knowledge—the earliest edition we have in Bodley weighs above one cwt.!—to the last issue of the *Encyclopædia Britannica*, writers have striven to transmit the stores of human knowledge. Such 'systems' have their day and then cease to be. The individual fares better than the encyclopaedia, but not often. The *Discoveries* of Ben Jonson, a timbered mosaic, so skilfully designed that even the glue is invisible, is dead. No one now reads the *Sylva Nuptialis* of Joannes Nevizano, a mere string of quotations; few have even heard of the *Zootomia* or *Moral Anatomy of the Living by the Dead*, by Richard Whitlock —though he was a Fellow of All Souls; or of scores of the sixteenth- and seventeenth-century patchworks. Only the golden compilation of Robert Burton lives, and lives by the law so well expressed in the lines:

> Sappho survives because we sing her songs,
> And Eschylus because we read his plays.

The silent, sedentary, solitary student (as he terms himself) in the most flourishing college of Europe, *augustissimo Collegio*, with Saturn lord of his geniture, to relieve a *gravidum cor*, swept all known literature into a cento. No book was ever so belied by its title as the *Anatomy of Melancholy*. In reality the anatomy of man in all possible relations, it is easy to read the secret of its salvation. The panorama of human life is sketched in broad, firm outlines by a man of keen humour and kindly satire. Though page after page is laden with what Milton calls 'horse loads of citation', the golden links are of Burton's own fashion-

ing. Even the dry bones of bibliography come to life as he pours
out a torrent of praise upon the 'world of books that offers itself
in all subjects, arts and sciences to the sweet content and capacity
of the reader'. Except Shakespeare, no writer has realized more
keenly that all thoughts, all passions, all delights, and whatever
stirs this mortal frame, minister to the one great moving impulse
of humanity. It is not a little surprising that from a student of
Christ Church, an old bachelor, and the Vicar of St. Thomas
the Martyr, should have come the most elaborate treatise ever
written upon love. There is no such collection of stories in all
literature, no such tributes to the power of beauty, no such
pictures of its artificial allurements, no such representation of
its power of abasement. The thoughts and words of more dead
writers are transmitted to modern readers by Burton than by
any other seventeenth-century author. That the *Anatomy* is not
in the cemetery of dead books is due to the saving salt of human
sympathy scattered through its pages. Burton comes within the
net of the Baconians, but it was much discussed by the late
Mr. George Parker, of the Bodleian, and Mr. M. S. Horr[1] of
Denver whether it was not more likely that he wrote the plays
of Shakespeare.

The melting-pot of the transmuters has changed the world.
They have been the alchemists at whose touch the base metal
of common knowledge has been turned to gold. Among them
Francis Bacon takes a high place, not so much for his inductive
philosophy, really a new creation, as for the convincing demonstration that the relief of man's estate was possible only through
a knowledge of the laws of nature. A great transformer of the
mind, he realized, as no one before had done, that 'within the
reach of the grasp of man lay the unexplored kingdom of knowledge if he will be but humble enough, and patient enough, and
truthful enough to occupy it'. With a Pisgah-sight of Palestine,
he lacked the qualities of a Joshua to enter himself upon cam-
paigns of conquest; but he was one of the world's seers with a

---

[1] 'Who wrote Shakespeare?' by '*Multum in Parvo*' (M. S. Horr), from the
Denver (Colorado) *Tribune-Republican*, 1885. 4 pp. (In Bodley.)

vision of the possibility of man's empire over nature. The singularly human admixture of greatness and littleness was in his works as well as in his life.

History repeats itself. Greek philosophy, lost in the wandering mazes of restless speculation, was saved by a steady methodical research into nature by Hippocrates and by Aristotle. While Bacon was philosophizing like a Lord Chancellor, two English physicians had gone back to the Greeks. 'Searching out nature by way of experiment' ('tis Harvey's phrase), William Gilbert laid the foundation of modern physical science, and William Harvey made the greatest advance in physiology since Aristotle. Recking not his own rede Bacon failed to see that these works of his contemporaries were destined to fulfil the very object of his philosophy—the one to give man dominion over the macrocosm, the world at large; the other to give him control of the microcosm, his own body. A more striking instance of mind blindness is not to be found in the history of science. Darkly wise and rudely great, Bacon is a difficult being to understand. Except the *Essays*, his books make hard reading. In the *Historia Naturalis*, a work of the compiler class, one would think that a consideration of Life and Death would so far fire the imagination as to save an author from the sin of dullness. Try to read it. A more nicely tasteless, more correctly dull treatise was never written on so fruitful a theme. There is good sense about medicine and nature, but with the exception of the contrast between youth and old age, which has a fine epigrammatic quality, the work is as dry as shoe-leather, and the dryness is all his own, as other authors are rarely quoted. Only a mollusc without a trace of red marrow or red blood could have penned a book without a page to stir the feelings and not a sentence with a burr to stick in the memory. Bacon students should study the lengthy consideration given in it to the spirits, and then turn to Schmidt's *Lexicon* to see how very different in this respect are the motions of Shakespeare's spirit. The truth is Bacon had in a singular degree what an old Carthusian (Peter Garnefelt) called 'the gift of infrigidation'.

What a contrast when a Creator deals with Life and Death! The thoughts of the race are crystallized for ever. From Galen to Laurentius, physicians have haggled over the divisions of the ages of man, but with a grand disregard of their teaching Shakespeare so settles the question that the stages are stereotyped in our minds. We can only think of certain aspects in terms of his description. The vicissitudes of every phase are depicted. The shuddering apprehension of death we can only express in his words.

The transmuters have given to man his world dominion. The raw ore of Leucippus and Democritus has been refined to radium by Crookes, Ramsay, and the Curies; the foundations of Krupp are laid in the *De Re Metallica* of Agricola; the defenders of Verdun use the expanded formulae of Archimedes and Apollonius; Lamarck and Darwin, Wallace and Mendel are only Anaximander, Empedocles, and Lucretius writ large; Poppy, Mandragora, and other drowsy syrups had been in use for centuries to make persons insensible to pain, but the great transmutation did not take place until 16 October 1846, when Morton demonstrated at the Massachusetts Hospital the practicability of ether anaesthesia; Pasteur, Koch, and Lister are Varro, Fracastorius, and Spallanzani in nineteenth-century garb. Only by the labours of transmuters has progress been made possible, and their works will fill the shelves of the concentrated *Bibliotheca Prima* of the future.

Whether the benches of this school would seat the members of our third group, the creators, would depend very much on the judgement of Prospero. Thus to Harvey claiming admission, he might say, 'You simply took the idea of a movement of the blood which had been current knowledge since Solomon, and by experiment demonstrated a motion in a circle and not by ebb and flow.' And this is true. Without Aristotle, Galen, and Fabricius there would have been no Harvey. Transforming their raw ores by methods all his own, he made the *De Motu Cordis*, 1628, a new creation in the world of science. Not by the material, not by the method of its manufacture, but by the

value of the finished product is the author's position to be
judged. In Science the best transmuters have been the fruitful
creators. The same law holds in Art and in Literature. The
Alchemy of Shakespeare made him a great creator. 'Self-school'd,
self-scann'd, self-honour'd, self-secure', in heaven-sent moments
he turned the common thoughts of life into gold. From Carlyle
and Emerson, the teachers who stirred our hearts, the youth of
my day had a final judgement upon Shakespeare. After the two
noble knights of literature[1] have spoken, it will be safer for
a layman to express his feelings in the words of one of these
masters:

What point of morals, of manners, of economy, of philosophy, of
religion, of taste, of the conduct of life, has he not settled? What
mystery has he not signified his knowledge of? What office, or function, or district of man's work, has he not remembered? What king
has he not taught state? What maiden has not found him finer than
her delicacy? What lover has he not outloved? What sage has he not
outseen? What gentleman has he not instructed in the rudeness of
his behaviour?—Emerson, *Shakespeare; or the Poet.*

Five thousand volumes in Bodley testify to a vast dominion
unequalled in the history of literature. Once before in the world
a poet held all the thoughts of his race. From Plutarch and
Lucian we can judge how an educated Greek was really con-
strained to express himself in Homer's words. Such universality
is to-day the prerogative of Shakespeare:

> All pains the immortal spirit must endure,
> All weakness which impairs, all griefs which bow,
> Find their sole speech in that victorious brow.

As a little needful leaven and just to indicate the very present
help he may be in these troublous times, let me quote Hotspur
—any officer to any wife:

> And, to conclude,
> This evening must I leave you, gentle Kate.
> I know you wise; but yet no further wise
> Than Harry Percy's wife: constant you are,

[1] Sir Walter Raleigh and Sir Sidney Lee.

> But yet a woman: and for secrecy,
> No lady closer; for I well believe
> Thou wilt not utter what thou dost not know;
> And so far will I trust thee, gentle Kate.

The exhibition which Bodley's Librarian and his Assistants have arranged with such care and the many celebrations the world over will have one good effect—a heightened appreciation of the value of Shakespeare in the education of the young. In life's perspective we seniors are apt to resent that the rising generation should work out its own salvation in ways that are not always our ways, and with thoughts that are not always our thoughts. One thing is in our power, to admix in due proportions with their present somewhat rickety bill of fare the more solid nourishment of the English Bible and of Shakespeare.

2

THE OLD HUMANITIES AND THE
NEW SCIENCE

I

EARLY in the sixteenth century a literary joke sent inextinguishable laughter through the learned circles of Europe. The *Epistolae Obscurorum Virorum* is great literature, to which I refer for two reasons—its standard is an exact gauge of my scholarship, and had *Magister Nostrandus Ortuinus Gratius* of Cologne, to whom most of the letters are addressed, been asked to join that wicked Erfurt Circle, he could not have been more surprised than I was to receive a gracious invitation to preside over this gathering of British scholars. I felt to have been sailing under false colours to have ever, by pen or tongue, suggested the possession of even the traditional small Latin and less Greek. Relieved by the assurance that in alternate years the qualification of your President was an interest in education and literature, I gladly accepted, not, however, without such anticipatory qualms as afflict an amateur at the thought of addressing a body of experts. Not an educated man in the Oxford sense, yet faint memories of the classics linger—the result of ten years of such study as lads of my generation pursued, memories best expressed in Tom Hood's lines:

> The weary tasks I used to con!
> The hopeless leaves I wept upon!
> Most fruitless leaves to me!

In a life of teaching and practice, a mere picker-up of learning's

---

The Presidential Address delivered before the Classical Association at Oxford, May 1919. Printed in the *British Medical Journal*, 1919, ii. Reprinted London, 1919; Boston, 1920, with an Introduction by Harvey Cushing.

crumbs is made to realize the value of the humanities in science not less than in general culture.

To have a Professor of Medicine in this Chair gives to the Oxford meeting an appropriate Renaissance—shall we say medieval?—flavour, and one may be pardoned the regret that the meeting is not being held in May 1519, to have had the pleasure of listening to an address from a real Oxford scholar-physician, an early teacher of Greek in this University, and the founder of the Royal College of Physicians, whose *Rudimenta Grammatices* and *De Emendata Structura Latini Sermonis* upheld for a generation, on the Continent at least, the reputation of English scholarship. These noble walls, themselves an audience—indeed, most appreciative of audiences—have storied memories of Linacre's voice, and the basis of the keen judgement of Erasmus may have been formed by intercourse with him in this very school. In those happy days, to know Hippocrates and Galen was to know disease and to be qualified to practise; and my profession looks back in grateful admiration to such great medical humanists as Linacre and Caius and Rabelais. Nor can I claim to speak for pure science, some salt of which remains from early association, and from a lifelong attempt to correlate with art a science which makes medicine, I was going to say the only—but it is more civil to say the most—progressive of the learned professions.

To have lived right through an epoch matched only by two in the story of the race, to have shared in its long struggle, to have witnessed its final victory (and in my own case, to be left, I trust, with wit enough to realize its significance)—to have done this has been a wonderful privilege. To have outgrown age-old theories of man and of nature, to have seen West separated from East in the tangled skein of human thought, to have lived in a world re-making—these are among the thrills and triumphs of the Victorian of my generation. To a childhood and youth came echoes of the controversy that Aristarchus began, Copernicus continued, and Darwin ended, that put the microcosm into line with the macrocosm, and for the golden age of Eden substituted the *tellus dura* of Lucretius. Think of the Cimmerian darkness out of which our generation has, at any rate, blazed a path! Picture the mental state of a community which could produce *Omphalos—an attempt to untie the geological knot!*[1] I heard warm clerical discussions on its main thesis, that the fossils were put into the earth's strata to test man's faith in the Mosaic account of the creation, and our Professor of Natural Theology lectured seriously upon it! The intellectual unrest of those days wrapped many in that 'divyne cloude of unknowynge', by which happy phrase Brother Herp designates medieval mysticism; and not a bad thing for a young man to live through, as sufficient infection usually remains to enable him to understand, if not to sympathize with, mental states alien or even hostile.

An Age of Force followed the final subjugation of Nature. The dynamo replaced the steam-engine, radiant energy revealed the hidden secrets of matter, to the conquest of the earth was added the control of the air and the mastery of the deep. Nor was it only an age of Force. Never before had man done so much for his brother, the victory over the powers of Nature meant also glorious victories of peace; pestilences were checked, the cry of the poor became articulate, and to help the life of the submerged half became the sacred duty of the other. How full we were of the pride of life! In 1910 at Edinburgh I ended an address on 'Man's Redemption of Man' with the well-known lines of Shelley beginning 'Happiness and Science dawn though late upon the earth'. And now! having survived the greatest war in history, and a great victory, with the wreckage of medieval autonomy to clear up, our fears are lest we may fail to control the fretful forces of Caliban, and our hopes are to rebuild Jerusalem in this green and pleasant land.

Never before in its long evolution has the race realized its full capacity. Our fathers have told us, and we ourselves have known, of glorious sacrifices; but the past four years have exhausted in every direction the possibilities of human effort.

[1] By the well-known naturalist, Philip Henry Gosse.

And, as usual, among the nations the chief burden has fallen on that weary Titan, the Motherland,

> Bearing on shoulders immense,
> Atlantean, the load,
> Wellnigh not to be borne,
> Of the too vast orb of her fate.

Not alone did she furnish the sinews of war, but she developed a spirit that made defeat impossible.

No wonder war has advocates, to plead the heroic clash of ideals, the purging of a nation's dross in the fire of suffering and sacrifice, and the welding in one great purpose of a scattered people. Even Montaigne, sanest of men, called it 'the greatest and most magnificent of human actions'; and the glamours of its pride, pomp, and circumstance still captivate. But there are other sides which we should face without shrinking. Why dwell on the horrors such as we doctors and nurses have had to see? Enough to say that war blasts the soul, and in this great conflict the finer sense of humanity has been shocked to paralysis by the helplessness of our civilization and the futility of our religion to stem a wave of primitive barbarism. Black as are the written and unwritten pages of history, the concentrated and prolonged martyrdom surpasses anything man has yet had to endure. What a shock to the proud and mealy-mouthed Victorian who had begun to trust that Love was creation's final law, forgetting that Egypt and Babylon are our contemporaries and of yesterday in comparison with the hundreds of thousands of years since the cave-dwellers left their records on walls and bones. In the mystic shadow of the Golden Bough, and swayed by the emotions of our savage ancestors, we stand aghast at the revelation of the depth and ferocity of primal passions which reveal the unchangeableness of human nature.

When the wild beast of Plato's dream becomes a waking reality, and a herd-emotion of hate sweeps a nation off its feet, the desolation that follows is wider than that in France and Belgium, wider even than the desolation of grief, and something worse—the hardened heart, the lie in the soul—so graphically described in Book II of the *Republic*—that forces us to do accursed things, and even to defend them! I refer to it because, as professors, we have been accused of sinning against the light. Of course we have. Over us, too, the wave swept, but I protest against the selection of us for special blame. The other day, in an address on 'The Comradeship of Letters' at Turin, President Wilson is reported to have said: 'It is one of the great griefs of this war that the universities of the Central Empires used the thoughts of science to destroy mankind; it is the duty of the universities of these states to redeem science from this disgrace, and to show that the pulse of humanity beats in the classroom, and that there are sought out not the secrets of death but the secrets of life.' A pious and worthy wish! but once in war a nation mobilizes every energy, and to say that science has been prostituted in discovering means of butchery is to misunderstand the situation. Slaughter, wholesale and unrestricted, is what is sought, and to accomplish this the discoveries of the sainted Faraday and of the gentle Dalton are utilized to the full, and to their several nations scientific men render this service freely, if not gladly. That the mental attitude engendered by science is apt to lead to a gross materialism is a vulgar error! Scientific men, in mufti or in uniform, are not more brutal than their fellows, and the utilization of their discoveries in warfare should not be a greater reproach to them than is our joyous acceptance of their success.

What a change of heart after the appalling experience of the first gassing in 1915! Nothing more piteously horrible than the sufferings of the victims has ever been seen in warfare.[1] Surely we could not sink to such barbarity! Is thy servant a dog? But martial expediency soon compelled the Allies to enlist the resources of chemistry; the instruction of our enemies was soon bettered, and before the armistice there were developments in technique and destructive force that would have delighted Nisroch, who first invented aerial 'machinations to plague the sons

---

[1] I am sorry to have seen Sargent's picture, 'Gassed', in this year's Academy. It haunts the mind like a nightmare.

of men'. A group of medical men representing the chief universities and medical bodies of the United Kingdom was innocent
enough to suggest that such an unclean weapon—the use of
lethal gases, 'condemning its victims to death by long-drawn-out
torture', and with infinite possibilities for its further development—should be for ever abolished. 'Steeped in folly by theories
and prepossessions', failure to read the 'lessons of war which
should have sufficed to convince a beetle'—such were among the
newspaper comments; and in other ways we were given to
understand that our interference in such matters was most
untimely. All the same, it is gratifying to see that the suggestion
has been adopted at the Peace Congress.

With what a howl of righteous indignation the slaughter of
our innocent women and children by the bombing of open towns
was received. It was a dirty and bloody business, worthy of the
Oxydracians, who by means of Levin-bolts and Thunders more
horrible, more frightful, more diabolical, maiming, breaking,
tearing, and slaying more folk, confounded men's senses and
threw down more walls than would a hundred thunderbolts
(Rabelais, Bk. IV, ch. lxi).

Against reprisals there was at first a strong feeling. Early in
1916 I wrote to *The Times*:

The cry for reprisals illustrates the exquisitely hellish state of mind
into which war plunges even sensible men. Not a pacifist, but a 'last
ditcher', yet I refuse to believe that as a nation, how bitter soever the
provocation, we shall stain our hands in the blood of the innocent.
In this matter let us be free from bloodguiltiness, and let not the
undying reproach of humanity rest on us as on the Germans.

Two years changed me into an ordinary barbarian. A detailed
tally of civilians killed by our airmen has not, I believe, been
published, but the total figures quoted are not far behind the
German. Could a poll have been taken a week before the armistice as to the moral justification of the bombing of Berlin—for
which we were ready—how we should have howled at the proposer
of any doubt. And many Jonahs were displeased that a city greater
than Nineveh, with more than the three score and ten thousand who

knew not the right hand from the left, had been spared. We may deplore the necessity and lament, as did a certain great personage:

> . . . yet public reason just—
> Honour and empire with revenge enlarged
> . . . compels me now
> To do what else, though damned, I should abhor.

All the same, we considered ourselves 'Christians of the best edition, all picked and culled', and the churches remained open, prayers rose to Jehovah, many of whose priests—even His bishops!—were in khaki, and quit themselves like men—yes, and scores died the death of heroes! Into such hells of inconsistency does war plunge the best of us!

Learning—new or old—seems a vain thing to save a nation, but possibly as a set-off science, as represented by cellulose and sulphuric acid, may yet prove the best bulwark of civilization. In his *History of the Origin of Medicine* (1778, p. 30) Lettsom maintains that the invention of firearms has done more to prevent the destruction of the human species than any other discovery. He says: 'Invention and discernment of mind have made it possible to reverse the ancient maxim that strength has always prevailed over wisdom.' Science alone may prevent a repetition of the story of Egypt, of Babylonia, of Greece, and of Rome. The suggestion seems brazen effrontery when we have not even given the world the equivalent of the Pax Romana. Ah! what a picture of self-satisfied happiness in Plutarch! One envies that placid life in the midst of the only great peace the world has known, spanning a period of more than two hundred years. And he could say, 'No tumults, no civil sedition, no tyrannies, no pestilences nor calamities depopulating Greece, no epidemic disease needing powerful and choice drugs and medicines', though as a Delphic priest there is a pathetic lament that the Pythian priestess has now only commonplace questions to deal with.[1] Surely those cultivated men of his circle must have felt that their house could never be removed. Has Science reached

[1] Why the Pythian priestess, &c. (Plutarch's *Morals*, vol. iii, p. 100, Goodwin's edition.)

such control over Nature that she will enable our civilization to escape the law of the Ephesian, written on all known records—*panta rei*? Perhaps so, now that material civilization is worldwide, cataclysmic forces, powerful enough in centres of origin, may weaken as they pass out in circles. Let this be our hope in the present crisis. At any rate, in the free democracies in which Demos with safety says *L'État c'est moi*, it has yet to be determined whether Science, as the embodiment of a mechanical force, can rule without invoking ruin. Two things are clear: there must be a very different civilization or there will be no civilization at all; and the other is that neither the old religion combined with the old learning, nor both with the new science, suffice to save a nation bent on self-destruction. The suicide of Germany, the outstanding fact of the war, followed an outburst of national megalomania. For she had religion—it may shock some of you to hear! I mean the people, not the writers or the thinkers, but the people for whom Luther lived and Huss died. Of the two devotional ceremonies which stand supreme in my memory one was a service in the Dom, Berlin, in which 'not the great nor well bespoke, but the mere uncounted folk' sang Luther's great hymn, *Ein' feste Burg ist unser Gott*.[1] With the Humanities Germany never broke, and the proportion of students in her schools and universities who studied Greek and Latin has been higher than in any other country. You know better than I the innumerable classical studies of her scholars. In classical learning relating to science and medicine she simply had the field, for one scholar in other countries she had a dozen, and the monopoly of journals relating to the history of these subjects. And she had science, and led the world in the application of the products of the laboratory to the uses of everyday life —in commerce, in the Arts, and in war. Withal, like Jeshurun, she waxed fat; and did ever such pride go before such destruction! What a tragedy that the successors of Virchow and Traube

---

[1] And the other, how different! The crowded Blue Mosque of Cairo, and the crowded streets with the thousands of kneeling Moslems awaiting the cry of the Muezzin from the tower.

and Helmholtz and Billroth should have made her a byword among the nations! 'Lilies that fester smell far worse than weeds.'

II

So much preliminary to the business before us, to meet changed conditions as practical men, with the reinforcement born of hope or with the strong resolution of despair.

For what does this Classical Association stand? What are these classical interests that you represent? Take a familiar simile. By a very simple trick, you remember, did Empedocles give Menippus in the moon-halt—the first stage of his memorable trip—such long and clear vision that he saw the tribes of men like a nest of ants, a seething mass going to and fro at their different tasks. Of the function of the classical members in this myrmecic community there can be no question. Neither warriors, nor slaves, nor neuters, you live in a well-protected social environment, heretofore free from enemies, and have been well taken care of. I hate to speak of you as larvae, but as such you perform a duty of the greatest importance in this trophidium stage of your existence. Let me explain. From earliest days much attention has been paid by naturalists to the incredible affection—'incredible στοργή', Swammerdam calls it—which ants display in feeding, licking, and attending the larvae. Disturb a nest, and the chief care is to take them to a place of safety. This attention is what our symphilic community—to use a biological term—bestows on you. So intensely altruistic, apparently, is this behaviour, that for the very word στοργή, which expresses the tenderest of all feelings, there is a difficulty in finding an equivalent; indeed, Gilbert White used it almost as an English word. The truth is really very different. It has been shown that the nursing function—or instinct— is really trophallactic. In the case of the ant the nurse places the larva on its back, and the broad ventral surface serves as a trough for the food, often pre-digested. The skill and devotion with which this is done are among the wonders in the life of the insect to which moralists have never tired of urging a visit. But listen to the sequel! The larva is provided with a pair of rich honey-bags in the shape of salivary glands, big exudatoria from which is discharged an ambrosia greedily lapped up by the nurse, who with this considers herself well paid for her care. In the same manner, when the assiduous V.A.D. wasp distributes food to the larvae, the heads of which eagerly protrude from their cells, she must be paid by a draught of nectar from their exudatoria, while if it is not forthcoming the wasp seizes the head of the larva in her mandibles and jams it back into its cell and compels it to pay up. The lazy males will play the same game and even steal the much sought liquid without any compensatory gift of nourishment.[1]

What does the community at large, so careful of your comforts, expect from you? Surely the honey-dew and the milk of paradise secreted from your classical exudatoria, which we lap up greedily in recensions, monographs, commentaries, histories, translations, and brochures. Among academic larvae you have for centuries absorbed the almost undivided interest of the nest, and not without reason, for the very life of the workers depends on the hormones you secrete. Though small in number, your group has an enormous kinetic value, like our endocrine organs. For man's body, too, is a humming hive of working cells, each with its specific function, all under central control of the brain and heart, and all dependent on materials called hormones (secreted by small, even insignificant-looking structures) which lubricate the wheels of life. For example, remove the thyroid gland just below the Adam's apple, and you deprive man of the lubricants which enable his thought-engines to work—it is as if you cut off the oil-supply of a motor—and gradually the stored acquisitions of his mind cease to be available, and within a year he sinks into dementia. The normal processes of the skin cease, the hair falls, the features bloat, and the paragon of animals is transformed into a shapeless caricature of humanity. These essential lubricators, of which a number are now known,

[1] Professor Wheeler in *Proceedings of Amer. Phil. Soc.*, vol. lvii, No. 4, 1918.

are called hormones—you will recognize from its derivation how appropriate is the term.

Now, the men of your guild secrete materials which do for society at large what the thyroid gland does for the individual. The Humanities are the hormones. Our friend Mr. P. S. Allen read before this Association a most suggestive paper on the historical evolution of the word Humanism. I like to think of the pleasant-flavoured word as embracing all the knowledge of the ancient classical world—what man knew of Nature as well as what he knew of himself. Let us see what this University means by the *Literae Humaniores*. The 'Greats' papers for the past decade make interesting study. With singular uniformity there is diversity enough to bear high tribute to the ingenuity of the examiners. But comparing the subjects in 1918 with those in the first printed papers of the School in 1831, one is surprised to find them the same—practically no change in the eighty-seven years! Compare them, again, with the subjects given in John Napleton's *Considerations*, 1773—no change! and with the help of Rashdall we may trace the story of the studies in Arts, only to find that as far back as 1267, with different names sometimes, they have been through all the centuries essentially the same— Greek and Latin authors, logic, rhetoric, grammar, and the philosophies, natural, moral, and metaphysical—practically the seven liberal Arts for which, as you may see by the name over the doors, Bodley's building provided accommodation. Why this invariableness in an ever-turning world? One of the marvels, so commonplace that it has ceased to be marvellous, is the deep rooting of our civilization in the soil of Greece and Rome— much of our dogmatic religion, practically all the philosophies, the models of our literature, the ideals of our democratic free-dom, the fine and the technical arts, the fundamentals of science, and the basis of our law. The Humanities bring the student into contact with the master minds who gave us these things—with the dead who never die, with those immortal lives 'not of now or of yesterday but which always were'. As true to-day as in the fifth century B.C. the name of Hellas stands no longer for the

name of a race, but as the name of knowledge; or, as more
tersely put by Maine, 'Except the blind forces of Nature, nothing
moves [intellectually, he means] in this world that is not Greek
in origin'. Man's anabasis from the old priest-ridden civilizations of the East began when 'the light of reason lighted up all
things', with which saying Anaxagoras expressed our modern
outlook on life.

The Humanities have been a subject of criticism in two directions. Their overwhelming prominence, it is claimed, prevents
the development of learning in other and more useful directions;
and the method of teaching is said to be antiquated and out of
touch with the present needs. They control the academic life of
Oxford. An analysis of the Register for 1919 shows that of the
257 men comprising the Heads and Fellows of the twenty-three
colleges (including St. Edmund Hall), only fifty-one are
scientific, including the mathematicians.

It is not very polite perhaps to suggest that as transmitters
and interpreters they should not bulk quite so large in a modern
university. 'Twas all very well

> ... in days when wits were fresh and clear
> And life ran gaily as the sparkling Thames—

in those happy days when it was felt that all knowledge had
been garnered by those divine men of old time, that there was
nothing left but to enjoy the good things harvested by such
universal providers as Isidore, Rabanus Maurus, and Vincent of
Beauvais, and those stronger dishes served by such artists as
Albertus Magnus and St. Thomas Aquinas—delicious blends
of such skill that only the palate of an Apicius could separate
Greek, Patristic, and Arabian savours.

It is not the dominance, but the unequal dominance that is a
cause of just complaint. As to methods of teaching—by their
fruits ye shall know them. The product of 'Greats' needs no
description in this place. Many deny the art to find the mind's
construction in the face, but surely not the possibility of diag-
nosing at a glance a 'first in Greats'! Only in him is seen that

altogether superior expression, that self-consciousness of having
reached life's goal, of having, in that pickled sentence of Dean
Gaisford's Christmas sermon, done something 'that not only
elevates above the common herd, but leads not unfrequently to
positions of considerable emolument'. 'Many are the wand-
bearers, few are the mystics', and a system should not be judged
by the exceptions. As a discipline of the mind for the few, the
system should not be touched, and we should be ready to sacrifice a holocaust of undergraduates every year to produce in each
generation a scholar of the type of, say, Ingram Bywater. 'Tis
Nature's method—does it not cost some thousands of eggs and
fry to produce one salmon?

But the average man, not of scholar timber, may bring one
railing accusation against his school and college. Apart from
mental discipline, the value of the ancient languages is to give
a key to their literatures. Yet we make boys and young men
spend ten or more years on the study of Greek and Latin, at the
end of which time the beauties of the languages are still hidden
because of the pernicious method in which they are taught. It
passes my understanding how the more excellent way of Montaigne, of Milton, and of Locke should have been neglected until
recently. Make the language an instrument to play with and to
play with thoroughly, and recognize that except for the few in
'Mods.' and 'Greats' it is superfluous to know how the instrument is constructed, or to dissect the neuro-muscular mechanism
by which it is played. It is satisfactory to read that the Greek
Curriculum Committee thinks 'it is possible in a comparatively
short time to acquire a really valuable knowledge of Greek, and
to learn with accuracy and fair fluency some of the most important works in Greek literature'. I am sure of it, if the teacher
will go to school to Montaigne and feed fat against that old
scoundrel Protagoras a well-earned grudge for inventing grammar—*pace* Mr. Livingstone, every chapter in whose two books
appeals to me, except those on grammar, against which I have
a medullary prejudice. I speak, of course, as a fool among the
wise, and I am not pleading for the 'Greats' men, but for the

average man whom to infect with the spirit of the Humanities is the greatest single gift in education. To you of the elect this is pure camouflage—the amateur talking to the experts; but there is another side upon which I feel something may be said by one whose best friends have been the old Humanists, and whose breviary is Plutarch, or rather Plutarch gallicized by Montaigne. Paraphrasing Mark Twain's comment upon Christian Science, the so-called Humanists have not enough Science, and Science sadly lacks the Humanities. This unhappy divorce, which should never have taken place, has been officially recognized in the two reports edited by Sir Frederic Kenyon,[1] which have stirred the pool, and cannot but be helpful. To have got constructive, anabolic action from representatives of interests so diverse is most encouraging. While all agree that neither in the Public Schools nor in the older Universities are the conditions at present in keeping with the urgent scientific needs of the nation, the specific is not to be sought in endowments alone, but in the leaven which may work a much needed change in both branches of knowledge.

III

The School of Literae Humaniores excites wonder in the extent and variety of the knowledge demanded, and there is everywhere evidence of the value placed upon the ancient models; but this wonder pales before the gasping astonishment at what is not there. Now and again a hint, a reference, a recognition, but the moving forces which have made the modern world are simply ignored. Yet they are all Hellenic, all part and parcel of the Humanities in the true sense, and all of prime importance in modern education. Twin berries on one stem, grievous damage has been done to both in regarding the Humanities and Science in any other light than complemental. Perhaps the anomalous position of Science in our philosophical school is due to the necessary filtration, indeed the preservation, of our

[1] *Education, Scientific and Humane*, 1917, and *Education, Secondary and University*, 1919.

classical knowledge, through ecclesiastical channels. Of this the
persistence of the Augustinian questions until late in the eighteenth century is an interesting indication. The moulder of
Western Christianity had not much use for Science, and the
Greek spirit was stifled in the atmosphere of the Middle Ages.
'Content to be deceived, to live in a twilight of fiction, under
clouds of false witnesses, inventing according to convenience,
and glad to welcome the forger and the cheat'—such, Lord
Acton somewhere says, were the Middle Ages. Strange, is it not,
that one man alone, Roger Bacon, mastered his environment
and had a modern outlook![1]

The practical point for us here is that in the only school
dealing with the philosophy of human thought, the sources of
the new science that has made a new world are practically
ignored. One gets even an impression of neglect in the Schools,
or at any rate of scant treatment, of the Ionian philosophers, the
very fathers of your fathers. Few 'Greats' men, I fear, could tell
why Hippocrates is a living force to-day, or why a modern
scientific physician would feel more at home with Erasistratus
and Herophilus at Alexandria, or with Galen at Pergamos, than
at any period in our story up to, say, Harvey. Except as a
delineator of character, what does the Oxford scholar know of
Theophrastus, the founder of modern botany, and a living force
to-day in one of the two departments of biology, and made
accessible recently to English readers—perhaps indeed to Greek
readers!—by Sir Arthur Hort.[2] Beggarly recognition or base
indifference is meted out to the men whose minds have fertilized
science in every department. The pulse of every student should
beat faster as he reads the story of Archimedes, of Hero, of
Aristarchus—names not even mentioned in the 'Greats' papers
in the past decade. Yet the methods of these men exorcised

---

[1] How modern Bacon's outlook was may be judged from the following
sentence: 'Experimental science has three great prerogatives over all other
sciences—it verifies conclusions by direct experiment, it discovers truths
which they could never reach, and it investigates the secrets of Nature and
opens to us a knowledge of the past and of the future.'

[2] Loeb Classics.

vagaries and superstitions from the human mind and pointed
to a clear knowledge of the laws of Nature. It is surprising that
some wag among the examiners has never relieved the grave
monotony of the papers by such peripatetic questions as 'How
long a gnat lives', 'To how many fathoms' depth the sunlight
penetrates the sea', and 'What an oyster's soul is like'—questions
which indicate whence the modern Lucian got his inspiration to
chaff so successfully Boyle and the Professors of Gresham College.

May I dwell upon two instances of shocking neglect? It really
is amusing in Oxford to assert neglect of 'the measurer of all
Art and Science, whose is all that is best in the passing sublunary
world', as Richard de Bury calls 'the Prince of the Schooles'. In
Gulliver's voyage to Laputa he paid a visit to the little island of
Glubbdubdrib, whose Governor, you remember, had an Endo-
rian command over the spirits, such as Sir Oliver Lodge or Sir
Arthur Conan Doyle might envy. When Aristotle and his commentators were summoned, to Gulliver's surprise they were
strangers, for the reason that having so horribly misrepresented
Aristotle's meaning to posterity, a consciousness of guilt and
shame kept them far away from him in the lower world. Such
shame, I fear, will make the shades of many classical dons of
this University seek shelter with the commentators when they
realize their neglect of one of the most fruitful of all the activities of the Master. In biology Aristotle speaks for the first time
the language of modern science, and indeed he seems to have
been first and foremost a biologist, and his natural history
studies influenced profoundly his sociology, his psychology, and
his philosophy in general. The beginner may be sent now to
Professor D'Arcy Wentworth Thompson's Herbert Spencer
Lecture, 1913, and he must be indeed a dull and muddy-
mettled rascal whose imagination is not fired by the enthusiastic
—yet true—picture of the founder of modern biology, whose
language is our language, whose methods and problems are our
own, the man who knew a thousand varied forms of life, of
plant, of bird, and animal, their outward structure, their metamorphosis, their early development; who studied the problems

of heredity, of sex, of nutrition, of growth, of adaptation, and of
the struggle for existence.[1] And the senior student, if capable
of appreciating a biological discovery, I advise to study the
account by Johannes Müller[2] (himself a pioneer in anatomy) of
his rediscovery of Aristotle's remarkable discovery of a special
mode of reproduction in one of the species of sharks. For two
thousand years the founder of the science of embryology had
neither rival nor worthy follower. There is no reference, I
believe, to the biological works in the Literae Humaniores
papers for the past ten years, yet they form the very foundations
of discoveries that have turned our philosophies topsy-turvy.

Nothing reveals the unfortunate break in Humanities more
clearly than the treatment of the greatest nature-poet in literature, a man who had 'gazed on Nature's naked loveliness'
unabashed, the man who united, as no one else has ever done,
the 'functions and temper and achievement of science and
poetry' (Herford). The golden work of Lucretius is indeed
recognized, and in Honour Moderations Books I–III and V
are set as one of seven alternatives in section D; and scattered
through the 'Greats' papers are set translations and snippets here
and there; but anything like adequate consideration from the
scientific side is to be sought in vain. Unmatched among the
ancients or moderns is the vision by Lucretius of continuity in
the workings of Nature—not less of *Le silence éternel de ces espaces
infinis* which so affrighted Pascal, than of 'the long limitless age
of days, the age of all time that has gone by'—

> . . . longa diei
> infinita aetas anteacti temporis omnis.

And it is in a Latin poet that we find up-to-date views of the
origin of the world and of the origin of man. The description of
the wild discordant storm of atoms (Book V) which led to the
birth of the world might be transferred verbatim to the accounts
of Poincaré or of Arrhenius of the growth of new celestial bodies

[1] Summarized from D'Arcy Wentworth Thompson.
[2] *Über den Glatten Hai des Aristoteles*, Berlin, 1842.

in the Milky Way. What an insight into primitive man and the beginnings of civilization! He might have been a contemporary and friend, and doubtless was a tutor, of Tylor. Book II, a manual of atomic physics with its marvellous conception of—

> . . . the flaring atom streams
> and torrents of her myriad universe,

can only be read appreciatively by pupils of Roentgen or of J. J. Thomson. The ring theory of magnetism advanced in Book VI has been reproduced of late by Parsons, whose magnetons rotating as rings at high speed have the form and effect with which this disciple of Democritus clothes his magnetic physics.

And may I here enter a protest? Of love-philtres that produce insanity we may read the truth in a chapter of that most pleasant manual of erotology, the *Anatomy of Melancholy*. Of insanity of any type that leaves a mind capable in lucid intervals of writing such verses as *De Rerum Natura* we know nothing. The sole value of the myth is its causal association with the poem of Tennyson. Only exsuccous dons who have never known the wiles and ways of the younger Aphrodite would take the intensity of the feeling in Book IV as witness to anything but an accident which may happen to the wisest of the wise, when enthralled by Vivien or some dark lady of the Sonnets!

In the School of Literae Humaniores the studies are based on classical literature and on history, 'but a large number of students approach philosophical study from other sides. Students of such subjects as mathematics, natural science, history, psychology, anthropology, or political economy, became naturally interested in philosophy, and their needs are at present very imperfectly provided for in this University.' This I quote from a Report to the Board of the Faculty of Arts made just before the (1914–18) war on a proposed new Honour School, the subject of which should be the principles of philosophy considered in their relation to the Sciences. That joint action of this kind should have been taken by the Boards of Arts and of Science indicates a widespread conviction that no man is cultivated up to the standard of his generation who has not an appreciation of how the greatest achievements of the human mind have been reached; and the practical question is how to introduce such studies into the course of liberal education, how to give the science school the leaven of an old philosophy, how to leaven the old philosophical school with the thoughts of science.[1]

It is important to recognize that there is nothing mysterious in the method of science, or apart from the ordinary routine of life. Science has been defined as the habit or faculty of observation. By such the child grows in knowledge, and in its daily exercise an adult lives and moves. Only a quantitative difference makes observation scientific—accuracy; in that way alone do we discover things as they really are. This is the essence of Plato's definition of science as 'the discovery of things as they really are', whether in the heavens above, in the earth beneath, or in the observer himself. As a mental operation, the scientific method is equally applicable to deciphering a bit of Beneventan script, to the analysis of the Commission on Coal-mines, a study of the mechanism of the nose-dive, or of the colour scheme in tiger-beetles. To observation, with reasoned thought, the Greek added experiment (but never fully used it in biology), the instrument which has made science productive, and to which the modern world owes its civilization. Our everyday existence depends on the practical application of discoveries in pure science by men who had no other motives than a search for knowledge of Nature's laws, a disinterestedness which Burnet claims to be the distinctive gift of Hellas to humanity. With the discovery of induced currents Faraday had no thought of the dynamo, Crookes's tubes were a plaything until Roentgen turned them into practical use with the X-rays. Perkin had no

[1] Since I wrote this lecture Professor J. A. Stewart has sent me his just-published essay on *Oxford after the War and a Liberal Education*, in which he urges with all the weight of his learning and experience that the foundations of a liberal education in Oxford should be 'No Humane Letters without Natural Science and no Natural Science without Humane Letters'.

thought of transforming chemical industry when he discovered aniline dyes. Priestley would have cursed the observation that an electrical charge produced nitrous acid had he foreseen that it would enable Germany to prolong the war, but he would have blessed the thought that it may make us independent of all outside sources for fertilizers.

The extraordinary development of modern science may be her undoing. Specialism, now a necessity, has fragmented the specialities themselves in a way that makes the outlook hazardous. The workers lose all sense of proportion in a maze of minutiae. Everywhere men are in small coteries intensely absorbed in subjects of deep interest, but of very limited scope. Chemistry, a century ago an appanage of the Chair of Medicine or even of Divinity, has now a dozen departments, each with its laboratory and literature, sometimes its own society. Applying themselves early to research, young men get into backwaters far from the main stream. They quickly lose the sense of proportion, become hypercritical, and the smaller the field, the greater the tendency to megalocephaly. The study for fourteen years of the variations in the colour scheme of the 1,300 species of tiger-beetles scattered over the earth may sterilize a man into a sticker of pins and a paster of labels; on the other hand, he may be a modern biologist whose interest is in the experimental modification of types, and in the mysterious insulation of hereditary characters from the environment. Only in one direction does the modern specialist acknowledge his debt to the dead languages. Men of science pay homage, as do no others, to the god of words whose magic power is nowhere so manifest as in the plastic language of Greece. The only visit many students pay to Parnassus is to get an intelligible label for a fact or form newly discovered. Turn the pages of such a dictionary of chemical terms as Morley and Muir, and you meet in close-set columns countless names unknown a decade ago, and unintelligible to the specialist in another department unless familiar with Greek, and as meaningless as the Arabic jargon in such medieval collections as the *Synonyma* of Simon Januensis or the Pandects of Mathaeus

Sylvaticus. As *Punch* put it the other day in a delightful poetical review of Professor West's volume:[1]

> Botany relies on Latin ever since Linnaeus' days;
> Biologic nomenclature draws on Greek in countless ways;
> While in Medicine it is obvious you can never take your oath
> What an ailment means exactly if you haven't studied both.
>
> (17. iv. 19.)

Let me give a couple of examples.

Within the narrow compass of the primitive cell from which all living beings originate, onomatomania runs riot. The process of mitosis has developed a special literature and language. Dealing not alone with the problems of heredity and of sex, but with the very dynamics of life, the mitotic complex is much more than a simple physiological process, and in the action and interaction of physical forces the cytologist hopes to find the key to the secret of life itself. And what a Grecian he has become! Listen to this account which Aristotle would understand much better than most of us.

The karyogranulomes, not the idiogranulomes or microsomenstratum in the protoplasm of the spermatogonia, unite into the idiosphaerosome, acrosoma of Lenhossék, a protean phase, as the idiosphaerosome differentiates into an idiocryptosome and an idiocalyptosome, both surrounded by the idiosphaerotheca, the archoplasmic vesicle; but the idioectosome disappears in the metamorphosis of the spermatid into a sphere, the idiophtharosome. The separation of the calyptosome from the cryptosome antedates the transformation of the idiosphaerotheca into the spermiocalyptrotheca.[2]

Or take a more practical if less Cratylean example. In our precious cabbage patches the holometabolous insecta are the hosts of parasitic polyembryonic hymenoptera, upon the prevalence of which rests the psychic and somatic stamina of our fellow-countrymen; for the larvae of *Pieris brassicae*, vulgarly cabbage butterfly, are parasitized by the *Apantales glomeratus*, which

---

[1]   *The Value of the Classics*, Princeton University Press, 1917.
[2]   Made up from a recent number of the *American Journal of Anatomy*, xxiv. 1.

in turn has a hyperparasite, the *Mesochorus pallidus*. It is tragic to think that the fate of a plant, the dietetic and pharmaceutical virtues of which have been so extolled by Cato, and upon which two of my Plinian colleagues of uncertain date, Chrysippus and Dieuches, wrote monographs—it fills one with terror to think that a crop so dear to Hodge (*et veris cymata!* the Brussels sprouts of Columella) should depend on the deposition in the ovum of the *Pieris* of another polyembryonic egg. The cytoplasm or ooplasm of this forms a trophoamnion and develops into a polygerminal mass, a spherical morula, from which in turn develop a hundred or more larvae, which immediately proceed to eat up everything in and of the body of their host. Only in this way does Nature preserve the Selenas, the Leas, and the Crambes, so dear to Cato and so necessary for the sustenance of our hard-working brawny-armed Brasserii.

From over-specialization scientific men are in a more parlous state than are the Humanists from neglect of classical tradition. The salvation of science lies in a recognition of a new philosophy —the *scientia scientiarum*, of which Plato speaks. 'Now when all these studies reach the point of intercommunion and connexion with one another and come to be considered in their mutual affinities, then I think, and not till then, will the pursuit of them have a value.' Upon this synthetic process I hesitate to dwell; since like Dr. Johnson's friend, Oliver Edwards, I have never succeeded in mastering philosophy—'cheerfulness was always breaking in'.

In the proposed Honour School the principles of philosophy are to be dealt with in relation to the sciences, and by the introduction of literary and historical studies, which George Sarton advocates so warmly as the new Humanism,[1] the student will gain a knowledge of the evolution of modern scientific thought. But to limit the history to the modern period—Kepler to the present time is suggested—would be a grave error. The scientific student should go to the sources and in some way be taught the connexion of Democritus with Dalton, of Archimedes with

[1] *Popular Science Monthly*, September, 1918, and *Scientia*, vol. xxiii. 3.

Kelvin, of Aristarchus with Newton, of Galen with John
Hunter, and of Plato and Aristotle with them all. And the
glories of Greek science should be opened in a sympathetic way
to 'Greats' men. Under new regulations at the public schools,
a boy of sixteen or seventeen should have enough science to
appreciate the position of Theophrastus in Botany, and perhaps
himself construct Hero's fountain. Science will take a totally
different position in this country when the knowledge of its
advances is the possession of all educated men. The time too is
ripe for the Bodleian to become a *studium generale*, with ten or
more departments, each in charge of a special sub-librarian.
When the beautiful rooms, over the portals of which are the
mocking blue and gold inscriptions, are once more alive with
students, the task of teaching subjects on historical lines will be
greatly lightened. What has been done with the Music-room,
and with the Science-room through the liberality of Dr. and
Mrs. Singer, should be done for classics, history, literature,
theology, &c., each section in charge of a sub-librarian who
will be Doctor perplexorum alike to professor, don, and undergraduate.

I wish time had permitted me to sketch even briefly the story
of the evolution of science in this old seat of learning. A fortunate opportunity enables you to see two phases in its evolution.
Through the kind permission of several of the Colleges, particularly Christ Church, Merton, St. John's, and Oriel, and with
the co-operation of the Curators of the Bodleian and Dr. Cowley,
Mr. R. T. Gunther of Magdalen College has arranged a loan
exhibition of the early scientific instruments and manuscripts.
A series of quadrants and astrolabes shows how Arabian instruments, themselves retaining much of the older Greek models,
have translated Alexandrian science into the Western world.
Some were constructed for the latitude of Oxford, and one was
associated with our astronomer-poet, Chaucer.

For the first time the instruments and works of the early
members of the Merton School of astronomer-physicians have
been brought together. They belong to a group of men of the

fourteenth century—Reed, Aschenden, Simon Bredon, Merle, Richard of Wallingford, and others—whose labours made Oxford the leading scientific University of the world.

Little remains of the scientific apparatus of the early period of the Royal Society, but through the kindness of the Dean and governing body of Christ Church, the entire contents of the cabinet of philosophical apparatus of the Earl of Orrery, who flourished some thirty years after the foundation of the Society, are on exhibit, and the actual astronomical model, the 'Orrery', made for him and called after his name.

The story of the free cities of Greece shows how a love of the higher and brighter things in life may thrive in a democracy. Whether such love may develop in a civilization based on a philosophy of force is the present problem of the Western world. To-day there are doubts, even thoughts of despair, but neither man nor nation is to be judged by the behaviour in a paroxysm of delirium. Lavoisier perished in the Revolution, and the Archbishop of Paris was butchered at the altar by the Commune, yet France was not wrecked; and Russia may survive the starvation of such scholars as Danielevski and Smirnov, and the massacre of Botkin. To have intelligent freemen of the Greek type with a stake in the State (not mere chattels from whose daily life the shadow of the workhouse never lifts), to have the men and women who could love the light put in surroundings in which the light may reach them, to encourage in all a sense of brotherhood reaching the standard of the Good Samaritan— surely the realization in a democracy of such reasonable ambitions should be compatible with the control by science of the forces of Nature for the common good, and a love of all that is best in religion, in art, and in literature.

Amid the smoke and squalor of a modern industrial city, after the bread-and-butter struggle of the day, 'the Discobolus has no gospel'. Our puritanized culture has been known to call the Antinous vulgar. Copies of these two statues, you may remember, Samuel Butler found stored away in the lumber-room of the Natural History Museum, Montreal, with skins, plants, snakes, and insects, and in their midst, stuffing an owl, sat 'the brother-in-law of the haberdasher of Mr. Spurgeon'. Against the old man[1] who thus blasphemed beauty, Butler broke into those memorable verses with the refrain 'O God! O Montreal!'

Let us not be discouraged. The direction of our vision is everything, and after weltering four years in chaos poor stricken humanity still nurses the unconquerable hope of an ideal state 'whose citizens are happy . . . absolutely wise, all of them brave, just and self-controlled . . . all at peace and unity, and in the enjoyment of legality, equality, liberty, and all other good things'. Lucian's winning picture of this 'Universal Happiness' might have been sketched by a Round Table pen or some youthful secretary to the League of Nations. That such hope persists is a witness to the power of ideals to captivate the mind; and the reality may be nearer than any of us dare dream. If survived, a terrible infection, such as confluent small-pox, seems to benefit the general health. Perhaps such an attack through which we have passed may benefit the body cosmic. After discussing the various forms of government, Plato concludes that 'States are as the men are, they grow out of human characters' (Rep. VIII), and then, as the dream-republic approached completion, he realized that after all the true State is within, of which each one of us is the founder, and patterned on an ideal the existence of which matters not a whit. Is not the need of this individual reconstruction the Greek message to modern democracy? and with it is blended the note of individual service to the community on which Professor Gilbert Murray has so wisely dwelt.

With the hot blasts of hate still on our cheeks, it may seem a mockery to speak of this as the saving asset in our future; but is it not the very marrow of the teaching in which we have been brought up? At last the gospel of the right to live, and the right to live healthy, happy lives, has sunk deep into the hearts of

---

[1] I knew him well—a dear old Cornishman named Passmore.

the people; and before the (1914–18) war, so great was the work
of science in preventing untimely death that the day of Isaiah
seemed at hand 'when a man's life should be more precious than
fine gold, even a man than the gold of Ophir'. There is a sentence in the writings of the Father of Medicine upon which all
commentators have lingered, 'ἤν γὰρ παρῇ φιλανθρωπίη, πάρεστι
καὶ φιλοτεχνίη'[1]—the love of humanity associated with the love
of his craft!—philanthropia and philotechnia—the joy of working joined in each one to a true love of his brother. Memorable
sentence indeed! in which for the first time was coined the
magic word *philanthropy*, and conveying the subtle suggestion that
perhaps in this combination the longings of humanity may find
their solution, and Wisdom—philosophia—at last be justified
of her children.

[1] *Œuvres complètes d'Hippocrates*, par E. Littré, ix. 258.

3

BOOKS AND MEN

How easily, how secretly, how safely in books do we make
bare without shame the poverty of human ignorance! These
are the masters that instruct us without rod and ferrule,
without words of anger, without payment of money or
clothing. Should ye approach them, they are not asleep; if
ye seek to question them, they do not hide themselves;
should ye err, they do not chide; and should ye show ignorance, they know not how to laugh. O Books! ye alone are
free and liberal. Ye give to all that seek, and set free all that
serve you zealously.

RICHARD DE BURY, *Philobiblon*, Grolier Club Edition, vol. ii,
p. 22.

Books delight us when prosperity sweetly smiles; they stay to
comfort us when cloudy fortune frowns. They lend strength
to human compacts, and without them grave judgments
may not be propounded.   Ibid., p. 113.

For Books are not absolutely dead things, but do contain a
potency of life in them to be as active as that soul was whose
progeny they are; nay, they do preserve as in a vial the purest
efficacy and extraction of that living intellect that bred them.

JOHN MILTON, *Areopagitica*.

THOSE of us from other cities who bring congratulations
this evening can hardly escape the tinglings of envy
when we see this noble treasure house; but in my own
case the bitter waters of jealousy which rise in my soul
are at once diverted by two strong sensations. In the first place
I have a feeling of lively gratitude towards this library. In 1876
as a youngster interested in certain clinical subjects to which I
could find no reference in our library at McGill, I came to
Boston, and I here found what I wanted, and I found moreover
a cordial welcome and many friends. It was a small matter I had

---

Remarks made at the opening of the Boston Medical Library, 12 January
1901. *Boston Medical and Surgical Journal*, 1901, cxliv. 60–1. Reprinted in
Aequanimitas.

in hand but I wished to make it as complete as possible, and I have always felt that this library helped me to a good start. It has been such a pleasure in recurring visits to the library to find Dr. Brigham in charge, with the same kindly interest in visitors that he showed a quarter of a century ago. But the feeling which absorbs all others is one of deep satisfaction that our friend, Dr. Chadwick, has at last seen fulfilled the desire of his eyes. To few is given the tenacity of will which enables a man to pursue a cherished purpose through a quarter of a century— *Ohne Hast, aber ohne Rast* ('tis his favourite quotation); to fewer still is the fruition granted. Too often the reaper is not the sower. Too often the fate of those who labour at some object for the public good is to see their work pass into other hands, and to have others get the credit for enterprises which they have initiated and made possible. It has not been so with our friend, and it intensifies a thousandfold the pleasure of this occasion to feel the fitness, in every way, of the felicitations which have been offered to him.

It is hard for me to speak of the value of libraries in terms which would not seem exaggerated. Books have been my delight these thirty years, and from them I have received incalculable benefits. To study the phenomena of disease without books is to sail an uncharted sea, while to study books without patients is not to go to sea at all. Only a maker of books can appreciate the labours of others at their true value. Those of us who have brought forth fat volumes should offer hecatombs at these shrines of Minerva Medica. What exsuccous, attenuated off-spring they would have been but for the pabulum furnished through the placental circulation of a library. How often can it be said of us with truth, *Das beste was er ist verdankt er Andern!*

For the teacher and the worker a great library such as this is indispensable. They must know the world's best work and know it at once. They mint and make current coin the ore so widely scattered in journals, transactions, and monographs. The splendid collections which now exist in five or six of our cities and the unique opportunities of the Surgeon-General's Library have done much to give to American medicine a thoroughly eclectic character.

But when one considers the unending making of books, who does not sigh for the happy days of that thrice happy Sir William Browne[1] whose pocket library sufficed for his life's needs, drawing from a Greek testament his divinity, from the aphorisms of Hippocrates his medicine, and from an Elzevir Horace his good sense and vivacity. There should be in connexion with every library a corps of instructors in the art of reading, who would, as a labour of love, teach the young idea how to read. An old writer says that there are four sorts of readers: 'Sponges which attract all without distinguishing; Howre-glasses which receive and powre out as fast; Bagges which only retain the dregges of the spices and let the wine escape, and Sives which retaine the best onely.' A man wastes a great many years before he reaches the 'sive' stage.

For the general practitioner a well-used library is one of the few correctives of the premature senility which is so apt to overtake him. Self-centred, self-taught, he leads a solitary life, and unless his everyday experience is controlled by careful reading or by the attrition of a medical society it soon ceases to be of the slightest value and becomes a mere accretion of isolated facts, without correlation. It is astonishing with how little reading a doctor can practise medicine, but it is not astonishing how badly he may do it. Not three months ago a physician living within an hour's ride of the Surgeon-General's Library brought to me his little girl, aged twelve. The diagnosis of infantile myxoedema required only a half glance. In placid contentment he had been practising twenty years in 'Sleepy Hollow' and not even when his own flesh and blood was touched did he rouse from an apathy deep as Rip Van Winkle's sleep. In reply to questions: No, he had never seen anything in the journals

---

[1] In one of the Annual Orations at the Royal College of Physicians he said: 'Behold an instance of human ambition! not to be satisfied but by the conquest, as it were, of three worlds, lucre in the country, honour in the college, pleasure in the medicinal springs.'

about the thyroid gland; he had seen no pictures of cretinism or myxoedema; in fact his mind was a blank on the whole subject. He had not been a reader, he said, but he was a practical man with very little time. I could not help thinking of John Bunyan's remarks on the elements of success in the practice of medicine.

Physicians [he says] get neither name nor fame by the pricking of wheals or the picking out thistles, or by laying of plaisters to the scratch of a pin; every old woman can do this. But if they would have a name and a fame, if they will have it quickly, they must do some great and desperate cures. Let them fetch one to life that was dead, let them recover one to his wits that was mad, let them make one that was born blind to see, or let them give ripe wits to a fool —these are notable cures, and he that can do thus, if he doth thus first, he shall have the name and fame he deserves; he may lie abed till noon.

Had my doctor friend been a reader he might have done a great and notable cure and even have given ripe wits to a fool! It is in utilizing the fresh knowledge of the journals that the young physician may attain quickly to the name and fame he desires.

There is a third class of men in the profession to whom books are dearer than to teachers or practitioners—a small, a silent band, but in reality the leaven of the whole lump. The profane call them bibliomaniacs, and in truth they are at times irresponsible and do not always know the difference between *meum* and *tuum*. In the presence of Dr. Billings or of Dr. Chadwick I dare not further characterize them. Loving books partly for their contents, partly for the sake of the authors, they not alone keep alive the sentiment of historical continuity in the profession, but they are the men who make possible such gatherings as the one we are enjoying this evening. We need more men of their class, particularly in this country, where every one carries in his pocket the tape-measure of utility. Along two lines their work is valuable. By the historical method alone can many problems in medicine be approached profitably. For example, the student who dates his knowledge of tuberculosis from Koch may have a very correct, but he has a very incomplete, appreciation of the

subject. Within a quarter of a century our libraries will have
certain alcoves devoted to the historical consideration of the
great diseases, which will give to the student that mental perspective which is so valuable an equipment in life. The past is
a good nurse, as Lowell remarks, particularly for the weanlings
of the fold.

> 'Tis man's worst deed
> To let the things that have been, run to waste
> And in the unmeaning Present sink the Past.

But in a more excellent way these *laudatores temporis acti* render
a royal service. For each one of us to-day, as in Plato's time,
there is a higher as well as a lower education. The very marrow
and fatness of books may not suffice to save a man from becoming
a poor, mean-spirited devil, without a spark of fine professional
feeling, and without a thought above the sordid issues of the
day. The men I speak of keep alive in us an interest in the great
men of the past and not alone in their works, which they cherish,
but in their lives, which they emulate. They would remind us
continually that in the records of no other profession is there
to be found so large a number of men who have combined
intellectual pre-eminence with nobility of character. This higher
education so much needed to-day is not given in the school, is
not to be bought in the market place, but it has to be wrought
out in each one of us for himself; it is the silent influence of
character on character and in no way more potent than in the
contemplation of the lives of the great and good of the past, in
no way more than in 'the touch divine of noble natures gone'.

I should like to see in each library a select company of the
Immortals set apart for special adoration. Each country might
have its representatives in a sort of alcove of Fame, in which
the great medical classics were gathered. Not necessarily books,
more often the epoch-making contributions to be found in
ephemeral journals. It is too early, perhaps, to make a selection
of American medical classics, but it might be worth while to
gather suffrages in regard to the contributions which ought to
be placed upon our Roll of Honour. A few years ago I made out

a list of those I thought the most worthy which I carried down to 1850, and it has a certain interest for us this evening. The native modesty of the Boston physician is well known, but in certain circles there has been associated with it a curious psychical phenomenon, a conviction of the utter worthlessness of the *status praesens* in New England, as compared with conditions existing elsewhere. There is a variety to-day of the Back Bay Brahmin who delights in cherishing the belief that medically things are everywhere better than in Boston, and who is always ready to predict 'an Asiatic removal of candlesticks', to borrow a phrase from Cotton Mather. Strange indeed would it have been had not such a plastic profession as ours felt the influences which moulded New England into the intellectual centre of the New World. In reality, nowhere in the country has the profession been adorned more plentifully with men of culture and of character—not voluminous writers or exploiters of the products of other men's brains—and they manage to get a full share on the Roll of Fame which I have suggested. To 1850, I have counted some twenty contributions of the first rank, contributions which for one reason or another deserve to be called American medical classics. New England takes ten. But in medicine the men she has given to the other parts of the country have been better than books. Men like Nathan R. Smith, Austin Flint, Willard Parker, Alonzo Clark, Elisha Bartlett, John C. Dalton, and others carried away from their New England homes a love of truth, a love of learning, and above all a proper estimate of the personal character of the physician.

Dr. Johnson shrewdly remarked that ambition was usually proportionate to capacity, which is as true of a profession as it is of a man. What we have seen to-night reflects credit not less on your ambition than on your capacity. A library after all is a great catalyser, accelerating the nutrition and rate of progress in a profession, and I am sure you will find yourselves the better for the sacrifice you have made in securing this home for your books, this workshop for your members.

4

SIR THOMAS BROWNE

As a boy it was my good fortune to come under the influence of a parish priest of the Gilbert White type, who followed the seasons of Nature no less ardently than those of the Church, and whose excursions into science had brought him into contact with physic and physicians. Father Johnson, as his friends loved to call him, founder and Warden of the Trinity College School, near Toronto, illustrated that angelical conjunction (to use Cotton Mather's words) of medicine and divinity more common in the sixteenth and seventeenth centuries than in the nineteenth. An earnest student of Sir Thomas Browne, particularly of the *Religio Medici*, he often read to us extracts in illustration of the beauty of the English language, or he would entertain us with some of the author's quaint conceits, such as the man without a navel (Adam), or that woman was the rib and crooked piece of man. The copy which I hold in my hand (J. T. Fields's edition of 1862), my companion ever since my schooldays, is the most precious book in my library. I mention these circumstances in extenuation of an enthusiasm which has enabled me to make this almost complete collection of the editions of his works I show you this evening, knowing full well the compassionate feeling with which the bibliomaniac is regarded by his saner colleagues.

I. THE MAN

The little Thomas was happy in his entrance upon the stage, 19 October 1605. Among multiplied acknowledgements, he

An Address delivered at the Physical Society, Guy's Hospital, London, 12 October 1905. Published *British Medical Journal*, 1905, ii. 993–8; as The 'Religio Medici' in the *Library*, London, 1906, vii. 1, and reprinted at the Chiswick Press, 1906; as 'Sir Thomas Browne' in *An Alabama Student*.

could lift up one hand to Heaven (as he says) that he was born of honest parents, 'that modesty, humility, patience, and veracity lay in the same egg, and came into the world' with him. Of his father, a London merchant, but little is known. There is at Devonshire House a family picture which shows him to have been a man of fine presence, looking not unworthy of the future philosopher, a child of three or four years, seated on his mother's knee. She married a second time, Sir Thomas Dutton, a man of wealth and position, who gave his stepson every advantage of education and travel. We lack accurate information of the early years—of the schooldays at Winchester, of his life at Broadgate Hall, now Pembroke College, Oxford, and of the influences which induced him to study medicine. Possibly he got his inspiration from the Regius Professor of Medicine, the elder Clayton, the Master of Broadgate Hall and afterwards of Pembroke College. That he was a distinguished undergraduate is shown in his selection at the end of the first year in residence to deliver an oration at the opening of Pembroke College. Possibly between the years 1626, when he took the B.A., and 1629, when he commenced M.A., he may have been engaged in the study of medicine; but Mr. Charles Williams, of Norwich, who is perhaps more familiar than any one living with the history of our author, does not think it likely that he began until he went abroad. In these years he could at least have 'entered upon the physic line' and could have proceeded to the M.B. He was too early to participate in the revival of science in Oxford, but even after that had occurred Sydenham flung the cruel reproach at his Alma Mater that he would as soon send a man to her to learn shoemaking as practical physic. It was possible, of course, to pick up a little knowledge of medicine from the local practitioners and from the Physic Garden, together with the lectures of the Regius Professor, who, as far as we know, had not at any rate the awkward failing of his more distinguished son, who could not look upon blood without fainting, and in consequence had to hand over his anatomy lectures to a deputy.

Clayton's studies and work would naturally be of a somewhat

mixed character, and at that period even many of those whose chief business was theology were interested in natural philosophy, of which medicine formed an important part. Burton refers to an address delivered about this time by Clayton dealing with the mutual relations of mind and body. The *Anatomy of Melancholy*, which appeared in 1621, must have proved a stimulating *bonne-bouche* for the Oxford men of the day, and I like to think of the eagerness with which so ardent a student as Browne of Pembroke would have pounced on the second and enlarged edition which appeared in 1624. He may, indeed, have been a friend of Burton, or he may have formed one of a group of undergraduates to watch Democritus Junior leaning over the bridge and laughing at the bargees as they swore at each other. It is stated, I know not on what authority, that Browne practised in Oxford for a time.

After a visit to Ireland with his stepfather he took the grand tour—France, Italy, and Holland—spending two years in study. Of his continental trip our knowledge is very meagre. He went to Montpellier, still famous, but failing, where he probably listened to the teaching of Rivière, whose *Praxis* was for years the leading text-book in Europe—thence to Padua, where he must have heard the celebrated Sanctorius of the Medicina Statica—then on to Leyden, just rising into prominence, where it is said he took his doctor's degree in 1633. Of this, however, there is no certainty. A few years ago I looked through the register of that famous University, but failed to find his name. At the end of two years' travel he may have had cobwebs in his pocket, and the Leyden degree was expensive, as that quaint old contemporary of Browne, the Rev. John Ward, of Stratford-on-Avon, tells us (*Diary*): 'Mr. Burnet had a letter out of the Low Countries of the charge of a doctor's degree, which is at Leyden about £16, besides feasting the professors; at Angers in France, not above £9, and feasting not necessary neither.' No doubt the young Englishman got of the best that there was in the teaching of the day, and from the *Religio* one learns that he developed from it an extraordinary breadth of culture, and a charity not always granted to travellers. He pierced beneath the shell of nationalism into the heart of the people among whom he lived, feeling at home everywhere and in every clime; hence the charity, rare in a Protestant, expressed so beautifully in the lines: 'I can dispense with my hat at the sight of a cross, but scarce with the thought of my Saviour.'

He must have made good use of his exceptional opportunities; as he was able to boast, in a humble way it is true, that he understood six languages.

Returning to England in 1634 he settled at Shibden Dale, close to Halifax, not, as Mr. Charles Williams has pointed out, to practise his profession, but to recruit his health, somewhat impaired by shipwreck and disease. Here, in Upper Shibden Hall, he wrote the *Religio Medici*, the book by which to-day his memory is kept green among us. In his travels he had doubtless made many observations on men, and in his reading had culled many useful memoranda. He makes it quite clear—and is anxious to do so—that the book was written while he was very young. He says: 'My life is a miracle of thirty years.' 'I have not seen one revolution of Saturn.' 'My pulse hath not beat thirty years.' Indeed, he seems to be of Plato's opinion that the pace of life slackens after this date, and there is a note of sadness in his comment, that while the radical humour may contain sufficient oil for seventy, 'in some it gives no light past thirty', and he adds that those dying at this age should not complain of immaturity. In the quiet Yorkshire valley, with 'leisurable hours for his private exercise and satisfaction', the manuscript was completed, 'with', as he says, 'such disadvantages that (I protest) from the first setting pen to paper I had not the assistance of any good book'. 'Communicated to one it became common to many', and at last in 1642, seven years after its completion, reached the press in a depraved form.

In 1637, at the solicitation of friends, Browne moved to Norwich, with which city, so far as we know, he had no previous connexion. At that date the East Anglian capital had not become famous in the annals of medicine. True, she had given Caius to the profession, but he had only practised there for a short time and does not seem to have had any special influence on her destinies. Sir Thomas Browne may be said to be the first of the long list of worthies who have in the past two and a half centuries made Norwich famous among the provincial towns of the kingdom. Here for forty-five years he lived the quiet, uneventful life of a student-practitioner, absorbed, like a sensible man, in his family, his friends, his studies, and his patients. It is a life of singular happiness to contemplate. In 1641 he married Dorothy Mileham, 'a lady of such a symmetrical proportion to her worthy husband—that they seemed to come together by a kind of natural magnetism'. In the *Religio* he had said some hard things of the gentle goddess and had expressed himself very strongly against Nature's method for the propagation of the race. He believed, with Milton, that the world should have been populated 'without feminine', and in almost identical words they wish that some way less trivial and vulgar had been found to generate mankind. Dame Dorothy proved a good wife, a fruitful branch, bearing ten children. We have a pleasant picture of her in her letters to her boys and to her daughter-in-law, in a spelling suggestive of Pitman's phonetics. She seems to have had in full measure the simple piety and the tender affection mentioned on her monument in St. Peter's Church. The domestic correspondence (Wilkin's edition of the *Works*) gives interesting glimpses of the family life, the lights and shadows of a cultured English home. The two boys were all that their father could have wished. Edward, the elder, had a distinguished career, following his father's footsteps in the profession and reaching the dignity of the Presidency of the Royal College of Physicians. Inheriting his father's tastes, as the letters between them prove, his wide interests in natural history and archaeology are shown in his well-known book of *Travels*, and I am fortunate in possessing a copy of the *Hydriotaphia* with his autograph.

Edward's son, the 'Tommy' of the letters, the delight of his grandfather, also became a physician, and practised with his father. He died in 1710 in rather unfortunate circumstances,

and with him the male line of Sir Thomas ended. Of the younger
son we have, in the letters, a charming picture—a brave sailor-
lad with many of his father's tastes, who served with great
distinction in the Dutch wars, in which he met (it is supposed)
a sailor's death. The eldest daughter married Henry Fairfax,
and through their daughter, who married the Earl of Buchan,
there are to-day among the Buchans and Erskines the only
existing representatives of Sir Thomas.

The waves and storms of the Civil War scarcely reached the
quiet Norwich home. Browne was a staunch Royalist, and his
name occurs among the citizens who in 1643 refused to contribute to a fund for the recapture of the town of Newcastle. It is
astonishing how few references occur in his writings to the
national troubles, which must have tried his heart sorely. In
the preface to the *Religio* he gives vent to his feelings, lamenting
not only the universal tyranny of the Press, but the defamation
of the name of his Majesty, the degradation of Parliament, and
the writings of both 'depravedly, anticipatively, counterfeitedly,
imprinted'. In one of the letters he speaks of the execution of
Charles I as 'horrid murther', and in another he calls Cromwell
a usurper. In civil wars physicians of all men suffer least, as the
services of able men are needed by both parties, and time and
again it has happened that an even-balanced soul, such as our
author, has passed quietly through terrible trials, doing the
day's work with closed lips. Corresponding with the most active
decades of his life, in which his three important works were
issued, one might have expected to find in them reference to
the Civil War, or, at least, echoes of the great change wrought
by the Commonwealth, but, like Fox, in whose writings the
same silence has been noticed, whatever may have been his
feelings, he preserved a discreet silence. His own rule of life,
no doubt, is expressed in the advice to his son: 'Times look
troublesome, but you have an honest and peaceable profession
which may employ you, and discretion to guide your words and
actions.'

Busy with his professional work, interested in natural history, in archaeology, and in literature, with a wide circle of scientific friends and correspondents, the glimpses of Browne's life, which we have from the letters, are singularly attractive. He adopted an admirable plan in the education of his children, sending them abroad, and urging them to form early habits of independence. His younger boy, Thomas, he sent at the age of fourteen to France, alone, and he remarks in one of his letters to him: 'He that hath learnt not in France travelleth in vain.' Everywhere in the correspondence with his children there is evidence of good, practical sense. He tells one of the boys to 'cast off *pudor rusticus,* and to have a handsome garb of his body'. Even the daughters were taken to France. In his souvenir of Sir Thomas Browne, Mr. Charles Williams has given an illustration of his house, a fine old building which was unfortunately torn down some years ago, though the handsome mantelpiece has been preserved.

An interesting contemporary account has been left by Evelyn, who paid a visit to Sir Thomas in 1673. He says:

. . . the whole house being a paradise and a cabinet of rarities, and that of the best collections, especially medails, books, plants, and natural things. Amongst other curiosities, Sir Thomas had a collection of the eggs of all the foule and birds he could procure, that country, especially the promintory of Norfolck, being frequented, as he said, by several kinds which seldom or never go further into the land, as cranes, storkes, eagles, and a variety of other foule.

After Dr. Edward Browne was established in London, the letters show the keen interest Sir Thomas took in the scientific work of the day. Writing of his son's lecture on anatomy at the Chirurgical Hall, he warns him that he would have more spectators than auditors, and after that first day, as the lecture was in Latin, 'very many will not be earnest to come here-after'. He evidently takes the greatest interest in his son's progress, and constantly gives him suggestions with reference to new points that are coming up in the literature. Here and there are references to important medical cases, and comments upon modes of treatment. It is interesting to note the prevalence of agues, even of

the severe haemorrhagic types, and his use of Peruvian bark.
In one of the letters a remarkable case of pneumothorax is
described: 'A young woman who had a julking and fluctuation
in her chest so that it might be heard by standers-by.' Evidently
he had a large and extensive practice in the Eastern Counties,
and there are numerous references to the local physicians. There
is a poem extolling his skill in the despaired-of case of Mrs. E. S.,
three or four of the lines of which are worth quoting:

> He came, saw, cur'd! Could Caesar's self do more;
> Galen, Hippocrates, London's four-score
> Of ffamous Colledge . . . had these heard him read
> His lecture on this Skeliton, half dead;
> And seen his modest eye search every part,
> Judging, not seeing.

The correspondence with his son is kept up to the time of his
death. Only part of the letters appear in Wilkin's *Life,* and there
are many extant worthy of publication.

In 1671 he was knighted by Charles II. In 1664 he was made
an honorary Fellow of the Royal College of Physicians, with
which, through his son, he had close affiliations. His name does
not appear in the roll of the Royal Society, with the spirit and
objects of which he must yet have had the warmest sympathy.
He was in correspondence with many of the leading men of the
day—Evelyn, Grew, Elias Ashmole, Dugdale, Paston, Aubrey,
and others. The letters deal with a remarkable variety of subjects
—natural history, botany, chemistry, magic and archaeology,
&c. The *Pseudodoxia Epidemica* (1646) extended his reputation
among all classes and helped to bring him into close relationship
with the virtuosi of the period. There is in the Bodleian a
delightful letter from Mr. Henry Bates, a wit of the court, a
few extracts from which will give you an idea of the extravagant
admiration excited by his writings:

Sir,—Amongst those great and due acknowledgements this horizon
owes you for imparting your sublime solid phansie to them in that
incomparable piece of invention and judgement, R. M. give mee
leave, sir, here at last to tender my share, which I wish I could make

proportionable to the value I deservedly sett upon it, for truly, sir, ever since I had the happiness to know your religion I have religiously honoured you; hug'd your Minerva in my bosome, and voted it my *vade mecum*. . . . I am of that opinion still, that next the *Legenda Dei*, it is the master piece of Christendome; and though I have met sometimes with some *omnes sic ego vero non sic* men, prejudicating pates, who bogled at shadowes in 't, and carpt at atoms, and have so strappadoed me into impatience with their senseless censures, yet this still satisfied my zeal toward it, when I found *non intelligunt* was the nurse of their *vituperant*, and they onely stumbled for want of a lanthorne.[1]

While interested actively in medicine, Browne does not seem to have been on intimate terms with his great contemporaries —Harvey, Sydenham, or Glisson—though he mentions them, and always with respect. He was a prudent, prosperous man, generous to his children and to his friends. He subscribed liberally to his old school at Winchester, to the rebuilding of the Library of Trinity College, Cambridge, and to the repairs at Christ Church, Oxford. A life placid, uneventful, and easy, without stress or strain, happy in his friends, his family, and his work, he expressed in it that harmony of the inner and of the outer man which it is the aim of all true philosophy to attain, and which he inculcated so nobly and in such noble words in the *Religio Medici* and in the *Christian Morals*.

A description of him given by his friend, the Rev. John Whitefoot, is worth quoting:

He was never seen to be transported with mirth or dejected with sadness; always cheerful but rarely merry, at any sensible rate; seldom heard to break a jest, and when he did he would be apt to blush at the levity of it. His gravity was natural, without affectation.

The end came unexpectedly in his seventy-seventh year, after a sharp attack of colic, on his birthday, 19 October 1682—a curious possibility of which he speaks in the *Letter to a Friend*:

But in persons who outlive many years, and when there are no less than 365 days to determine their lives every year—that the first day

[1] Wilkin, vol. i, p. 353.

should make the last, that the tail of the snake should return into its mouth precisely at that time, and they should wind up upon the day of their nativity—is, indeed, a remarkable coincidence, which, though astrology hath taken witty pains to solve, yet hath it been very wary in making predictions of it.

There are three good portraits of Sir Thomas; one in the College of Physicians, London, which is the best known and has been often reproduced, and from which is taken the frontispiece in Greenhill's edition of the *Religio Medici*; a second is in the Bodleian, and this also has frequently been reproduced; the third is in the vestry of St. Peter Mancroft, Norwich. In many ways it is the most pleasing of the three, and Browne looks in it a younger man, closer to the days of the *Religio*. There is a fourth picture, the frontispiece to the fifth edition of the *Pseudodoxia*, but it is so unlike the others that I doubt very much if it could have been Sir Thomas. If it was, he must have suffered from the artist, as did Milton, whose picture in the frontispiece to the *Poems*, 1645, is a base caricature; but Browne has not had the satisfaction of Milton's joke and happy revenge.

II. THE BOOK

As a book the *Religio Medici* has had an interesting history. Written at 'leisurable hours and for his private exercise and satisfaction', it circulated in manuscript among friends, 'and was by transcription successively corrupted, until it arrived in a most depraved copy at the press'. Two surreptitious editions were issued by Andrew Crooke in 1642, both in small octavo, with an engraved frontispiece by Marshall representing a man falling from a rock (the earth) into the sea of eternity, but caught by a hand issuing from the clouds, under which is the legend, *A Coelo Salus*. Johnson suggests that the author may not have been ignorant of Crooke's design, but was very willing to let a tentative edition be issued—'a stratagem by which an author panting for fame, and yet afraid of seeming to challenge it, may at once gratify his vanity and preserve the appearance of modesty'.

There are at least six manuscripts of the *Religio* in existence, all presenting minor differences, which bear out the author's contention that by transcription they had become depraved. One in the Wilkin collection, in the Castle Museum, Norwich, is in the author's handwriting. Had Browne been party to an innocent fraud, he would scarcely have allowed Crooke to issue within a year a second imperfect edition—not simply a second impression, as the two differ in the size and number of the pages, and present also minor differences in the text. The authorized edition appeared in the following year by the same publisher and with the same frontispiece, with the following words at the foot of the plate: 'A true and full copy of that which was most imperfectly and surreptitiously printed before under the name of *Religio Medici*.' It was issued anonymously, with a preface, signed 'A. B.'; 'To such as have or shall peruse the observations upon a former corrupt copy of this Booke.' A curious incident here links together two men, types of the intellectual movement of their generation—both students, both mystics—the one a quiet observer of nature, an antiquary, and a physician; the other a restless spirit, a bold buccaneer, a politician, a philosopher, and an amateur physician. Sir Kenelm Digby, committed to Winchester House by the Parliamentarians, had heard favourably from the Earl of Dorset of the *Religio Medici*. Though late in the day, 'the magnetic motion', as he says, 'was impatience to have the booke in his hands', so he sent at once to St. Paul's churchyard for it. He was in bed when it came.

This good natur'd creature I could easily perswade to be my bedfellow and to wake me as long as I had any edge to entertain myselfe with the delights I sucked in from so noble a conversation. And truly I closed not my eyes till I had enricht myselfe with (or at least exactly surveyed) all the treasures that are lapt up in the folds of those new sheets.

Sir Kenelm holds the record for reading in bed; not only did he read the *Religio* through, but he wrote *Observations* upon it the same night in the form of a letter to his friend, which extends to three-fourths of the size of the *Religio* itself. As

Johnson remarks, he 'returned his judgement of it not in the form of a letter but of a book'. He dates it at the end 'the 22nd (I think I may say the 23rd, for I am sure it is morning and I think it is day) of December, 1642'. Johnson says that its principal claim to admiration is that it was written within twenty-four hours, of which part was spent in procuring Browne's book and part in reading it. Sir Kenelm was a remarkable man, but in connexion with his statements it may be well to remember the reputation he had among his contemporaries, Stubbs calling him 'the Pliny of our age for lying'. However this may be, his criticisms of the work are exceedingly interesting and often just. This little booklet of Sir Kenelm has floated down the stream of literature, reappearing at intervals attached to editions of the *Religio*, while his weightier tomes are deep in the ooze at the bottom.

The *Religio Medici* became popular with remarkable rapidity. As Johnson remarks, 'It excited attention by the novelty of paradoxes, the dignity of sentiment, the quick succession of images, the multitude of abstrusive allusions, subtility of disquisition, and the strength of language.' A Cambridge student, Merryweather, travelling in Europe, translated it into Latin, and it was published in 1644 by Hackius at Leyden in a very neat volume. A second impression appeared in the same year, and also a Paris edition, a reprint of the Leyden. The continental scholars were a good deal puzzled, and not altogether certain of the orthodoxy of the work. Merryweather, in a very interesting letter (1649), says that he had some difficulty in getting a printer at Leyden. Salmasius, to whom Haye, a book merchant, took it for approbation, said 'that there was in it many things well said, but that it contained also many exorbitant conceptions in religion and would probably find much frowning entertainment, especially amongst the ministers'. Two other printers also refused it. The most interesting continental criticism is by that distinguished member of the profession, Gui Patin, professor in the Paris Faculty of Medicine. In a letter to Charles Spon of Lyons, dated Paris, 21 October 1644, he mentions having received a little book called the *Religio Medici*, written by an Englishman, 'a very mystical book containing strange and ravishing thoughts'. In a letter, dated 1645, he says, 'the book is in high credit here; the author has wit, and there are abundance of fine things in the book. He is a humorist whose thoughts are very agreeable, but who, in my opinion, is to seek for a master in religion may in the end find none.' Patin thought the author in a parlous state, and as he was still alive he might grow worse as well as better. Evidently, however, the work became a favourite one with him, as in letters of 1650–3–7 he refers to it again in different editions. It is remarkable that he nowhere mentions the author by name, but subsequently, when Edward Browne was a student in Paris, Patin sends kindly greetings to his father.

Much discussion occurred on the Continent as to the orthodoxy of the *Religio*. It is no slight compliment to the author that he should have been by one claimed as a catholic, by another denounced as an atheist, while a member of the Society of Friends saw in him a likely convert. The book was placed on the 'Index'. In England, with the exception of Digby's *Observations*, there were no adverse criticisms of any note. Alexander Ross, that interesting old Southampton schoolmaster, who seems always to have been ready for an intellectual tilt, wrote a criticism entitled *Medicus Medicatus, or the Physician's Religion cured by a Lenitive or Gentle Potion*.

In England there were two reprints in 1645, and it appeared again in the years 1656, 1659, 1669, 1672, and in 1682, the year of Browne's death. A comparison of the early editions shows that all have the same frontispiece and are, with slight variations, reprints of that of 1643. The work also began to be reprinted with the *Pseudodoxia Epidemica* (third edition, 1659). The Latin editions followed each other rapidly. As I mentioned, it first appeared at Leyden in 1644, and was reprinted the same year there and in Paris; then in 1650 in Leyden again, in 1652 in Strasburg, and in the same place in 1665 and 1667. The most important of these editions was that of Strasburg, 1652, with elaborate notes by Moltkius, of which Gui Patin speaks as 'miserable examples of pedantry', and indeed stigmatizes the commentator as a fool. The Dutch translation appeared in 1665 and a French in 1668, so that altogether during the author's lifetime there were at least twenty editions of the work.

In the seventeenth century there were in all twenty-two editions. In the eighteenth century there were four English editions, one Latin, and one German. Then a long interval of seventy-seven years elapsed, until in 1831 Thomas Chapman, a young Exeter College man, brought out a neat little edition. In the same year the first American edition was published, edited by the Rev. Alexander Young, of Boston. In 1838 appeared an excellent edition by J. A. St. John, 'traveller, linguist, author, and editor', and in 1844 Longmans' edition by John Peace, the librarian of the City Library, Bristol. This edition was republished in America by the house of Lea & Blanchard,[1] Philadelphia, the only occasion, I believe, on which the *Religio* has been issued by a firm of medical publishers. In 1845 appeared Pickering's beautiful edition, edited, with many original notes, by the Rev. Henry Gardiner, in many ways the most choice of nineteenth-century issues. In 1862 James Ticknor Fields, the well-known Boston scholar and publisher, brought out a very handsome edition, of which, for the first time in the history of the book, an *édition de luxe* was printed on larger paper. In 1869 appeared Sampson Low & Co.'s edition by Willis Bund; and in 1878 Rivingtons' edition edited by W. P. Smith. Then in 1881 there came what must always remain the standard edition, edited by Dr. Greenhill for the Golden Treasury Series, and reprinted repeatedly by Macmillan & Co. To his task Dr. Greenhill brought not only a genuine love of Sir Thomas Browne, but the accuracy of an earnest, painstaking scholar. Since the year 1881 a dozen or more editions have appeared, of which I may mention the excellent one by Dr. Lloyd Roberts, of Manchester. I may finish this dry summary by noting the

---

[1] They did not issue an edition in 1848, as is stated by Greenhill on the authority of J. T. Fields.

contrast between the little parchment-covered surreptitious edition of 1642 and the sumptuous folio of the Vale Press. In all,
including those which have appeared with the collected works,
there have been about fifty-five editions. Browne states that the
work had also been translated into High Dutch and into Italian,
but I can find no record of these editions, nor of a German
translation, 1680, mentioned by Watt.

Space will allow only a brief reference to Browne's other
writings. *Pseudodoxia Epidemica: or, Enquiries into very many received
Tenents and commonly presumed Truths,* appeared in 1646 in a small
folio. In extent this is by far the most pretentious of Browne's
works. It forms an extraordinary collection of old wives' fables
and popular beliefs in every department of human knowledge,
dealt with from the standpoint of the science of that day. In a
way it is a strong protest against general credulity and inexactness
of statement, and a plea for greater accuracy in the observation
of facts and in the recording of them. Walter Pater has drawn
attention to the striking resemblance between Browne's chapter
on the sources of Error and Bacon's doctrine of the Idola—shams
which men fall down and worship. He discusses cleverly the use
of doubts; but, as Pater remarks, 'Browne was himself a rather
lively example of entertainments of the Idols of the Cave—Idola
Specus—and, like Boyle, Digby, and others, he could not quite
free himself from the shackles of alchemy and a hankering for
the philosopher's stone.' The work was very popular, and extended the reputation of the author very widely. Indeed, in
1646 Browne was not known at large as the author of the *Religio*,
as his name had not appeared on the title-page of any edition
issued at that date. The *Pseudodoxia* was frequently reprinted, a
sixth edition being published in 1672, and it appeared in
French both in France and in Holland.

Equalling in popularity among certain people the *Religio*, certainly next to it in importance, is the remarkable essay known
as *Hydriotaphia—Urne-Buriall: or, A Discourse of the Sepulchrall
Urnes lately found in Norfolk* (1658). Printed with it is *The Garden
of Cyrus*, a learned discourse on gardens of all forms in all ages.

Naturally, when an unusual number of funeral urns were found at Walsingham, they were brought to the notice of Browne, the leading antiquary of the county. Instead of writing a learned disquisition upon their date—he thought them Roman, they were in reality Saxon—with accurate measurements and a catalogue of the bones, he touches upon the whole incident very lightly, but, using it as a text, breaks out into a noble and inspiring prose poem, a meditation upon mortality and the last sad rites of all nations in all times, with learned comments on modes of sepulchre, illustrated with much antiquarian and historical lore. Running through the work is an appropriate note of melancholy at the sad fate which awaits the great majority of us, upon whom 'the iniquity of oblivion blindly scattereth her poppy'. 'The greater part must be content to be as though they had not been, to be found in the register of God, not in the record of man.'

Nowhere in his writings does the prose flow with a more majestic roll. Take, for example, this one thought:

If the nearness of our last necessity brought a nearer conformity unto it, there were a happiness in hoary hairs and no calamity in half senses. But the long habit of living indisposeth us for dying, when avarice makes us the sport of death, when even David grew politically cruel, and Solomon could hardly be said to be the wisest of men. But many are too early old and before the days of age. Adversity stretcheth our days, misery makes Alcmena's nights, and time hath no wings unto it.

Closely connected in sentiment with the *Urne-Buriall* is the thin folio pamphlet—the rarest of all Browne's works, printed posthumously in 1690—*A Letter to a Friend, upon Occasion of the Death of his Intimate Friend*. It is a splendid dissertation on death and modes of dying, and is a unique study of the slow progress to the grave of a consumptive. It is written in his most picturesque and characteristic vein, with such a charm of diction that some critics have given it the place of honour among his works. Pater, in most enthusiastic terms, speaks of it with the *Urne-Buriall* as 'the best justification of Browne's literary reputation'.

The tender sympathy with the poor relics of humanity which Browne expresses so beautifully in these two meditations has not been meted to his own. 'Who knows the fate of his bones or how often he is to be buried?' he asks. In 1840, while workmen were repairing the chancel of St. Peter Mancroft, the coffin of Sir Thomas was accidentally opened, and one of the workmen took the skull, which afterwards came into the possession of Dr. Edward Lubbock, who deposited it in the Museum of the Norfolk and Norwich Infirmary. When I first saw it there in 1872 there was on it a printed slip with these lines from the *Hydriotaphia*: 'To be knaved out of our graves, to have our skulls made drinking-bowls, and our bones turned into pipes, to delight and sport our enemies, are tragical abominations escaped in burning burials.' The skull has been carefully described by Mr. Charles Williams, to whom I am indebted for the loan of photographs.[1]

In addition to the *Letter to a Friend*, there are three posthumous works, *Certain Miscellany Tracts* (1684), edited by Archbishop Tenison, and *Posthumous Works* (1712), containing chiefly papers of antiquarian interest. In the same year, 1712, appeared the *Christian Morals*, edited by Archdeacon Jeffrey of Norwich, from a manuscript found among Browne's papers. Probably a work of his later life, it forms a series of ethical fragments in a rich and stately prose which, in places, presents a striking parallelism to passages in the Hebrew poetry. The work is usually printed with the *Religio*, to which in reality it forms a supplement.

Of the collected editions of Browne's works, the first, a fine folio, appeared in 1686. In 1836, Simon Wilkin, himself a Norwich man, edited the works with the devotion of an ardent lover of his old townsman, and with the critical accuracy of a scholar. All students of Sir Thomas remain under a lasting debt to Mr. Wilkin, and it is pleasant to know that through the kindness of his daughter-in-law, Mrs. Wilkin, of Sidmouth, a Sir Thomas Browne Library has been founded in connexion with the Castle Museum, Norwich, in which Mr. Simon Wilkin's collections have been placed.

[1] The skull was reburied in 1922.—ED.

III. APPRECIATION

Critics from Johnson to Walter Pater have put on record their estimate of Browne and of his place in literature. Among these for keenness of appreciation Pater takes the first rank. Lamb and Coleridge dearly loved the old Norwich physician, in whom they found a kindred spirit. In America the New England writers, Ticknor, Fields, Holmes, and Lowell, were ardent students of his works. Lowell in particular is fond of apt quotations from him, and in one place speaks of him as 'our most imaginative mind since Shakespeare'. But no one has put so briefly and so clearly the strong characters of our author as the French critic, Taine:

> Let us conceive a kindred spirit to Shakespeare's, a scholar and an observer instead of an actor and a poet, who in place of creating is occupied in comprehending, but who, like Shakespeare, applies himself to living things, penetrates their internal structure, puts himself in communication with their actual laws, imprints in himself fervently and scrupulously the smallest details of their figure; who at the same time extends his penetrating surmises beyond the region of observation, discerns behind visible phenomena a world obscure yet sublime, and trembles with a kind of veneration before the vast, indistinct, but populous abyss on whose surface our little universe hangs quivering. Such a one is Sir Thomas Browne, a naturalist, a philosopher, a scholar, a physician, and a moralist, almost the last of the generation which produced Jeremy Taylor and Shakespeare. No thinker bears stronger witness to the wandering and inventive curiosity of the age. No writer has better displayed the brilliant and sombre imagination of the North. No one has spoken with a more elegant emotion of death, the vast night of forgetfulness, of the all-devouring pit of human vanity which tries to create an immortality out of ephemeral glory or sculptured stones. No one has revealed in more glowing and original expressions the poetic sap which flows through all the minds of the age.

The growing popularity of Browne's writings testifies to the assured position he holds, if not in the hearts of the many, at least in the hearts of that saving remnant which in each generation hands on the best traditions of our literature. We, who are members of his profession, may take a special pride in him. Among physicians, or teachers of physic, there is, perhaps, but one name in the very first rank. Rabelais stands apart with the kings and queens of literature. Among the princes of the blood there are differences of opinion as to rank, but Sir Thomas Browne, Holmes, and John Brown of Edinburgh form a group together high in the circle. Of the three, two were general practitioners; Oliver Wendell Holmes only in the early part of his life, and for forty years a teacher of anatomy; but all three have far closer ties with us than Goldsmith, Smollett, or Keats, whose medical affiliations were titular rather than practical.

Burton, Browne, and Fuller have much in common—a rare quaintness, a love of odd conceits, and the faculty of apt illustrations drawn from out-of-the-way sources. Like Montaigne's— Burton's even more—Browne's bookishness is of a delightful kind, and yet, as he maintains, his best matter is not picked from the leaves of any author, but bred among the 'weeds and tares' of his own brain. In his style there is a lack of what the moderns call technique, but how pleasant it is to follow his thoughts, rippling like a burn, not the stilted formality of the technical artist in words, the cadences of whose precise and mechanical expressions pall on the ear.

As has been remarked, the *Religio Medici* is a *tour de force*, an attempt to combine daring scepticism with humble faith in the Christian religion. Sir Thomas confesses himself to be 'naturally inclined to that which misguided zeal terms superstition'. He 'cannot hear the Ave Maria bell without an elevation'. He has no prejudices in religion, but subscribes himself a loyal son of the Church of England. In clear language he says, 'In brief, where the Scripture is silent the Church is my text; where that speaks it is but my comment. When there is a joint silence of both, I borrow not the rules of my religion from Rome or Geneva, but from the dictates of my own reason.' He is hard on the controversialist in religion—'every man is not a proper champion for truth, nor fit to take up the gauntlet in the cause of verity', &c. While he disclaims any 'taint or tincture' of heresy, he confesses to a number of heretical hopes, such as the ultimate salvation of the race, and the efficacy of prayers for the dead. He freely criticizes certain seeming absurdities in the Bible narrative. His travels have made him cosmopolitan and free from all national prejudices.

I feel not in myself those common antipathies that I can discover in others, those national repugnancies do not touch me, nor do I behold with prejudice the French, Italian, Spaniard, or Dutch; but where I find their actions in balance with my countrymen's, I honour, love, and embrace them in the same degree. I was born in the eighth climate, but seem for to be framed and constellated unto all. I am no plant that will not prosper out of a garden; all places, all airs, make unto me one country; I am in England, everywhere, and under any meridian.

Only the 'fool multitude' that chooses by show he holds up to derision as 'that numerous piece of monstrosity, which, taken asunder, seem men, and the reasonable creatures of God; but confused together, make but one great beast, and a monstrosity more prodigious than Hydra'. He has a quick sympathy with the sorrows of others, and, though a physician, his prayer is with the husbandman and for healthful seasons. No one has put more beautifully the feeling which each one of us has had at times about patients:

Let me be sick myself, if sometimes the malady of my patient be not a disease unto me; I desire rather to cure his infirmities than my own necessities; where I do him no good, methinks it is scarce honest gain; though I confess 'tis but the worthy salary of our well-intended endeavours.

He has seen many countries, and has studied their customs and politics. He is well versed in astronomy and botany. He has run through all systems of philosophy but has found no rest in any. As death gives every fool gratis the knowledge which is won in this life with sweat and vexation, he counts it absurd to take pride in his achievements, though he understands six languages besides the patois of several provinces.

As a scientific man Browne does not take rank with many of his contemporaries. He had a keen power of observation, and in the *Pseudodoxia* and in his letters there is abundant evidence that he was an able naturalist. He was the first to observe and describe the peculiar substance known as adipocere, and there are in places shrewd flashes, such as the suggestion that the virus of rabies may be mitigated by transmission from one animal to another. But we miss in him the clear, dry light of science as revealed in the marvellous works of his contemporary, Harvey. Busy as a practical physician, he was an observer, not an experimenter to any extent, though he urges: 'Join sense unto reason and experiment unto speculation, and so give life unto embryon truths and verities yet in their chaos.' He had the highest veneration for Harvey, whose work he recognized as epoch making—'his piece, *De Circul. Sang.*, which discovery I prefer to that of Columbus'. He recognized that in the faculty of observation the old Greeks were our masters, and that we must return to their methods if progress were to be made. He had a much clearer idea than had Sydenham of the value of anatomy, and tells his young friend, Power of Halifax, to make *Autopsia* his *fidus Achates*.

That he should have believed in witches, and that he should have given evidence in 1664 which helped to condemn two poor women, is always spoken of as a blot on his character; but a man must be judged by his times and his surroundings. While regretting his credulity, we must remember how hard it was in the sixteenth and seventeenth centuries not to believe in witches —how hard, indeed, it should be to-day for anyone who believes implicitly the Old Testament!—and men of the stamp of Reginald Scot and Johannes Wierus, who looked at the question from our point of view, were really anomalies, and their strong presentation of the rational side of the problem had very little influence on their contemporaries.

For the student of medicine the writings of Sir Thomas Browne have a very positive value. The charm of high thoughts clad in beautiful language may win some readers to a love of good literature; but beyond this is a still greater advantage. Like the 'Thoughts of Marcus Aurelius' and the *Enchiridion* of Epictetus, the *Religio* is full of counsels of perfection which appeal to the mind of youth, still plastic and unhardened by contact with the world. Carefully studied, from such books come subtle influences which give stability to character and help to give a man a sane outlook on the complex problems of life. Sealed early of this tribe of authors, a student takes with him, as *compagnons de voyage,* lifelong friends whose thoughts become his thoughts and whose ways become his ways. Mastery of self, conscientious devotion to duty, deep human interest in human beings—these best of all lessons you must learn now or never: and these are some of the lessons which may be gleaned from the life and from the writings of Sir Thomas Browne.[1]

[1] Since Osler vainly searched the Leyden register (p. 42), Browne's M.D. has been recognized under the disguise, 'Braun, Thomas, Anglus Londinensis, 3 Dec. 1633'; the Castle Museum MS. (p. 50) is no longer believed to be autograph; and the witches (p. 60) are now known to have been condemned in spite of, not with the help of, Browne's evidence.—ED.

5

GUI PATIN

ONE physician we know thoroughly, and one only—Gui Patin, Dean of the Faculty of Medicine, Paris. His ways and works, his inmost thoughts, his children, his wife, his mother-in-law (!), his friends, his enemies—the latter *very well*—his books and pictures, his likes and dislikes, joys and sorrows, all the details of a long and busy life, are disclosed in a series of unique letters written to his intimates between 1630 and 1672. But this is not a biographical note—I wish only to lodge a protest and to express a hope.

Editions of the famous letters are common, from that of Frankfort, 1683, to the three volumes of Reveillé-Parise, 1846 —fourteen in all, and all imperfect, many garbled. A unique and priceless contribution, general and medical, to the history of the seventeenth century, 'forming', as Triaire says, 'a veritable diary improvised day by day, a mordant chronicle of the times by one of the most brilliant, the most alert, the most spirituel and the most satyric of the period'. The worst possible luck has dogged all attempts to issue a definitive edition. Formey, of the Berlin Academy, in 1770, conceived the design to issue the correspondence complete with notes, but nothing came of it.

The edition of Reveillé-Parise, the only one of the nineteenth century, while a great improvement upon and much fuller than any other, had many errors, and perhaps deserved the severe handling given to it by Sainte-Beuve. MM. de Montaiglon and Tamisey de la Roque had collected material, collated the letters, and had one volume ready when, in 1893, a fire destroyed every page of their manuscripts. Not a whit discouraged by the ill-success of his predecessors, Dr. Paul Triaire, of Tours, already

Between 1912 and 1914 Osler sent twenty-five short notes to the *Canadian Medical Association Journal* under the heading 'Men and Books'. This is number X (*Canad. Med. Ass. J.*, 1912, ii. 429).

well known for his biographical writings, undertook the task, and in 1907 issued one splendid volume containing the letters from 1630 to 1648. As illness overtook him, the work could not be completed, and the death of the accomplished editor has just been announced. It is a sad loss, a calamity in the world of letters.

Now for my protest: it is not often that a Frenchman makes a mistake in matters literary, but there is one Pierre Pic, whom I would like to shake for the disappointment caused by a wretched abortion which has seen the light under the title of *Gui Patin, avec 74 portraits ou documents*, Paris, G. Steinheil, 1911. Pic has the shamefacedness to acknowledge that he does not know much of his subject—'Mais mon bagage à son sujet n'était pas lourd.' This is evident. From two old editions which he has picked up he has sorted various extracts from the letters, but he has never even looked into—so he says, and one can well believe him—the edition of Reveillé-Parise, or the delightful first volume of Triaire with the early letters; and he appears to be ignorant of the important collection of letters in the Bibliothèque Nationale. One is not surprised at his judgement—'Gui Patin has been abominably over-rated. He is a bore. . . .' It is a pity for M. Pic's reputation that he had not left him alone. Had he devoted a little appreciative study to his author, he might have come to the conclusion of his great countryman, Fleurens, who saw the *man* through all his faults:

Gui Patin has really written nothing but his 'letters': and these 'letters', in spite of a boldness of view which is sometimes extreme, in spite of language which is often common, in spite of many errors of judgement, of many prejudices against certain men—these letters are a brilliant expression of a proud and lofty soul, and in them he will live, for there is in them what never dies—style. Gui Patin is the most 'spirituel' doctor who has ever written, unless one includes Rabelais, in whom, however, medicine was hardly more than '*la qualité externe*'.

But the chief object of this note is to make an appeal, to express a hope, that the Paris Faculty will at once arrange for the completion of M. Triaire's edition. Much of the work has been done, and it should not be difficult to find someone with the necessary qualifications. They owe it to the memory of one of the greatest of their deans. When completed, an English edition should be forthcoming. From one of the old editions a translation has already been made by Dr. Blodgett, of Boston, who, at my request, has withheld it from the press awaiting the completion of Triaire's work.

6

ROBERT BURTON

THE MAN, HIS BOOK, HIS LIBRARY

I. THE MAN

MELANCHOLY may be defined as a state of mind in which a man is so out of touch with his environment that life has lost its sweetness. Galen speaks of it as 'a malady that injures the mind, associated with profound depression and aversion from the things one loves best'. Burton himself nowhere defines it, but quotes definitions from Fernelius, Fuchsius, and other authors. And great minds are not free from it: 'nullum magnum ingenium sine mixtura dementiae', says Aristotle; to defend the truth of which thesis Reveillé-Parise has written an interesting monograph. Unfortunately from birth melancholy marks some for her own: those unhappy souls who at every stage smell the mould above the rose, and sing, with Lady Mary Wortley Montagu, 'With toilsome steps I pass thro life's dull road'. From the transitory form, the 'blues' or low spirits, 'no man living', as our author says, 'is

Reprinted from the *Proceedings and Papers of the Oxford Bibliographical Society*, 1925, i. 163–90. In a Prefatory Note Falconer Madan wrote: 'The following three articles by Sir William Osler on Burton's *Anatomy* (the Writer, his Book and his Library) have had diverse fates, and are now printed together and in full for the first time. The original manuscript of all three is in the Osler Library, and has been made use of by Lady Osler's permission. The first two papers were fused into one, with omissions, to form a lecture on Burton's *Anatomy* delivered at Yale, and printed in the *Yale Review* of January 1914 (vol. iii, pp. 251–71). The Proprietors of the Review have kindly given permission for use of the form there printed, which has been compared with the original manuscript and supplemented therefrom, as well as divided into its two original parts. It is in Osler's *Collected Reprints*, vi, no. 304. The third was read before the (London) Bibliographical Society on November 15, 1909, and a summary (only) is printed in the Society's *Transactions*, vol. xi, pp. 4–6, as well as in its News-sheet for December 1909. . . .'

free, no stoic, none so wise, none so happy, none so patient, so generous, so godly, so divine that can vindicate himself; so well composed but more or less some time or other he feels the smart of it'. Life is a mixed glukupicric passion. Into this infernal gulf we must all wade; happy those who do not get beyond the shallows; but when the habit becomes 'a settled humour, a chronic or continuate disease', the unfortunate victim cries aloud with the Psalmist, 'All thy waves and storms have gone over me'.

Of the 'eighty-eight varieties' said to exist, Burton will treat only the severer, inveterate, fixed forms, not the passing melancholy which is more or less a character of mortality. Naturally a malady of such universal prevalence has a literature of corresponding importance. A glance through the titles of the Index Catalogue of the [U.S.A.] Surgeon General's Library gives some idea of its extent in medicine: books, monographs, journal articles by the score have been written on the subject. There is scarcely an ancient author of note who has not dealt with some aspect of it. But among them all, one only has the touchstone of time declared to be of enduring, of supreme, merit; the centuries have made Burton's book a permanent possession of literature.

The main facts of Robert Burton's life are in the book. He was born at Lindley in Leicestershire of a family of which he was justly proud and to the members of which he not infrequently refers in his book. At the end of the 'Digression of Air Rectified', mentioning pleasant high places in England, as [Glastonbury Tower], &c., he speaks of Oldbury 'in the confines of Warwickshire, where I have often looked about me with great delight, at the foot of which hill I was born', and the marginal note[1] adds 'at Lindley in Leicestershire, the possession and dwelling place of Ralph Burton Esquire, my late deceased Father'. The pedigree and full account of the family, which was one of importance, is given very fully in Nichols's *History of Leicestershire*. Possibly it was from his mother that he got his love for the study of medicine. He states that she had 'excellent skill

---

[1] The reference to his father is first found in the 2nd edition, 1624.

in chirurgery, sore eyes, aches, &c., and such experimental medicines, as all the country where she dwelt can witness, to have
done many famous and good cures upon divers poor folks that
were otherwise destitute of help'. He seems delighted to have
found that one of her cures for ague, an amulet of a spider in a
nutshell lapped in silk, was mentioned by Dioscorides and
approved by Matthiolus. He went to school at Nuneaton, as he
states in his Will, and at Sutton Coldfield in Warwickshire, to
the excellent air of which he bears testimony. He had not a
happy school life, and in Part I (2. 4. 2) remarks that he once
thought there was no slavery in the world like that of a Grammar
Scholar. He came fourth in a family of nine children, one of
whom, his elder brother, William, became the distinguished
Leicestershire antiquary. A picture of the home at Lindley is
given in the *Description of Leicestershire* [by W. Burton]; but the
house no longer stands. Robert Burton followed his brother
William, in 1593, to Brasenose College, Oxford, as a commoner.
In 1599 he was elected a Student of Christ Church, which he
calls the most flourishing college of Europe, and where he lived,
as he says, 'a silent, sedentary, solitary, private life', trying to
learn wisdom, 'penned up most part in my study'. He never
travelled, but he took a great delight in the study of cosmography;
and for his recreation he would wander round about the world
in map or card. He had neither wife nor children, good or bad,
to provide for; he was neither rich nor poor; he had little and
wanted nothing. All his treasure was in Minerva's tower. He
was all his life *aquae potor*. He was a mere spectator of others'
fortunes and adventures, and so he rubbed on through his forty-
seven years of college life, '*privus privatus*; as I have still lived,
so I now continue, *statu quo prius*, left to a solitary life, and mine
own domestic discontents; saving that sometimes, *ne quid mentiar*,
as Diogenes went into the city, and Democritus to the haven,
to see fashions, I did for my recreation now and then walk
abroad, look into the world, and could not choose but make
some little observation, *non tam sagax observator ac simplex recitator*,
not as they did to scoff or laugh at all, but with a mixed passion.'

After his appointment at Christ Church, Burton took orders and did the ordinary work of a college tutor. He was also Vicar of St. Thomas's, and from 1630(?) Rector of Segrave in Leicestershire. Unfortunately we do not know his rooms at the House, nor have we any letters or documents from which we could gather a picture of his daily life. Wood's character of him is very happily drawn:

He was an exact mathematician, a curious calculator of nativities, a general read scholar, a thro' pac'd philologist, and one that understood the surveying of lands well. As he was by many accounted a severe student, a devourer of authors, a melancholy and humorous person; so by others, who knew him well, a person of great honesty, plain dealing, and charity. I have heard some of the antients of Christ Church often say, that his company was very merry, facete and juvenile; and no man in his time did surpass him for his ready and dextrous interlarding his common discourses among them with verses from the poets, or sentences from classic authors; which being then all the fashion in the University, made his company more acceptable.

Burton's stay at Christ Church came under the deanships (among others) of Richard Corbet, Brian Duppa, and Samuel Fell, whom he remembers in his Will. That he took an active share in the college life is evidenced by the fact that he wrote many occasional verses and a Latin comedy called *Philosophaster*, which was acted on Shrove Monday, 16 February 1617–18.[1] We may infer from his Will that he was an intimate friend of Dean Fell and his family; and he remembers a number of his friends, so that, though an old bachelor, he was well looked after and doubtless much beloved in the community. His Will indicates also that he was on the best of terms with his family, to whom he left the greater part of his considerable estate. When the melancholy fits increased, 'nothing could make him laugh but going to the bridge-foot and hearing the ribaldry of the bargemen, which rarely failed to throw him into a violent fit of laughter'. He died on the 25th of January 1639–40, very

[1] Printed with Burton's occasional verses, for the Roxburghe Club in 1862. [Also, with English translation, San Francisco, 1931.]

near the time which he had some years before foretold from the
calculation of his nativity; and Wood remarks that this 'being
exact, several of the students did not forbear to whisper among
themselves, that rather than there should be a mistake in the
calculation, he sent up his soul to heaven thro' a slip [noose]
about his neck'. He was buried in the north aisle of Christ
Church Cathedral; and there is a handsome monument with his
bust, painted to the life, and the calculation of his nativity.

II. BURTON'S BOOK, THE 'ANATOMY'

For the writing of the *Anatomy of Melancholy* we have Burton's
full reasons. To escape melancholy he wrote upon it, to ease his
mind, for he had *gravidum cor, fœtum caput,* a kind of imposthume
in his head, of which he was desirous to be unladen, and he
could imagine no fitter evacuation. He calls melancholy his
Mistress, his Egeria; and he would comfort 'one sorrow with
another, idleness with idleness, *ut ex Vipera Theriacum,* make an
antidote out of that which was the prime cause of my disease'.
Many notable authors, he says, have done the same—Tully and
Cardan, for example; and he can speak from experience, and
would help others out of a fellow feeling. Though oppressed
with a vast chaos and confusion of books, so that his eyes ache
with reading and his fingers with turning, and though many
excellent physicians have written elaborate treatises on this subject, he will venture to weave the same web and twist the same
rope again. He has laboriously collected this *cento* out of divers
writers and that *sine injuria*. He can say with Macrobius, '*Omne
meum, nihil meum,* 'tis all mine and none mine'. At any rate, like
an honest man he cites and quotes his authors; but if, as Synesius
says, 'it is a greater offence to steal dead men's labours than their
clothes', what shall become of most authors? He must plead
guilty and hold up his hand at the bar with the rest. Still, the
method and composition is his own and he hopes it shows a
scholar. He realizes that this is a medical subject and that great
exception may be taken that he, a divine, has meddled with
physic. The apology must be given in his own words:

There be many other subjects, I do easily grant, both in humanity and divinity, fit to be treated of, of which had I written *ad ostentationem* only, to show myself, I should have rather chosen, and in which I have been more conversant, I could have more willingly luxuriated, and better satisfied myself and others; but that at this time I was fatally driven upon this rock of melancholy, and carried away by this by-stream, which, as a rillet, is deducted from the main channel of my studies, in which I have pleased and busied myself at idle hours, as a subject most necessary and commodious. Not that I prefer it before Divinity, which I do acknowledge to be the Queen of professions, and to which all the rest are as handmaids, but that in Divinity I saw no such great need. For had I written positively, there be so many books in that kind, so many commentators, treatises, pamphlets, expositions, sermons, that whole teams of oxen cannot draw them; and had I been as forward and ambitious as some others, I might have haply printed a Sermon at Paul's Cross, a Sermon in St. Mary's Oxon, a Sermon in Christ Church, or a Sermon before the Right Honourable, Right Reverend, a Sermon before the Right Worshipful, a Sermon in Latin, in English, a Sermon with a name, a Sermon without, a Sermon, a Sermon, etc. But I have been ever as desirous to suppress my labours in this kind, as others have been to press and publish theirs.

And the physicians, he says, must not feel aggrieved. Have not many of their sect taken orders—Marsilius Ficinus and T. Linacre, for example? And as this melancholy is 'a common infirmity of body and soul', 'a compound mixed malady', in which a divine can do little alone and a physician much less, he hopes it is not unbecoming in one who is by profession a divine, and by inclination a physician, and who was fortunate enough to have Jupiter in his sixth house, to write on the subject. But if the good reader be not satisfied and complains that the discourse is too medicinal or savours too much of humanity, he promises to make amends in some treatise of divinity. All the same, he hopes it may suffice when his reasons and motives are considered—'the generality of the disease, the necessity of the cure, and the commodity or common good that will arise to all men by the knowledge of it'.

The book itself, issued in 1621 in small thick quarto by the Oxford publisher Cripps, has had a chequered career. The first edition is now among the treasures of the bibliophile, and year by year the auction sales tell of its steady appreciation. It was sold at the sale of John Arthur's books in 1683 for three shillings; a good copy now brings from £50 to £60. For the quaint title-page Burton offers a full explanation: 'It is a kind of policy to prefix a phantastical title to a book which is to be sold.' And he cites honourable precedents as Anthony Zara's *Anatomy of Wit*,[1] in four sections, members, subsections, &c. And there were many Anatomies in those days—the Anatomy of Wit by Lilly (1581), Anatomy of Popery, Anatomy of Immortality, Anatomy of the Mass, Anatomy of Antimony, and among his books left to the Bodleian, the Anatomy of the Metamorphoses.

The first two editions have the motto *Omne meum, Nihil meum*, which is replaced in the subsequent editions by the larger one from Horace *Omne tulit punctum qui miscuit utile dulci*.

In explaining the adoption of the pseudonym, 'Democritus Junior', Burton says that he laughed and scoffed with Lucian and again he wept with Heraclitus; and he tells of the visit of Hippocrates to Abdera, where he found Democritus sitting under a shady bower, with a book on his knees, the subject of which was melancholy, and about him lay the carcasses of many beasts newly cut up in order to find the seat of the *atra bilis*, or melancholy, and how it was engendered. As this book is lost, our author undertakes *quasi succenturiator Democriti*, to revive it again, prosecute and finish it in this treatise. Burton's name does not occur in the title-page of any of the seventeenth-century editions; but at the end of the postscript, which is only in the first edition, is the name, Robert Burton, 'from my Studie in Christ Church, Oxon. Decemb. 5, 1620'. His anonymity has been respected in all subsequent editions until the one issued in 1806. The work was dedicated to George, Lord Berkeley, who [in 1630?] presented him with the living of Segrave. It is not surprising that the book at once had a great success: 'The

---

[1] *Anatomia Ingeniorum et Scientiarum*. Venetiis, MDCXV.

first, second, and third editions were suddenly gone, eagerly read', as Burton says in one place, when discussing the peevishness of men's judgements and the diversity of tastes in readers —'Pro captu lectoris habent sua fata libelli.' A lucky fate has followed the *Anatomy*, which has held its readers for wellnigh three centuries.

Five editions of the work appeared during Burton's lifetime. A sixth was issued in 1651, with a statement by Cripps that the author had left many alterations and corrections. A seventh appeared in 1660, and an eighth in 1676. With the exception of the first all were in folio with full page, but the eighth is in double columns. I have seen no eighteenth-century edition [before its last year, 1800]. Watt and Allibone are wrong in giving dates of 1728 and 1738. The studies of that learned physician, Dr. Ferriar of Manchester, had called the attention of writers at the end of the eighteenth century to the merits of Burton, and in his *Illustrations of Sterne* he had shown how this author had plagiarized wholesale from the *Anatomy*. It is not surprising then that a new edition which appeared in 1800 is rightly called the ninth. It is preceded by a Life, and contains a tragical frontispiece of a maniac. Other editions came in 1804, 1806, 1813, 1821, 1824, 1826, 1827, 1829, all in two volumes. In 1836 appeared a single octavo volume, with a reproduction of the famous frontispiece printed for B. Blake. Reissues of this are found in 1837 and 1838. Tegg's edition also, a thick octavo, appeared in 1843, and it too was frequently reprinted, and for the student is perhaps the most convenient edition. It is readily obtained second-hand. In 1893 appeared the three-volume edition edited by Shilleto. It is practically a reprint without any attempt at critical study of the text.[1]

From the second to the sixth edition the work received alterations and corrections from the author. In the second and third

---

[1] Osler overlooked the special features of Shilleto's edition. Shilleto 'was the first to start the labour of tracking the thousands of quotations to their sources and giving precise references'. Tegg's first edition is 1840, see *N. & Q.*, 9th S., i. 42, and *Bibliotheca Osleriana*, no. 7681.

editions these were very extensive, very much less in the fourth
and fifth. The sixth edition which was issued in 1651 is to all
intents a reprint of the 1638 [5th]. Cripps, in a 'Note to the
Reader' prefixed to the sixth edition, states that the ingenious
author left a copy exactly corrected with several additions by his
own hand. Here and there are verbal alterations, but the book
is practically a reprint and, as may readily be seen, the pages
correspond almost word for word; I have noted a few trifling
changes, but there could have been no very accurate revision by
the author, as the statement about the number of years at Christ
Church was not corrected from the fourth edition [of 1632].
Yet at p. 410 of the sixth edition (470 of Tegg) he says he has
added something to this light treatise, 'ut iam sexta vice cala-
mum in manum sumerem'. In earlier editions *tertia, quarta,
quinta* occur, and he begs Arethusa in all editions to smile on
this his 'last' labour.

It is said that Cripps made a large sum of money by the work
—which is very likely. A folio is naturally preferred by the
book-lover (and fortunately is not hard to get). Who will not
sympathize with the remark of Charles Lamb, 'I do not know
a more heartless sight than the reprint of the *Anatomy of Melancholy*. What need was there of unearthing the bones of that
fantastic old great man to expose them in a winding-sheet of
the newest fashion to modern censure? What hapless stationer
could dream of Burton ever becoming popular?' All the same,
Tegg's octavo one-volume edition, or that of 1893 in three
volumes, is very serviceable. It is to be hoped that before long
a proper edition of this classic will appear.

A few [more] remarks may be made upon the differences
and additions in the early editions. The second (1624) is in folio
with the same title-page and the same motto [as the first]. The
postscript is left out, but the material is largely incorporated
with the Introduction. The work is very greatly extended. There
is scarcely a page without additions, more particularly in the
introduction—'Democritus to the Reader'—which is greatly
enlarged. The sermon at the end on Despair was added at the

request of his brother, George Burton, and the author's quondam chamber-fellow and late fellow Student at Christ Church, James Whitehall. The third edition (1628) had a great many minor alterations in the text, and there are two special additions, the verses[1] and the engraved title-page, which appear in all the subsequent seventeenth-century editions. In the fourth edition there is very little change; only a few sentences added here and there, and in stating the length of time he has lived at Christ Church, he adds the additional years since the publication of the third edition. He had said in the third edition that he was resolved never to put this treatise out again, and that he would not alter, add, or retract; that he had done with it: and to all intents and purposes this is the case. The index, never a very satisfactory one, appears for the first time in the second edition, and Burton made a few alterations in the fourth and fifth.

The frontispiece is one of the most Burtonian features of the work. In the absence of information as to its origin, we may well suppose that the author himself prepared the design, which was carried out by a little-known engraver of the time, Charles Le Blon. The upper centre figure represents Democritus of Abdera as Hippocrates found him sitting in a garden in the suburbs with a book on his lap. Borage is growing in the garden, and on the wall there are pictures of animals—the cats and dogs of which he has made anatomy. The sign of Saturn is in the sky. To the left is a landscape of jealousy, and there are two fighting cocks (evidently bantams), a swan, a heron, and a kingfisher; and the verses state that there are two roaring bulls to be seen, but they are not visible in any of my folios. For the frontispiece of Tegg's edition, the engraver has taken liberties, as he has left out the fighting cocks and put in the tail, at any rate, of one of the bulls. A bird and a bat and a section of the moon appear in the sky. The third section at the top represents solitariness— animals alone in the desert with bats and owls hovering over them. In the next section is Inamorato inditing a ditty:

[1] The verse-argument of the Frontispiece first occurs in the *fourth* edition (1632).

> His lute and books about him lie,
> As symptoms of his vanity.
> If this do not enough disclose,
> To paint him, take thyself by th' nose.

Opposite is the Hypochondriac:

> About him pots and glasses lie,
> Newly brought from 's apothecary.
> This Saturn's aspects signify,
> You see them portray'd in the sky.

The next section represents the superstitious man, and opposite him is the madman naked in chains—a ghastly sight. Then below at the lower corners are the borage and hellebore, which were the 'Soveraign plants to purge the veins Of Melancholy' and, if well assayed, 'The best medicine that ere God made For this malady'. And lastly, a portrait of the author, which the verses tell us shows the habit which he wore and his image as he appeared to the world, though his mind would have to be guessed by his writings. It was neither pride nor vainglory made him put his picture here, but 'The Printer would needs have it so'.

To use his own expression, Burton was a minion of the Muses. I have already mentioned that his play, *Philosophaster*, was acted at Christ Church, and that there are a number of his occasional verses in the college collections of the period. In the third edition of the *Anatomy*, 1628, appeared the well-known poem on melancholy, the author's address to his book, and in 1632 the verses on the frontispiece. The poem presents all the shifting phases of this sweet and bitter passion in alternate verses of praise and condemnation. Let me quote the first and the last of the twelve stanzas. The first runs:

> When I go musing all alone,
> Thinking of divers things fore-known,
> When I build castles in the air,
> Void of sorrow and void of fear,
> Pleasing myself with phantasms sweet,
> Methinks the time runs very fleet.
> All my joys to this are folly,
> Naught so sweet as Melancholy.

And then the other picture:

> I'll change my state with any wretch,
> Thou canst from gaol or dunghill fetch;
> My pain's past cure, another hell,
> I may not in this torment dwell!
> Now desperate I hate my life,
> Lend me a halter or a knife.
> All my griefs to this are jolly,
> Naught so damn'd as Melancholy.

Warton remarked upon the similarity of idea in the contrast between these two dispositions in Milton's famous poems, *L'Allegro* and *Il Penseroso*—the 'Hence loathèd Melancholy', in the one, and the 'Hail! thou Goddess sage and holy, Hail! divinest Melancholy', in the other; and the antithesis maintained throughout the two poems may possibly have been suggested to Milton by the lines of Burton.

With appropriate verses, Democritus Junior sends his book into the open day, hoping its pleasant vein may save those who con its lore in city—or country—from twitches of care. Surely Catos will not love it, and grand dames will cry 'Pish!' and frown and yet read on. For dainty damsels, whom he confesses to love dear as life, he would spread his best stores. The melancholy wight or pensive lover will in its pages find himself in clover and gain both sense and laughter. The learned leech may find here no trifling prize, but to the crafty lawyer he cries 'Caitiff, avaunt!' Of his faults he asks the ripe scholar to be oblivious, but not refuse praise to his merit, in lines which have the ring of Matt Prior. Flippant spouter and empty prater will search his pages for polished words and verse; and the doggerel poet, his brother, is welcome to the jests and stories. He will fly from, and not reply to, sour critics and Scotch reviewers. To the friendly though severe censor who complains of his free and even licentious vein, he pleads with Catullus that his life is pure beyond the breath of scandal, and in any case he is ever willing to be improved by censure.[1]

[1] In the foregoing paragraph, as Professor Bensly points out, Osler is

Few writers show such familiarity as Burton with poetry ancient and modern; and his books at Christ Church and the Bodleian testify to his fondness for literature of this class. There are those who hold that Francis Bacon not only wrote Shakespeare's plays and Spenser's *Faerie Queene,* but also Burton's *Anatomy of Melancholy.* With the biliteral cipher, the whole story of Queen Elizabeth, Essex, and Bacon may be found in the pages of Democritus Junior! Is it not just as reasonable to suppose, as Mr. [George] Parker of Oxford suggested,[1] that Burton himself wrote the plays of Shakespeare? Does he not quote him several times, and are there not fine original editions of *Venus and Adonis* and *The Rape of Lucrece* among his books in the Bodleian?

The *Anatomy of Melancholy* consists of a long introduction, the subject-matter of melancholy, and three long digressions. The introduction occupies about one-tenth of the book. Burton states that he has had to do the whole business himself, that the book was composed out of a confused company of notes, that he had not time to lick it into shape as a bear does her whelps, and it was writ with as small deliberation as he ordinarily spoke, without any affectation of big words. He is, he says, a loose, plain, rude writer, and as free as loose. He calls a spade a spade, and his wit lacks the stimulus of wine, as he was a water-drinker. He warns those who are melancholy not to read the symptoms or prognosis, lest they should appropriate the things there spoken to their person and get more harm than good.

Then he is transported in imagination with Cyprian and Jerome to some place where he can view the whole world. He finds that 'kingdoms and provinces are melancholy, cities and families, all creatures, vegetall, sensible and rationall; that all sorts, sects, ages, conditions are out of tune'. He promises to bring arguments to show that most men are mad and have more need of a pilgrimage to the Anticyrae than to Loretto, more

making some use of a modern paraphrastic rendering of Burton's Latin verses, as if Burton's own. 'Scotch reviewers', for instance, and other expressions do not correspond to anything in the original.
[1] See *Bodleian Quarterly Record*, vol. ii, p. 102, 1918 (Mr. Horr's theory).

need of hellebore than of tobacco. And this he proceeds to prove abundantly from the Scriptures and from the writers of all time. Incidentally he gives the interesting story, probably apocryphal, of the visit of Hippocrates to Democritus. If the sage of Abdera could return and see the religious follies, the bloody wars, the injustice, the oppression, he would think us as mad as his fellow townsmen. Page after page he piles up with illustrations of human folly, and asks every now and then how would Democritus have been confounded. Would he think you or any man else well in their wits? Can all the hellebore in the Anticyrae cure these men—no, sure—an acre of hellebore alone could do it!

Then he descends to particulars, and heaps up examples drawn from every possible source. Coming to England, he speaks of its flourishing condition, and its many particular advantages, and then proceeds to speak of the evils, and remarks that idleness is the evil genius of the nation. Burton was a warm advocate for home industries, a tariff reformer, and would not allow England to be made a dumping-ground for foreign manufactures. The paragraph is worth quoting: 'We send our best commodities beyond the seas, which they make good use of to their necessities, set themselves a work about, and severally improve, sending the same to us back at dear rates; or else make toys and baubles of the tails of them, which they sell to us again, at as great a reckoning as they bought the whole.' He is full of sensible suggestions about the improvements of roads, and the drainage of bad lands, and the neglect of the navigable rivers. Following the example of Plato and of More, he sketches his own Utopia, a new Atlantis, a poetical commonwealth. As his predecessor, Democritus, was a politician and recorder of Abdera, why should not he presume to do as much? Then follows a delightful sketch, based in part upon More's *Utopia* and full of common-sense, practical suggestions. He is a strong advocate for old-age pensions. Why should a smith, a carpenter, a husbandman, who has spent his time in continual labour and without whom we cannot live—why should he be left in his old age to beg or starve and lead a miserable life? The introduction ends with a serio-comical address to the reader, saying if he is denied this liberty of speech he will take it; he owes him nothing, he looks for no favour at his hand, he is independent, and may say anything he wishes in the guise of Democritus. Then of a sudden he comes to himself: 'No, I recant, I will not, I care, I fear, I confess my fault, acknowledge a great offence'; and he promises a more sober discourse in the future. In a later edition a small section of a few lines follows the introduction, in which Burton again admonishes the careless reader, not to asperse, calumniate, or slander Democritus Junior; and this is followed by five Latin elegiac couplets, in which he concludes that a thousand Heraclituses and a thousand Democrituses are needed, and that all the world must be sent to the Anticyrae to graze on helle-bore.

The treatise itself is divided into three main partitions, and each of these into sections, members, and subsections. A synopsis precedes each partition, bristling with the brackets which learned writers in his time loved to use. There are many books written entirely in this synoptical way, and Burton had many models in his own library. This is a feature of the book which at once attracts attention and is, I believe, unique among books reprinted at the present day. It is impossible to give more than the briefest sketch of the way in which Burton deals with the subject; but the first partition is taken up almost entirely with the causes, symptoms, and prognostics of melancholy. The second partition deals with the cure, and the third with love melancholy and religious melancholy. Three important digressions occur, on anatomy, on air rectified, and on the nature of spirits.

The anatomy and physiology are those of the early part of the seventeenth century before the great discovery by Harvey; and it is remarkable that in the fourth or fifth edition he did not refer to the circulation of the blood. The four humours of the body—blood, phlegm, bile, and serum—play an important part, particularly the black bile which was supposed to cause melan-choly. The natural, vital, and animal spirits of the old writers are everywhere evident. The subject is treated in a most systematic manner, and nothing could be more irrational than the criticism of Hallam that the volumes are apparently 'a great sweeping of miscellaneous literature from the Bodleian library'. As it is difficult to make a proper division of melancholy, Burton first deals with the subject in a general manner and then proceeds to speak of the particular species—head melancholy, hypochondriacal melancholy, and melancholy from the whole body. The third partition, as was said, is devoted entirely to the subjects of love and religious melancholy. The causes are discussed at great length and under fifteen subsections, ranging from bad diet to over-much study. This part of the work is really a psychological treatise with illustrations from history and literature. A most attractive section is on the love of learning as a cause, with a digression on the misery of scholars. For two main reasons students are more subject than others to this malady—the sedentary, solitary life in which health is neglected, and continuous meditation in the head, which leaves the stomach and liver destitute. The symptoms and prognosis are dealt with at great length.

About one-fourth of the work—the second partition—is taken up with the cure of melancholy. This is a strictly medical treatise, in which the author has collected all the known information about the treatment of mental disorders; the entire pharmacopoeia is brought in, and Burton writes prescriptions like a physician. There is scarcely a medical author of note who is not quoted. It is in this section that there occurs the delightful digression on air rectified, the first English tractate on climatology. Burton here shows that he was a great student of geography and revelled in travellers' tales. He starts off in a most characteristic way:

As a long-winged Hawk, when he is first whistled off the fist, mounts aloft, and for his pleasure fetcheth many a circuit in the Air, still soaring higher and higher till he be come to his full pitch, and in the end, when the game is sprung, comes down amain, and stoops upon a sudden: so will I, having now come at last into these ample fields of Air, wherein I may freely expatiate and exercise myself for my recreation, a while rove, wander round about the world, mount aloft to those ethereal orbs and celestial spheres, and so descend to my former elements again. In which progress I will first see whether that relation of the friar of *Oxford* be true, concerning those northern parts under the Pole (if I meet *obiter* with the wandering *Jew*, *Elias Artifex*, or *Lucian's Icaromenippus*, they shall be my guides), whether there be such *four Euripuses*, and a great rock of Loadstones which may cause the needle in the Compass still to bend that way, and what should be the true cause of the variation of the Compass. Is it a magnetical rock, or the pole-star, as *Cardan* will?

One would scarcely have expected from a Student of Christ Church, much less from an old bachelor and a divine, the most elaborate treatise on love that has ever been written. It is not surprising that Burton apologizes that many will think the subject too light for a divine and too comical a subject, fit only for a wanton poet or some idle person; but he declares that an old, grave, discreet man is fittest to discourse of love matters, that he has had more experience, has a more staid judgement, and can give better cautions and more solid precepts. He says:

I will examine all the kinds of Love, his nature, beginning, difference, objects, how it is honest or dishonest, a virtue or vice, a natural passion or a disease, his power and effects, how far it extends: of which, although something hath been said in the first partition, in those sections of Perturbations (for Love and hatred are the first and most common passions, from which all the rest arise, and are attendant, as *Piccolomineus* holds, or as *Nich. Caussinus*, the *primum mobile* of all other affections, which carry them all about them), I will now more copiously dilate, through all his parts and several branches, that so it may better appear what Love is, and how it varies with the objects, how in defect, or (which is most ordinary and common) immoderate, and in excess, causeth melancholy.

And he keeps his promise.

There is no such collection of stories of love and its effect in all literature; no such tribute to the power of beauty; no such picture of the artificial allurements; no such representations of its power of debasement. And what a section on jealousy!—

its causes, its symptoms, and its cure. One could almost write
the history of every noted woman from his pages:

> All the golden
> Names of olden
> Women yet by men's love cherished.

Burton says that after the harsh and unpleasant discourse of
melancholy which had molested the patience of the reader and
tired the author, he will ask leave to recreate himself in this
kind, and promises to tell such pretty stories that foul befall
him that is not well pleased with them. Nor does he propose to
mince matters: 'He will call a spade a spade, and will sound all
the depths of this inordinate love of ours, which nothing can
withstand or stave off.' All the love stories, pure and impure,
of literature are here. Jacob and Rachel, Sichem and Dinah,
Judah and Tamar, Samson and Delilah, David and Bathsheba,
Am[n]on and Tamar; the stories of Esther, Judith, and Susannah;
the loves of the Gods—the fopperies of Mars and Venus, of
Neptune and Amymone; Jupiter and his amorous escapades.
Modest Matilda, Pretty Pleasing Peg, Sweet Singing Susan,
Mincing Merry Moll, Dainty Dancing Doll, Neat Nancy, Jolly
Joan, Nimble Nell, Kissing Kate, Bouncing Bess with black
eyes, Fair Phyllis with fine white hands—all flit across Burton's
pages as he depicts the vagaries of the great passion, not a single
aspect of which is omitted.

Religious melancholy is a form which Burton made peculiarly
his own. Many writers had dealt with other aspects of the subject,
but he very rightly says of religious melancholy: In this 'I have
no pattern to follow, no man to imitate. No physician hath as
yet distinctly written of it, as of the other.' Then he deals with
the varied effects of religion in a remarkable way. He says:

Give me but a little leave, and I will set before your eyes in brief
a stupendous, vast, infinite ocean of incredible madness and folly: a
sea full of shelves and rocks, sands, gulfs, Euripuses and contrary tides,
full of fearful monsters, uncouth shapes, roaring waves, tempests,
and Siren calms, halcyonian seas, unspeakable misery; such comedies

and tragedies, such absurd and ridiculous, feral and lamentable fits, that I know not whether they are more to be pitied or derided, or may be believed, but that we daily see the same still practised in our days, fresh examples, *nova novitia*, fresh objects of misery and madness, in this kind, that are still represented to us, abroad, at home, in the midst of us, in our bosoms.

Heretics, old and new, schismatics, schoolmen, prophets, enthusiasts, martyrs, are all discussed, with their several vagaries. This section concludes with the address to those who are in a state of religious despair, written at the instigation of his brother.

Though it smells of the lamp, 'The Anatomy' has a peculiar fragrance of its own, blended with that aroma so dear to the student of old times which suggests the alcoves in Duke Humphrey or the benches at Merton Library. Burton himself acknowledges that he is largely the purveyor of other men's wits; but, as he says, he has wronged no author and given every man his own. He is certainly the greatest borrower in literature. Others perhaps have borrowed nearly as freely, but have concealed it. He has not the art of Ben Jonson, in whose *Discoveries* whole sentences from authors are woven together with such great skill that it is only lately that both thoughts and form have been assigned to their lawful owners. A careless reader might suppose that certain sections represented what Lowell called

> A mire ankle deep of deliberate confusion
> Made up of old jumbles of classic allusion,—

but one has not to go far before seeing a method in this apparent confusion; and the quotations are marshalled in telling order. Page after page of the *Anatomy* is made up of what Milton would call 'horse loads of citations', the opinions of authors in their own words, Burton acting as a conjunction. Take, for example, a page which I opened at random—p. 300 of Tegg's edition. There are twenty-one references covering the whole range of ancient and modern learning. The Bible, the Fathers of the Church, particularly St. Augustine; the fathers of medicine, Hippocrates, Galen, the Alexandrians, the Arabians, and every sixteenth-century medical writer of note; Plato, Aristotle, Seneca, the poets of all ages, the travellers in all climes, the mystical writers, the encyclopaedists—all are laid under contribution in this vast emporium. Well indeed could he say—'non meus hic sermo —'tis not my speech.' What has become of his common-place books? He says that the book was first written 'in an extemporaneous style . . . out of a confused company of notes'. In no copies of the early editions can I find marginal notes, and there are very few in his books at Christ Church and in the Bodleian.

His own style is often delightful, and one cannot but regret that we have not more of Burton and less of Bodley. An apology which he makes gives a good idea of his vigour:

And for those other faults of barbarism, Doric dialect, extempora-nean style, tautologies, apish imitation, a rhapsody of rags gathered together from several dung-hills, excrements of authors, toys and fopperies confusedly tumbled out, without art, invention, judgement, wit, learning, harsh, raw, rude, phantastical, absurd, insolent, indis-creet, ill-composed, indigested, vain, scurrile, idle, dull, and dry; I confess all ('tis partly affected), thou canst not think worse of me than I do of myself. 'Tis not worth the reading, I yield it, I desire thee not to lose time in perusing so vain a subject, I should be per-adventure loath myself to read him or thee so writing.

In another place he says that he is studying entirely to inform his reader's understanding, not to please his ear:

So that as a river runs, sometimes precipitate and swift, then dull and slow; now direct, then *per ambages*; now deep, then shallow; now muddy, then clear; now broad, then narrow; doth my style flow: now serious, then light; now comical, then satirical; now more elaborate, then remiss, as the present subject required, or as at that time I was affected. And if thou vouchsafe to read this treatise, it shall seem no otherwise to thee, than the way to an ordinary traveller, sometimes fair, sometimes foul, here champaign, there enclosed; barren in one place, better soil in another: by woods, groves, hills, dales, plains, &c.

The result is that Burton often tells a story in a charming fashion. I do not know that there is anything much better in

literature than the following tale of the poor scholar who would
become a prebendary, a cathedral official with a good stipend:

In *Moronia Pia*, or *Moronia Felix*, I know not whether, nor how long
since, nor in what Cathedral Church, a fat prebend fell void. The
carcass scarce cold, many suitors were up in an instant. The first had
rich friends, a good purse, and he was resolved to outbid any man
before he would lose it, every man supposed he should carry it. The
second was my Lord Bishop's chaplain (in whose gift it was) and he
thought it his due to have it. The third was nobly born, and he
meant to get it by his great parents, patrons, and allies. The fourth
stood upon his worth, he had newly found out strange mysteries in
chemistry, and other rare inventions, which he would detect to the
public good. The fifth was a painful preacher, and he was com-
mended by the whole parish where he dwelt, he had all their hands
to his certificate. The sixth was the prebendary's son lately deceased,
his father died in debt (for it, as they say), left a wife and many poor
children. The seventh stood upon fair promises, which to him and
his noble friends had been formerly made for the next place in his
lordship's gift. The eighth pretended great losses, and what he had
suffered for the Church, what pains he had taken at home and
abroad, and besides, he brought noblemen's letters. The ninth had
married a kinswoman, and he sent his wife to sue for him. The tenth
was a foreign doctor, a late convert, and wanted means. The eleventh
would exchange for another, he did not like the former's site, could
not agree with his neighbours and fellows upon any terms, he would
be gone. The twelfth and last was (a suitor in conceit) a right honest,
civil, sober, man, an excellent scholar, and such a one as lived private
in the university, but he had neither means nor money to compass it;
besides, he hated all such courses, he could not speak for himself, neither
had he any friends to solicit his cause, and therefore made no suit, could
not expect, neither did he hope for, or look after it. The good Bishop,
amongst a jury of competitors thus perplexed, and not yet resolved
what to do, or on whom to bestow it, at the last, of his own accord,
mere motion, and bountiful nature, gave it freely to the university
student, altogether unknown to him but by fame; and, to be brief,
the academical scholar had the prebend sent him for a present. The
news was no sooner published abroad but all good students rejoiced,
and were much cheered up with it, though some would not believe

it; others, as men amazed, said it was a miracle; but one amongst the rest thanked God for it, and said, *Nunc iuvat tandem studiosum esse, et Deo integro corde servire* [i.e. At last there is some advantage in being studious, and in serving God with integrity!] You have heard my tale, but alas! it is but a tale, a mere fiction, 'twas never so, never like to be, and so let it rest. [II. 3. 7.]

No book of any language presents such a stage of moving pictures—kings and queens in their greatness and in their glory, in their madness and in their despair; generals and conquerors with their ambitions and their activities; the princes of the Church in their pride and in their shame; philosophers of all ages, now rejoicing in the power of intellect, and again grovelling before the idols of the tribe; the heroes of the race who have fought the battle of the oppressed in all lands; criminals, small and great, from the petty thief to Nero with his unspeakable atrocities; the great navigators and explorers with whom Burton travelled so much in map and card, and whose stories were his delight; the martyrs and the virgins of all religions, the deluded and fanatics of all theologies; the possessed of devils and the possessed of God; the beauties, frail and faithful, the Helens and the Lucretias, all are there. The lovers, old and young; the fools who were accounted wise, and the wise who were really fools; the madmen of all history, to anatomize whom is the special object of the book; the world itself, against which he brings a railing accusation—the motley procession of humanity sweeps before us on his stage, a fantastic but fascinating medley at which he does not know whether to weep or to laugh.

Which age of the world has been most subject to this feral passion, so graphically portrayed by Burton, is a question to be asked but not easily answered. I believe that the improved conditions of modern life have added enormously to the world's cheerfulness. Few now sigh for love, fewer still for money; and it is no longer fashionable to air our sorrows in public. In spite of this, the worries and stress of business, the pangs of misprized love, the anguish of religious despair, make an increasing number of unhappy ones choose death rather than a bitter life. With the exception of a monograph by the great Dean of St. Paul's,[1] I know of no more interesting discussion on Suicide than that with which the first part of the book closes. Only one who had himself made the descent into the hell could have written the tender passage with which the section closes:

Thus of their goods and bodies we can dispose; but what shall become of their souls, God alone can tell; his mercy may come *inter pontem et fontem, inter gladium et jugulum*, betwixt the bridge and the brook, the knife and the throat. *Quod cuiquam contigit, cuivis potest.* Who knows how he may be tempted? It is his case, it may be thine. *Quae sua sors hodie est, cras fore vestra potest.* We ought not to be so rash and rigorous in our censures, as some are; charity will judge and hope the best: God be merciful unto us all.

The greatest gift that nature or grace can bestow upon a man is the *aequus animus*, the even-balanced soul; but unfortunately nature rather than grace, disposition rather than education, determines its existence. I cannot agree with William King, the last of the Oxford Jacobites, in his assertion that it is not to be acquired. On the contrary, I maintain that much may be done to cultivate a cheerful heart, but we must begin young if we are to have the Grecian rather than the Hebrew outlook on life.

A recognition of the possible depths of this affection should make us bear with a light heart those transient and unavoidable disappointments in life which we are rather apt to nurse than to shake off with a smile. With the prayer of Themistocles for forgetfulness on our lips, let us bury the worries of yesterday in the work of to-day. Some little tincture of Saturn may be allowed in our hearts, but never in our faces. Sorrow and sadness must come to each one—it is our lot:

> We look before and after
>   And pine for what is not:
> Our sincerest laughter
>   With some pain is fraught;
> Our sweetest songs are those that tell of saddest thought.

[1] Dr. John Donne.

We can best oppose any tendency to melancholy by an active life of unselfish devotion to others; and with the advice with which Burton ends the book, I will close:

'Give not way to solitariness and idleness . . .
Sperate Miseri;
Cavete Fœlices.'

(If unhappy, have hope;
If happy, be cautious.)

III. THE LIBRARY OF ROBERT BURTON

The buried libraries in which Oxford is so rich recall the memories of the great collectors, as Rawlinson, Gough, and Douce; princely bishops like Laud; great lawyers like Selden; wise students like Malone; errant sons like Kenelm Digby. They make the Bodleian what it is, and it is no slight merit of the University and College Libraries to keep alive the names of grateful sons who have left their treasures to Alma Mater.

Naturally great interest surrounds the library of the Anatomist of Melancholy, of whose immortal work more truly than of any other it may be said that it is a mine of quotations.

In 1599 there migrated from Brasenose College to Christ Church Robert Burton, aged 22, a member of a good Leicester-shire family, whose brother William, also a Brasenose man, is still remembered as the author of a work on the antiquities of his native county. Robert thus epitomizes his life:

I have lived a silent, sedentary, solitary, private life, *mihi et musis* in the University, as long almost as Xenocrates in Athens, *ad senectam fere*, to learn wisdom as he did, penned up most part in my study. For I have been brought up a student in the most flourishing College in Europe, *augustissimo collegio*, and can brag with Jovius, almost, *in ea luce domicilii Vaticani, totius orbis celeberrimi, per 37 annos multa opportunaque didici*; for thirty years I have continued (having the use of as good libraries as ever he had) a scholar, and would be therefore loth, either by living as a drone, to be an unprofitable or unworthy member of so learned and noble a society, or to write that which should be any way dishonourable to such a royal and ample foundation.

The libraries to which he refers were the Bodleian, of which his friend Rous was the Keeper, and (as a foot-note mentions) the Christ Church library, which he says had been lately revived by Otho Nicholson.

Though a College Tutor [and Librarian], and Vicar of St. Thomas's, he confesses to a roving humour, and like a ranging spaniel that barks at any bird he sees, leaving his game he has followed all saving that which he should. He has read many books, but to little purpose for want of good method, tumbling over confusedly the divers authors with small profit for want of order, memory, and judgement. With a competency he lived the monastic life of a collegiate student, sequestered from the tumults and troubles of the world, a mere spectator of other men's fortunes and adventures; and so, to continue the abstract, he rubbed on *privus privatus*, occasionally going abroad into the world and making some little observations, now laughing and scoffing with Lucian, and again lamenting with Heraclitus. Such a description would fit many a college Don to-day; but Burton had the misfortune, for us the good fortune, to have Saturn as lord of his geniture; and, fatally driven as he says upon the rock of melancholy, to ease his mind and comfort one sorrow with another, idleness with idleness, to make an antidote out of that which was the prime cause of his disease, he composed the *Anatomy of Melancholy*. Undertaken partly to do himself good, partly out of a fellow feeling for others, he spent his time and knowledge in laboriously collecting out of the vast chaos and confusion of books a *cento* for the consolation of the afflicted in spirit. That which others heard and read of he had felt and practised himself; they got their knowledge by books, he his by melancholizing.

For forty years he lived in Christ Church, dying on the 25th of January 1639/40, very near the time which he had some years before foretold from the calculation of his nativity. Wood remarks that this 'being exact, several of the students did not forbear to whisper among themselves, that rather than there should be a mistake in the calculation, he sent up his soul to heaven thro' a slip [noose] about his neck'. The inscription, his own composition, on his tomb at Christ Church bears out the suggestion.

> Paucis notus, paucioribus ignotus,
> Hic jacet DEMOCRITUS junior
> Cui vitam dedit et mortem
> Melancholia.

To appreciate the character of his library a word must be said upon the *Anatomy of Melancholy*, which, much misunderstood and misinterpreted, has been thought to be only

> A mire ankle deep of deliberate confusion
> Made up of old jumbles of classic allusion.

A medical treatise, the greatest indeed written by a layman, it deals with all types and forms of mental aberration. Though called by the author a *cento*, a patchwork, this is by no means a correct designation, for the *Anatomy* is orderly in arrangement, serious in purpose, and weighty beyond belief with authorities. Scores of works on the subject written by seventeenth-century worthies more learned than Burton have long since sunk in the ooze; neither system, matter, nor form has sufficed to float them to our day. Nor would the *Anatomy* have survived the first edition if its vitality had depended on the professional picture; but Burton enriched a subject of universal interest with deep human sympathy, in which soil the roots have struck so deep that the book still lives.

Just as every man is a quotation from his ancestors, so, says Emerson, is every book a quotation, but of no work in any language is this so literally true as of the *Anatomy of Melancholy*. Burton wrought from his daily reading illustrative passages to serve his turn, but borrowed so profusely that the author is everywhere obscured by his quotations—one cannot see the wood for the trees. Montaigne, whose *Essays* Burton knew, though not so deeply as often to quote, apologizes for his borrowed ornaments, attributing them to idleness, and the humour of age. Burton's *cento* is collected from others *sine injuria*, as he says, and, honest man, when he cites he quotes his authors, unlike in this respect his great contemporary Ben Jonson, whose *Discoveries* turn out to be in great part wholesale loans taken from other writers by an ingenious method of adaptation and translation. Only the man who has written much can appreciate the truth of the remark: 'Das Beste was er ist verdankt er Andern'.

The *Anatomy of Melancholy* appeared in a small quarto form in 1621; subsequent editions appeared in 1624, 1628, 1632, 1638, 1651, 1660, and 1676. The second and third received many, the fourth and fifth a few additions from the author's hand. So laden with quotations is the *Anatomy* that it has been called 'The Sweepings of the Bodleian'. Though, as I said, it is in the first place a medical treatise, it is much more, for so roving a humour had Burton, that he levied upon all literature, ancient and modern, sacred and profane.

From an appendix to his Will, dated 15 August 1639, we learn of the disposal of his library in the following terms:

If I have any books the University Library hath not, let them take them. If I have any books our own library hath not, let them take them. I give to Mrs. Fell all my English books of husbandry, one excepted. . . . To Mrs. Iles my Gerard's Herball, to Mrs. Morris my Country Farme translated out of French, and all my English Physick Books. . . . To all my fellow students Master in Arts a book in fol. or two apiece, as Master Morris Treasurer or Mr. Dean shall appoint, whom I request to be the overseer of this appendix and give him for his pains Atlas Geografer and Ortelius Theatrum Mundi. . . . To Thomas Iles, Doctor Iles his son, student, Salmuth's Panciroli and Lucian's works in four tomes. If any books be left, let my executors dispose of them, with all such books as are written with my own hands, and half my *Melancholy* Copy, for Crips hath the other half. To Mr. Jones Chaplin and Chanter my surveying books and instruments.

The note of the books thus acquired by the Bodleian is given under the date 1639, the entry of which is in Rous's own handwriting. The list in the Benefaction Book is followed by this sentence: 'Porro [dono dedit] comoediarum, tragediarum, et schediasmatum ludicrorum (praesertim idiomate vernaculo) aliquot centurias, quas propter multitudinem, non adjecimus.' Macray in his *Annals of the Bodleian Library*, speaking of the lighter works in Burton's collection, says they were just the classes of books, the admission of which the Founder had almost prohibited, namely, 'Almanacks, plays and an infinite number that are daily printed'. 'Even if some little profit might be reaped (which God knows is very little) out of some of our play-books, the benefit thereof will nothing near countervail the harm that the scandal will bring upon the Library, when it shall be given out that we stuffed it full of baggage books.' In consequence of this well-meant but mistaken resolution, the Library was bare of just those books which Burton's collection could afford, and which now form some of its rarest and most curious divisions. The books have remained undisturbed, a few in the Duke Humphrey's portion of the Library, but most in the Arts and Selden Ends. Not collected together, the identity of a large proportion of them might easily have been lost, had Burton not followed the useful custom of writing his name or initials on each volume. Mr. R. A. Abrams has collected them for me, and the individual titles extend to 581 in number. Christ Church, which took what the Bodleian did not want, received in all 473 books. With the permission of the Governing Body of the College I have had them placed in one portion of the Library, surrounding a copy of the Brasenose portrait of their owner.

Before speaking of Burton's Books it may be well to refer to his signature, by which they have been so readily identified. The name is always written on the title-page, usually across the middle, and either 'Robertus Burton', frequently followed by 'ex Aede Christi'; sometimes 'R. Burton', or 'Ro: Burton', or 'R. B.' Most frequently the name is written out in full. Almost without exception at the bottom of the page there is a curious mark, a sort of hieroglyphic or cypher, which Mr. Madan tells me has usually been supposed to represent the three 'R's' in his name joined together.[1] I have had a number of the forms photographed. As a rule the three letters are united, but in a few cases only the upper two, and sometimes all three may be seen to be separate. There is often a dot in the middle. He had begun using his personal mark quite early, as it occurs in a book which he had purchased in 1600; and also in one purchased on 9 October 1594, while he was still an undergraduate at Brasenose. In one of these early copies there are four of the hieroglyphics, three at one corner, and the other in the usual situation at the bottom of the page. Now and then a Burton book turns up at Sotheby's, readily identified by the initials and cypher.

Burton was not a copious annotator. In his books, all of which have been looked over, scraps of writing occur here and there, usually in the form of marginal notes, which are more frequent perhaps in the medical books. In one or two there are prescriptions, or lists of references to pages. On the whole there is very little writing of any moment. On a blank leaf of a volume of memorial verses there is an obituary verse for the tomb of King James. Burton as is well known wrote poems, the best of which is his Abstract of Melancholy, published in the *Anatomy*. He contributed also to the Memorial volumes of verse issued by members of the University on the occasions of the deaths of Elizabeth and James. His play *Philosophaster* was published by the Roxburghe Club in 1862, the MS. of which, once in the possession of the Regius Professor of Greek, has now gone to America.[2] The only book with any large amount of writing in it (4° R 9 Art., Bodleian), an astronomical work of Ptolemy, is dated in Burton's writing 1603, and has a long list of astronomers from Adam who comes first in order; an extract from a letter from Dr. Dee to Mercator; three folios of astronomical writing by Dee himself; a number of astrological notes; a horoscope of Queen Elizabeth; and, most important of all, Burton's

---

[1] RobeRt ⎫ but the late Dr. P. H. Aitken suggested a reference to the buRton ⎭ three talbots' heads in Burton's arms, R being *littera canina*: see the *Athenaeum*, 1912, p. 13.

[2] A second MS. was sold in the Mostyn Sale in 1920.

own horoscope, practically the same as that on his monument in Christ Church.

With but few exceptions the sources of the Burton river are easily traced, and they drain the whole territory of literature, ancient and modern, sacred and profane, only a trifling portion of which is now represented in Burton's own library. Professor Bensly, who has made a very thorough study of the sources of the *Anatomy*, groups them as follows:

Medical writers of all periods, and scientific works; the Bible, the Fathers, theologians; Greek and Latin classics (the former 'cited out of their interpreters'): some few are largely or wholly neglected, such as Aeschylus: to others, such as Horace, he has frequent recourse; historians and chroniclers; travels, descriptions of cities and countries (Burton was 'ever addicted to the study of cosmography'); treatises on government and politics; the *miscellanea* of scholars and Latin *belles lettres* from the revival of learning; poems, orations, epistles, satires, *facetiae* and the like; English poetry; Chaucer, Spenser, Marlowe, Shakespeare, Jonson, Daniel, Drayton; Harington's *Ariosto*, Florio's *Montaigne*, Rabelais and others.

The various sections into which the *Anatomy* may be divided are very unequally represented in his books. The famous introduction, 'Democritus to the Reader', in which, from a survey of the state of the world, he concludes that not only man, but kingdoms, provinces and politic bodies, even 'Vegetals and sensibles' are subject to melancholy, shows Burton's wide reading in history and geography and current politics. The Bodleian section of his library is rich in the pamphlet literature of the day from which much of this information is derived. There are *Delectable Histories*, *Plain Descriptions*, *Strange Voyages*, *Strange Chronicles*, *True Discoveries*, *True Narrations*, *News from France*, *News from Aleppo*, *News of the Netherlands*, *True News*, *New Newes*, *More Strange News*, of *Horrible Murders*, of *Flouds in England*, of *Witches*, of *Journeys*, of *Accidents*, &c.—the pamphlet literature of the seventeenth century which gave the current news of the day such as we get from newspapers. The Christ Church section is rich in geographical and descriptive works. In 'an inimitable

passage Burton tells us how the news of the world comes streaming in to him in his solitary quiet life at Christ Church. It is in
the introduction that he makes a poetical commonwealth of his
own, a Utopia, a New Atlantis—a remarkable document full of
good sense, in which we may note that he urges strongly old-age
pensions and tariff reform.

Of the three partitions into which the book is divided, two
are strictly medical and deal with every aspect of mental aberration. The elaborate synopses which precede each partition were
much in vogue in Burton's day, and whole books were written
in this form. He may have got the idea from Wecker's *Medicae
Syntaxes* (1582), a work in the Christ Church section from which
he quotes very often. There are about ninety works on medicine
in the collection, but the English Physick Books were given
away, and his fellow students had each the choice of one or two
folios. There is scarcely an author of any note from Hippocrates
to Harvey from whom Burton does not quote. No works of the
fathers of medicine are found in the collection, but he knew
thoroughly Hippocrates, Galen, Avicenna, the members of the
Arabian School, the Alexandrians, the Byzantine writers, and
all the sixteenth- and seventeenth-century authors. A few of the
writers on melancholy such as Arnoldus de Villanova are found
among his books, but there is not the treatise of his contemporary, Timothy Bright, to which he frequently refers. A few of
his prime favourites, such as Felix Platter, Gesner, and Matthiolus are represented. It is strange not to find any one of the many
works of Jerome Cardan whom he quotes so frequently. Some
of his references are to medical writers of great obscurity whom
it has been exceedingly difficult to trace, and copies of whose
works are not now in the Bodleian or indeed in England; but it
is to be remembered that Burton very often quotes second-hand.

It may be mentioned that his physiology was largely that of
Galen, and even in the editions which appeared after Harvey's
great discovery (1628) no change is made in the Galenic views
upon the circulation of the blood.

Amid much that is stale and dry, in the first partition occurs the delightful digression upon 'Air rectified', one of the earliest and best discussions upon soil and climate in relation to health. Among his books are scores which bear upon this subject, *Relations, Voyages, Strange Voyages, Plain Descriptions*, as well as the larger works on geography. The Introduction may be said to show Burton's wide knowledge of history, and of the existing state of Europe; Partitions i and ii show him to have been an encyclopaedic student of medicine, while Partition iii reveals the lighter side of his reading. One[1] would have scarcely expected from a Student of Christ Church, much less from an old bachelor, the most elaborate treatise on Love that has ever been written, but the greater portion of the last section is a monograph dealing with every aspect of the gentle passion, and with which there is nothing in literature to be compared. It is not surprising that he apologizes that many will think the subject too light and too comical, fit only for a wanton poet or some idle person, but he declares that an old, grave, discreet man is fittest to discuss of love matters, and that he has had more experience, has a more staid judgement, and can give better cautions and more solid precepts. He says:

I will examine all the kinds of love, his nature, beginning, difference, objects, how it is honest or dishonest, a vertue or vice, a natural passion or a disease, his power and effects, how far it extends; of which, although something hath been said in the first Partition, in those sections of perturbations ('for love and hatred are the first and most common passions, from which all the rest arise, and are attendant', as Piccolomineus holds, or as Nich. Caussinus, the *primum mobile* of all other affections, which carry them all about them), I will now more copiously dilate, through all his parts and several branches, that so it may better appear what Love is, and how it varies with the objects, how in defect, or (which is most ordinary and common) immoderate, and in excess, causeth melancholy.

[1] [From *One would have scarcely* to *which is omitted* occurs also above at pp. 81–2, as part of Osler's second paper, but may stand in both. An interesting passage will bear reading twice, and in style it contains an example of *Oslerus Burtonizatus*, though the 'Modest Matilda' and other following names are from *Anatomy* 3. 2. 6. 3. Its original and proper place is *here*. The reader will notice other repetitions.]

And he keeps his promise! There is no such collection of stories of love and its effect in all literature; no such tribute to the power of beauty; no such picture of the artificial allurements; no such representations of its power of debasement. And what a section on jealousy, its causes, its symptoms, and its cure! One could almost write the history of every noted woman from his pages.

> All the golden
> Names of olden
> Women yet by men's love cherished.

He says that after the harsh and unpleasant discourse of melancholy which had molested the patience of the reader and tired the author, he will ask leave to recreate himself in this kind after such laborious studies and the promise to tell such pretty stories that foul befall him that is not well pleased with them. Nor does he propose to mince matters. 'He will call a spade a spade, and will sound all the depths of this inordinate love of ours, which nothing can withstand or stave off.' All the love stories, pure and impure, of literature are here. Jacob and Rachel, Sichem and Dinah, Judah and Tamar, Samson and Delilah, David and Bathsheba, Am[n]on and Tamar. The stories of Esther, Judith, and Susannah; the loves of the Gods; the fopperies of Mars and Venus, of Neptune and Amymone; Jupiter and his amorous escapades. Modest Matilda, Pretty Pleasing Peg, Sweet Singing Susan, Mincing Merry Moll, Dainty Dancing Doll, Neat Nancy, Jolly Joan, Nimble Nell, Kissing Kate, Bouncing Bess with black eyes, Fair Phyllis with fine white hands—all flit across his page as he depicts the vagaries of the great passion, not a single aspect of which is omitted. Aretine's Lucretia is a prime favourite, and her biography and that of her suitors might almost be gleaned from his pages. Nothing is omitted. . . .

Such a section, too, on kissing and kisses, everything from the lines of Catullus to the interdiction of the Church! Well indeed might the Vicar of St. Thomas's and the grave Student of Christ Church conclude abruptly: 'But what have I to do with this?'

From the most valuable part of the Bodleian section, the contemporary plays and pamphlets, we can see where he got part of his education in these matters. Greene's *Quip for an Upstart Courtier*, the 1602 edition of Shakespeare's *Venus and Adonis*, *The Merry Devill of Edmonton*, Heywood's *Challenge for Beautie*, Fletcher's *Rule a Wife and Have a Wife*, Rowley's *Match at Midnight*, Beaumont's *Knight of the Burning Pestle*, *A Groats Worth of Witte*, and many others indicate his love of lighter literature. From one of these pamphlets, bound in the same volume with the famous *Quip for an Upstart Courtier*, Burton may have got the idea of Democritus Junior. It is called *Tyros Roring Megge. Planted against the Walls of Melancholy*, London 1598. One of the verses in the dedication to Master John Lucas is very suggestive:

> Naithlesse, prickt on with foolish hardiment,
> I put into those gratious handes of thine
> These looser numbers: fitter to be rent,
> Or swept away, like deft Arachnes twine,
> Than to be read: yet (deerest) list a while
> Unto thy Tyros Democriticke stile.

And then he says:

I was altogether terrestriall, or rather melancholicke. . . . Resolved to be the grater that should chase the sad humour to crums, I became Subsizar to Democritus, being well content to be no longer mal-content.

Among his favourite English poets, Chaucer, Spenser, Daniel, Buchanan, Drayton, Sidney, Marlowe, Tofte, Chaloner, Ben Jonson, and Wither, only a majority are represented.

As he says in one place, he was only a divine by profession, by inclination he was a physician. In the Bodleian list about a third deal with theology, in the Christ Church collection not so many. Out of these, in part at least, he has gathered the wonderful section on religious melancholy, one of the first and ablest treatises on the subject. Neither Plutarch nor Seneca is represented, though he loved them as did Montaigne. Doubtless these would be the very volumes selected by his fellow students.

The 'fantastic old great man' seems to have read everything
that had been written to 1639. And the volumes which we
have recounted represent but a small fraction of the raw material
of the *Anatomy*, in whose pages, as in no other book, sweeps
before us the panorama of humanity: Kings and Queens in their
greatness and in their glory, in their madness and in their
despair; generals and conquerors with their ambitions and
their activities; the Princes of the Church in their pride and in
their shame; philosophers of all ages, now rejoicing in the power
of intellect, and again grovelling before the idols of the tribe; the
heroes of the race who have fought the battle of the oppressed
in all lands; criminals small and great, from the petty thief to
Nero with his unspeakable atrocities; the great navigators and
explorers with whom he travelled so much in map and card,
and whose stories were his delight; the martyrs and the virgins
of all religions, the deluded and the fanatics of all theologies;
the possessed of devils and the possessed of God; the beauties,
frail and faithful, the Helens and the Lucretias, all are there;
the lovers old and young; the fools who were accounted wise,
and the wise who were really fools; the madmen of all history,
to anatomize whom is the special object of the book; the world
itself, against which he brings a railing accusation—the motley
procession of humanity sweeps before us on his stage, a fantastic
but fascinating medley at which Burton hesitates whether to
weep or to laugh—'Fleat Heraclitus, an rideat Democritus?'

7

MICHAEL SERVETUS

I

THE year 1553 saw Europe full of tragedies, and to the earnest student of the Bible it must have seemed as if the days had come for the opening of the second seal spoken of in the Book of Revelation, when peace should be taken from the earth and men should kill one another. One of these tragedies has a mournful interest this year, the four hundredth anniversary of the birth of its chief actor; yet it was but one of thousands of similar cases with which the history of the sixteenth century is stained. On 27 October shortly after twelve o'clock, a procession started from the town-hall of Geneva—the chief magistrates of the city, the clergy in their robes, the *Lieutenant Criminel* and other officers on horseback, a guard of mounted archers, the citizens, with a motley crowd of followers, and in their midst, with arms bound, in shabby, dirty clothes, walked a man of middle age, whose intellectual face bore the marks of long suffering. Passing along the rue St. Antoine through the gate of the same name, the cortège took its way towards the Golgotha of the city. Once outside the walls, a superb sight broke on their view: in the distance the blue waters and enchanting shores of the Lake of Geneva, to the west and north the immense amphitheatre of the Jura, with its snow-capped mountains, and to the south and west the lovely valley of the Rhône; but we may well think that few eyes were turned away from the central figure of that sad procession. By his side, in earnest entreaty, walked the aged pastor, Farel, who had devoted a long and useful life to the service of his fellow citizens. Mounting the hill, the field of Champel was reached,

This address did double duty—at the Johns Hopkins Medical School Historical Club, and as an Extension lecture in the Summer School, Oxford. Oxford University Press, 1909, with 10 illustrations. In *Johns Hopkins Hospital Bulletin*, 1910, xxi. 1–11.

and here on a slight eminence was the fateful stake, with the
dangling chains and heaping bundles of faggots. At this sight
the poor victim prostrated himself on the ground in prayer. In
reply to the exhortation of the clergyman for a specific confession
of faith, there was the cry, 'Misericordia, misericordia! Jesu,
thou Son of the eternal God, have compassion upon me!' Bound
to the stake by the iron chain, with a chaplet of straw and green
twigs covered with sulphur on his head, with his long dark face,
it is said that he looked like the Christ in whose name he was
bound. Around his waist were tied a large bundle of manuscript
and a thick octavo printed book. The torch was applied, and as
the flames spread to the straw and sulphur and flashed in his
eyes, there was a piercing cry that struck terror into the hearts of
the bystanders. The faggots were green, the burning was slow,
and it was long before in a last agony he cried again, 'Jesu, thou
Son of the eternal God, have mercy upon me!' Thus died, in
his forty-fourth year, Michael Servetus Villanovanus, physician,
physiologist, and heretic. Strange, is it not, that could he have
cried, 'Jesu, thou Eternal Son of God!' even at this last moment,
the chains would have been unwound, the chaplet removed,
and the faggots scattered; but he remained faithful unto death
to what he believed was the *Truth* as revealed in the Bible.

The story of his life is the subject of my address.

Michael Servetus, known also as Michel Villeneuve, or
Michael Servetus Villanovanus, or, as he puts in one of his
books, *alias* Revès, was a Spaniard born at Villanueva de Sigena,
in the present province of Huesca. When on trial at Vienne, he
gave Tudela, Navarre, as his birthplace, at Geneva, Villanueva
of Aragon; and at one place he gave as the date of his birth 1509,
and at the other 1511. The former is usually thought to be the
more correct.[1] As at Villanueva de Sigena there are records of
his family, and as the family altar, made by the father of Servetus, still exists, we may take it that at any rate the place of his
birth is settled. The altar-screen is a fine piece of work, with

---

[1] [Alex. Gordon in the *Encyclopaedia Britannica*, 1911, reverses this opinion.
—W. W. F.]

ten paintings. Servetus seems to have belonged to a good family in easy circumstances, and at his trial he said he came of an ancient race, living nobly.

From the convent school he probably went to the neighbouring University of Saragossa. Possibly he may have studied for the priesthood, but however that may be, there is evidence that he was a precocious youth, and well read in Latin, Greek, and Hebrew, the last two very unusual accomplishments at that period.

We next hear of him at Toulouse, studying canon and civil law. He could not have been twenty when he entered the service of the Friar Quintana, confessor to the Emperor Charles V, apparently as his private secretary. In the suite of the Emperor he went to Italy, and was present when Pope and Emperor entered Bologna, and 'he saw the most powerful prince of the age at the head of 20,000 veterans kneeling and kissing the feet of the Pope'. Here he had his first impression of the worldliness and mercenary character of the Papacy, hatred of which, very soon after, we find to have become an obsession.

In the summer of 1530 the Emperor attended the Diet of Augsburg, where the Princes succeeded in getting Protestantism recognized politically. Such a gathering must have had a profound influence on the young student, already, we may suppose, infected with the new doctrines. Possibly at Saragossa, or at Toulouse, he may have become acquainted with the writings of Luther. Such an expression of opinion as the following, written before his twenty-first year, could scarcely have been of a few months' growth:

For my own part, I neither agree nor disagree in every particular with either Catholic or Reformer. Both of them seem to me to have something of truth and something of error in their views; and whilst each sees the other's shortcomings, neither sees his own. God in his goodness give us all to understand our errors, and incline us to put them away. It would be easy enough, indeed, to judge dispassionately of everything, were we but suffered without molestation by the churches freely to speak our minds. (Willis.)

How far he held any personal communication with the German reformers is doubtful. It is quite possible, and Tollin, his chief biographer, makes him visit Luther. We do not know how long he held service with Quintana, Tollin thinks a year and a half. It is not unlikely that the good friar was glad to get rid of a young secretary infected with heresy so shocking as that contained in his first book, published in 1531; indeed, there is a statement to the effect that a monk in the suite of Quintana found the book in a shop at Ratisbon and hastened to tell the confessor of its terrible contents. Servetus had plunged headlong into studies of the most dangerous character, and had even embooked them in a small octavo volume, entitled *De Trinitatis Erroribus*, which appeared without the printer's name, but on the title-page as author, 'Per Michaelem Serveto, *aliâs* Reves ab Aragonia, Hispanum', and with the date MDXXXI. In the innocency of his heart he thought the work would be a good introduction to the more liberal of the Swiss reformers, but they would have none of it, and were inexpressibly shocked at its supposed blasphemies. Nor did he fare better at Strasburg; and even the kind-hearted Bucer said that the author of such a work should be disembowelled and torn in pieces.

In thorny theological questions a layman naturally seeks shelter, and I am glad to quote the recent opinion of a distinguished student of the period, Professor Emerton,[1] on this youthful phase of the life of Servetus.

He would not admit that the eternal Son of God was to appear as man, but only that a man was to come who should be the Son of God. This is the earliest intimation we have as to the speculations which were occupying the mind of the young scholar. It is highly significant that from the start he was impressed with what we should now call the historical view of theology. As he read the Old Testament, its writers seemed to him to be referring to things that their hearers would understand. Their gaze into the future was limited by the fortunes of the people at the moment. To imagine them possessed of all the divine mysteries, and to have in mind the person of the

[1] *Harvard Theological Review*, April 1909.

man Jesus as the ultimate object of all their prophetic vision, was to reflect back the knowledge of history into a past to which such knowledge was impossible. So far as I can understand him, this is the key to all Servetus's later thought. His manner of expressing himself is confusing and intricate to the last degree, so much so that neither in his own time nor since has any one dared to say that he understood it. To his contemporaries he was a half-mad fanatic; to those who have studied him, even sympathetically, his thought remains to a great extent enigmatical; but this one point is fairly clear: that he grasped, as no one up to his time had grasped, this one central notion, that, whatever the divine plan may have been, it must be revealed by the long, slow movement of history—that, to understand the record of the past, it must be read, so far as that is possible, with the mind of those to whom it was immediately addressed, and must not be twisted into the meanings that may suit the fancy of later generations.

To have seized upon such an idea as this—an idea which has begun to come to its rights only within our memories—was an achievement which marks this youth of twenty as at all events an extraordinary individual, a disturbing element in his world, a man who was not likely to let the authorities rest calmly in possession of all the truth there was.

In the following year, 1532, two dialogues appeared, explanatory and conciliatory, a little book which only aggravated the offence, and feeling the Protestant atmosphere too hot, Servetus went to Paris. Dropping this name by which he had been known, and closing this brief but stormy period, for the next twenty-one years we now follow Michel Villeneuve, or Michael Villanovanus, in a varied career as student, lecturer, practitioner, author, and editor, still nursing the unconquerable hope that the world might be reformed could he but restore the primitive doctrine of the Church.

II

We know very little of this his first stay in Paris. Possibly he found employment as teacher, or as reader to the press. At this period his path first crossed that of Calvin, then a young student.

Of about the same age, both ardent students, both on the high road of emancipation from the faith of their birth, they must have had many discussions on theological questions. One may conclude from the reproachful sentence of Calvin many years later, 'Vous avez fuy la lutte', that arrangements had been made for a public debate.

After a short stay at Avignon and Orleans, we next find Servetus at Lyons, in the employ of the Trechsel brothers, the famous printers. Those were the days of fine editions of the classics and other books, which required the assistance of scholarly men to edit and correct. He brought out a splendid folio of Ptolemy's Geography, 1535, with commentaries on the different countries, which show a wide range of knowledge in so young a man. It is marked also by many examples of independent criticism, as, when speaking of Palestine, he says that the 'Promised Land' was anything but a 'promising land', and instead of flowing with milk and honey, and a land of corn, olives, and vineyards, it was inhospitable and barren, and the stories about its fertility nothing but boasting and untruth. He seems to have been brought to task for this, as in the second edition, 1541, this section does not exist. For this work he was paid by the Trechsels 500 crowns.

It is possible that Servetus and 'Rabelais may have met at Lyons, as at this time the 'great Dissimulator' was physician to the Hôtel-Dieu, but there is nothing in the writings of either to indicate that their paths crossed. The man who had the greatest influence upon him at Lyons was Symphorien Champier, one of the most interesting and distinguished of the medical humanists of the early part of the sixteenth century. Servetus helped him with his French Pharmacopoeia, and Pastor Tollin will have it that Champier even made a home for the poor scholar. An ardent Galenist, an historian, the founder of the hospital and of the medical school, Champier had the usual predilection of the student of those days for astrology. Probably from him Servetus received his instructions in the subject. At any rate, when the distinguished Professor of Medicine of

Tübingen, Fuchsíus, attacked Champier on the ground of his astrological vagaries, Servetus took up his pen and replied in defence with a pamphlet entitled 'In Leonhardum Fuchsium defensio apologetica pro Symphoriano Campeggio', an exceedingly rare item, the only one indeed of the writings of Servetus that I have not seen in the original.

Stimulated doubtless by the example and precept of Champier, Servetus returned to Paris to study medicine. Fairly rich in pocket with the proceeds of his literary work, he attached himself first to the College of Calvi, and afterwards to that of the Lombards, and it is said that he took the degrees of M.A. and M.D., but of this I am told that there is no documentary evidence.

Of his life in Paris we have very little direct evidence, except in connexion with a single incident. We know that he came into intimate contact with three men—Guinther of Andernach, Jacobus Sylvius, and Vesalius. Guinther and Sylvius must have been men after his own heart, ripe scholars, ardent Galenists, and keen anatomists. In the *Institutiones Anatomicae* (Basel, 1539), Guinther speaks of Servetus in connexion with Vesalius, who was at this time his fellow prosector. 'And after him by Michael Villanovanus, distinguished by his literary acquirements of every kind, and scarcely second to any in his knowledge of Galenical doctrine.' With their help he states that he has examined the whole body, and demonstrated to the students all of the muscles, veins, arteries, and nerves. There was at this time a very keen revival in the study of anatomy in Paris, and to have been associated with such a young genius as Vesalius, already a brilliant dissector, must have been in itself a liberal education in the subject. It is easy to understand whence was derived the anatomical knowledge upon which was based the far-reaching generalization with which the name of Servetus is associated in physiology.

But the Paris incident of which we know most is connected with certain lectures on judicial astrology. We have seen that at Lyons, Servetus had defended his friend and patron Symphorien

Champier, through whom he had doubtless become familiar
with its practice. Though forbidden by the Church, judicial
astrology was still in favour in some universities, and was practised largely by physicians occupying the most distinguished
positions. In those days few were strong minded enough to
defy augury, and in popular belief all were 'servile to skiey
influences'. It was contrary to the regulations of the Paris
Faculty to lecture on the subject, though at this time the king
had in his employ a professional astrologist, Thibault. Shortly
after reaching Paris Servetus began a course of lectures on the
subject, which very soon brought him into conflict with the
authorities.

The admirable practice for the Dean to write out each year
his report has preserved for us the full details of the procedure
against Servetus. Duboulay, in his *History of the University of
Paris*, vol. vi, has extracted the whole affair from the Dean's
Commentary, as it is called, of the year. He says that a certain
student of medicine, a Spaniard, or, as he says, from Navarre,
but with a Spanish father, had taught for some days in Paris in
1537 judicial astrology or divination. After having found out
that this was condemned by the Doctors of the Faculty, he
caused to be printed a certain apology in which he attacked
the doctors, and moreover declared that wars and pests and all the
affairs of men depended on the heavens and on the stars, and he
imposed on the public by confounding true and judicial astrology. The Dean goes on to state that, accompanied by two of his
colleagues, he tried to prevent Villanovanus from publishing
the apology, and met him leaving the school where he had been
making a dissection of the body with a surgeon, and in the
presence of several of the scholars, and of two or three doctors,
he not only refused to stop the publication, but he threatened
the Dean with bitter words.

The Faculty appears to have had some difficulty in getting
the authorities to move in the matter. Possibly we may see here
the influence of the court astrologer, Thibault. After many
attempts, and after appealing to the Theological Faculty and

the Congregation of the University, the question was taken up by Parliament. The speeches of counsel for the Faculty, for the University, for Villanovanus, and for the Parliament are given in full. The Parliament decided that the printed apology should be recalled, the booksellers were forbidden to keep them, the lectures on astrology were forbidden, and Villanovanus was urged to treat the Faculty with respect. But on their part they were asked to deal with the offender gently, and in a parental fashion. It is a very interesting trial, and the Dean evidently enjoyed his triumph. He says that he took with him three theologians, two doctors in medicine, the Dean of the Faculty of Canonical Law, and the Procurator-General of the University. The affair was discussed by Parliament with closed doors.

The *Apologetica disceptatio pro astrologia*, the rarest of the Servetus items, the only copy known being in the Bibliothèque Nationale, is an eight-leaf pamphlet, without title-page, pagination, or printer's name. The friends of the Faculty must have been very successful in their confiscation of the work. Tollin, who discovered the original, has reprinted it (Berlin, 1880). It was not hard for Servetus to cite powerful authorities on his side, and he summons in his defence the great quartette, Plato, Aristotle, Hippocrates, and Galen. A practical star-gazer, he took his own observations, and the pamphlet records an eclipse of Mars by the moon. He must, too, have been a student of the weather, as he speaks of giving in his lectures public predictions which caused great astonishment. The influence of the moon in determining the critical days of diseases, a favourite doctrine of Galen, is fully discussed, and he says that Galen's opinion should be written in letters of gold. He rests content with these great authorities, referring very briefly to one or two minor lights. He scoffs at the well-known bitter attack on divination by Picus.

It took several generations to eradicate completely from the profession a belief in astrology, which lingered well into the seventeenth century. In his *Vulgar Errors*, discussing the

'Canicular' or 'Dog Days', Sir Thomas Browne expresses his opinion of astrology in the most characteristic language.

Nor do we hereby reject or condemn a sober and regulated Astrology; we hold there is more truth therein than in Astrologers; in some more than many allow, yet in none so much as some pretend. We deny not the influence of the Starres, but often suspect the due application thereof; for though we should affirm that all things were in all things; that heaven were but earth celestified, and earth but heaven terrestrified, or that each part above had an influence upon its divided affinity below; yet how to single out these relations, and duly to apply their actions, is a work oft times to be effected by some revelation, and Cabala from above, rather than any Philosophy, or speculation here below.

Among the auditors of Servetus was a young man, Pierre Paulmier, the Archbishop of Vienne, who appears to have befriended him in Paris, and who a few years later asked him to be his body physician. The astrology trial was settled in March 1537.

Servetus cannot have been very long a student of medicine, but never lacking in assurance, he came before the world as a medical author in the little treatise on Syrups and their use. Association with Champier, whom he had helped in an edition of his French Pharmacopoeia, had made him familiar with the subject. The first three chapters are taken up with the views on 'Concoctions' or 'Digestions', of which at that time a series, from the first to the fourth, was recognized. He pleads for a unity of the process, and, as Willis remarks, he makes the very shrewd remark at that day, 'that diseases are only perversions of natural functions and not new entities introduced into the body'. The greater part of the treatise is taken up with theoretical discussions on the opinions of Galen, Hippocrates, and Avicenna. The 'Composition and use of the Syrups' is deferred to the fifth and a concluding (sixth) chapter.

The little book appears to have been popular, and was reprinted twice at Venice, 1545 and 1548, and twice at Lyons, 1546 and 1547.

III

Whether the adverse decision of Parliament disgusted him with Paris, or whether through some friend the opportunity to settle in practice had offered, we next hear of Villeneuve at Charlieu, a small town about twelve miles from Lyons, where he spent a year, or part of the years 1538–9. Here his old Paris friend Paulmier sought him and induced him to settle at Vienne, offering him apartments in the palace, and an appointment as his body physician. After nearly ten years of wandering, at last, in a peaceful home in the fine old Roman city, with its good society, and under the protection of the Primate of all France, Servetus spent the next fourteen years as a practising physician.

Few details of his life are known. He retained his association with the Trechsels, the printers, who had set up a branch establishment in Vienne. In 1541 he brought out a new edition of Ptolemy, with a dedication to the Archbishop. From the preface we have a glimpse of a genial group of companions, all interested in the new studies. Several critical items in the edition of 1535 disappear in the new one of 1541, e.g. the scoffing remarks about Palestine; and in mentioning the royal touch, instead of, 'I have myself seen the King touching many with this disease (i.e. scrofula), but I have not seen that they were cured', he says, 'I have heard that many were cured'. Perhaps he felt it unbecoming in a member of an ecclesiastical circle, and living under the patronage of the Archbishop, to say anything likely to give offence.

In the following year he issued an edition of Pagnini's Bible in a fine folio. Its chief interest to us is the testimony that Servetus was still deep in theological studies, for the commentaries in the work place him among the earliest and boldest of the higher critics. The prophetic psalms, and the numerous prophecies in Isaiah and Daniel are interpreted in the light of contemporary events, but as Willis remarks: 'These numerous excessively free and highly heterodox interpretations appear to have lost Villeneuve neither countenance nor favour at Vienne.'

For another Lyons publisher, Frelon, he edited a number of educational works, and through him the Vienne physician was put in correspondence with the Geneva reformer.

A dreamer, an enthusiast, a mystic, Servetus was possessed with the idea that could but the doctrines of the Church be reformed the world could be won to a primitive, simple Christianity. We have already seen his attempt to bring the Swiss reformers into what he thought correct views upon the Trinity. He now began a correspondence with Calvin on this subject, and on the question of the Sacraments. The letters, which are extant, in tone and contents shocked and disgusted Calvin to such a degree that in a communication to Farel, dated February 1546, after stating that Servetus had offered to come to Geneva, he adds: 'I will not pledge my faith to him, for did he come if I have any authority here I should never suffer him to go away alive.'

For years Servetus had in preparation the work which he fondly hoped would restore primitive Christianity. Part of a manuscript of this he had sent to Calvin. Having tried in vain to get it published, he decided to print it privately at Vienne. Arrangements were made with a local printer, who set up a separate press in a small house, and in a few months 1,000 copies were printed. The title-page of this *Christianismi Restitutio* has the date 1553, and on the last page are the initials of his name, 'M.S.V.'

He must have known that the work was likely to cause great commotion in the Church, but he hoped that the identity of the author would be as little suspected as that the Vienne physician, Michel Villeneuve, was the Michael Servetus of the heretical *de Trinitatis Erroribus*. Intended for distribution in Germany, Switzerland, and Italy, the work was made up into bales of 100 copies for distribution to the trade. Probably from their mutual friend Frelon Calvin received a couple of copies. The usual story is that through one Guillaume de Trye as a medium, Calvin denounced Villeneuve to the inquisition at Vienne. This was the view of Servetus himself, and is supported by Willis,

Tollin, and others; but advocates of Calvin continue to deny that there is sufficient evidence of his active participation at this stage.

There was at this time at Lyons the well-known inquisitor Orry, who ten years before had brought Étienne Dolet to the stake. No sooner had he got scent of the affair than he undertook the prosecution with his customary zeal, and Servetus was arrested. The preliminary trial at Vienne is chiefly of interest on account of the autobiographical details which Servetus gives. The evidence against him was so overwhelming that he was committed to prison. Surrounded by his friends, who must have been greatly shocked and distressed to find their favourite physician in so terrible a plight, abundantly supplied with money, with the prison discipline very lax as the jailer was his friend, it is not surprising that the day after his commitment Servetus escaped, greatly no doubt to the relief of the Archbishop and the authorities. The inquisitor had to be content with burning an effigy of the heretic with some 500 copies of his work.

After 7 April Servetus disappears from view, and we next meet with him, of all places in the world, at Geneva. [Arriving there on the morning of 13 August, he was recognized that afternoon and immediately arrested.] Why he should have run this risk has been much discussed, but the explanation given by Guizot is probably the correct one. At that time the Liberals, or 'Libertines', as they were called because of their hostility to Calvin, fully expected to triumph.

One of their leaders, Ami Perrin, was first Syndic: a man of their party, Gueroult, who had been banished from Geneva, had been corrector of the press at the time when the *Restoration of Christianity* was published, and thanks to the influence of his patrons, the Libertines, he had returned to Geneva, and would naturally be the medium between them and Servetus. Taking a comprehensive view of the whole case and the antecedents of all those concerned in it, I am convinced that Servetus, defeated at Vienne, went to Geneva, relying on the support of the Libertines, whilst they on their side expected to obtain efficacious help from him against Calvin.

The full account of this famous heresy trial has lost much of its interest so far as the doctrinal details are concerned. At this distance, with our modern ideas, the procedure seems very barbarous. Servetus was cruelly treated in prison, and there is a letter from him which speaks of his shocking condition, without proper clothing, and a prey to vermin. Mademoiselle Roch has well depicted this phase of the martyr's career in her fine statue which has been erected at Annemasse. The full report of the trial may be followed in the account given by Willis, and the *procès-verbal* is in existence at Geneva in manuscript.

One thing seems clear, that while at first the accusations were largely concerned with the heretical views of Servetus, later the public prosecutor laid more stress upon the political side of the case, accusing him of conspiracy with the Libertines. The trial divided Geneva into hostile camps, and it sometimes looked as though Calvin, quite as much as Servetus, was on trial. To strengthen their hands the clerical party appealed to the Swiss churches. The answer, strong enough in condemning the heresy and blasphemy, refrained from specifying the kind of punishment.

Accustomed in France to hear the Swiss reformers branded as the worst type of heretics, Servetus appears never to have understood why he should not have been received with open arms by the Protestants, whose one desire was the same as his own, the restoration of primitive faith and practice. He made a brave fight, and brought strong countercharges against Calvin, whom he accused specifically of causing his arrest at Vienne. He offered to discuss the questions at issue publicly, an offer which Calvin would have accepted had the syndics allowed. The whole city was in a ferment, and Sunday after Sunday Calvin and the other pastors thundered from their pulpits against the blasphemies of the Spaniard. After dragging its weary length for nearly two months, the public feeling veered strongly to the side of Calvin, and on 26 October the Council, by a majority vote, resolved that in consideration of his great errors and blasphemies, the prisoner should be burnt alive.

Servetus appears to have been a curious compound of audacity and guilelessness. The announcement of the condemnation appears to have completely stunned him, as he seems never to have considered its possibility. He sent for Calvin and asked his pardon, but there was bitterness in the heart of the great reformer whose account of the interview is not very pleasant reading.

On the morning of the 27th, the Tribunal assembled before the porch of the Hôtel de Ville to read to the prisoner his formal condemnation, under ten separate heads, the two most important of which relate to the doctrine of the Trinity, and Infant Baptism. It is curious that under one of the headings he should be denounced as an arrogant innovator, and an inventor of heresies against Popery! The entreaty of Servetus for a more merciful mode of death (for which, to his credit, be it said, Calvin also pleaded) was in vain. The procession at once formed to the place of execution.

Nothing in his life, it may be said, became him like the leaving of it. As Guizot remarks: 'The dignity of the philosopher triumphed over the weakness of the man, and Servetus died heroically and calmly at that stake the very thought of which had at first filled him with terror.'

There will be dedicated next year at Vienne a monument commemorating the services of Servetus as an independent spirit in theology, and as a pioneer in physiology.

It has been said that Sappho survives because we sing her songs, and Aeschylus because we read his plays, but it would be difficult to explain the widespread interest in Servetus from any knowledge men have of his writings. The pathos of his fate, which scandalized Gibbon more profoundly than all the human hecatombs of Spain or Portugal, accounts for it in part. Then there is the limited circle of those who regard him as a martyr to the Unitarian confession; while scientific men have a very definite interest in him as one of the first to make a substantial contribution to our knowledge of the circulation of the blood. His theological and physiological views call for brief comments.

IV

Next to theology itself the study of medicine has been a great heresy breeder. From the days of Arnold of Villanova and Peter of Abano, there have been noted heretics in our ranks. Bossuet defines a heretic as 'One who has opinions'. Servetus seems to have been charged with opinions like a Leyden jar. His most notable ones concerned the Trinity and Infant Baptism. Wracked almost to destruction in the third and fourth centuries on the subject of the Trinity, the final conquest of Arianism found its expression in that magnificent human document the Athanasian Creed, with which the Catholic Church has for ever settled the question, in language which sends a cold shudder down the backs of heretics. But there have always been turbulent souls who could not rest satisfied, and who would bring up unpleasant points from the Bible—men who were not able to accept Dante's wise advice: 'Mad is he who hopes that our reason can traverse the infinite way which one Substance as Three Persons holds. Be content, O human race, with the *Quia*.'

The doctrine has been a great breeding ground of heretics, the smoke of whose burning has been a sweet savour in the nostrils alike of Catholics and Protestants. Even to-day, so deeply ingrained is the Catholic creed, that nearly everything in the way of doctrinal vagary is forgiven save denial of the Trinity, which is thought to put a man outside the pale of normal Christianity. If this is the feeling to-day, imagine what it must have been in the middle of the sixteenth century!

Servetus wrote two theological works—*de Trinitatis Erroribus*, published in 1531, followed by a supplement in 1532. To these I have already referred. Living a double life at Vienne, to the inhabitants he was the careful and kind practitioner of medicine, to whom they had become devoted, but all the while, nourishing the dream of his youth, he had in preparation a work which he believed would win the world to Christ by purifying the Church from grave errors in doctrine.

I have already spoken of the printing of the *Christianismi*

Restitutio. Mainly concerned with most abstruse questions concerning the Trinity and Infant Baptism, it is a most difficult work to read, and, as theologians confess, a still more difficult one to understand. Professor Emerton, in his article from which I have already quoted, gives in a few paragraphs the essence of his views.

He finds the central fact of Christian speculation, not in the doctrine of the Trinity as formulated by the schools, but in the fact of the divine incarnation in the person of Jesus. He admits the divine birth, explaining it as in harmony with a general law of divine manifestation whereby the spiritual is revealed in the material. He would not accept the idea of an eternal sonship, except in this sense, that the divine Word, the Logos, had always been active as the expression in outward form of the divine activity. So, in the fullness of time, this same Logos produced a being from a human mother upon whom at the moment of his birth the divine Spirit was breathed. Obviously this is not the 'eternal Son' of the creeds, and herein lay the special theological crime of Servetus. In his criticism of the church order, of the papal government, of the sacramental system, he does not differ essentially from the more radical of the reformers. On the essential matters of baptism and the Eucharist he goes quite beyond the established reforming churches. In both cases he invokes the principle of plain reason. He rejects Infant Baptism on the ground that the infant can have no faith, and that the practice is therefore mere incantation. He denies transubstantiation on the rational basis that substances and accidents may not be separated, and does not spare the reforming leaders for what seemed to him their half-hearted attitude on this point. His language throughout is harsh and violent, except where, as at the close of his chapters, he passes over into the forms of devotion and closes his diatribes with prayers of great beauty and spirituality.

The Christian Church early found out that there was only one safe way of dealing with heresy. From the end of the fourth century, when the habit began, to its climax on St. Bartholomew's Day, it was universally recognized that only dead heretics ceased to be troublesome. History affords ample evidence of the efficacy of repressive measures, often carried out on a scale of noble proportions. France is Catholic because of a root and branch policy; England's Protestantism is an enduring testimony to the thoroughness with which Henry VIII carried out his measures. As De Foe says in his famous pamphlet, *Shortest way with Dissenters*, if a man is obstinate and persists in having an opinion of his own, contrary to that held by a majority of his fellows, and if the opinion is pernicious and jeopardizes his eternal salvation, it is much safer to burn him than to allow his doctrines to spread! For 1,200 years this policy kept heresy within narrow limits until the great outbreak. The very best men of the day were consenting to the death of heretics. The spirit of Protestantism was against it; Luther nobly so. Judged by his age Servetus was a rank heretic, and as deserving of death as any ever tied to a stake. We can scarcely call him a martyr of the Church.—What Church would own him? All the same, we honour his memory as a martyr to the truth as he saw it.

Servetus was a student of medicine in Paris with Sylvius and Guinther, two of the most ardent of the revivers of the Galenic anatomy. More important still, he was a fellow student and prosector with Vesalius. He wrote one little medical book of no special merit. The works which he edited, which brought him more money than fame, indicate an independent and critical spirit. Vienne was a small town, in which we cannot think there was any scientific stimulus, though it was in a region noted for its intellectual activity.

In possession of a fact in physiology of the very first moment, Servetus described it with extraordinary clearness and accuracy. But so little did he think of the discovery, of so trifling importance did it appear in comparison with the great task in hand of restoring Christianity, that he used it simply as an illustration when discussing the nature of the Holy Spirit in his work *Christianismi Restitutio*. The discovery was nothing less than that of the passage of the blood from the right side of the heart to the left through the lungs, what is known as the pulmonary, or lesser circulation.

In the year 1553 the views of Galen everywhere prevailed.

The great master had indeed effected a revolution in the knowledge of the circulation almost as great as that made by Harvey
in the seventeenth century. Briefly stated there were two bloods,
the natural and the vital, in two practically closed systems, the
veins and the arteries. The liver was the central organ of the
venous system, the 'shop' as Burton calls it, in which the chylus
was converted into blood and from which it was distributed by
the veins to all parts of the body for nourishment. The veins
were rather vessels containing the blood than tubes for its
transmission—irrigating canals Galen called them. Galen knew
the structure of the heart, the arrangement of its valves, and
the direction in which the blood passed, but its chief function
was not, as we suppose, mechanical, but in the left ventricle,
the seat of life, the vital spirits were generated, being a mixture
of inspired air and blood. By an alternate movement of dilatation
and collapse of the arteries the blood with the vital spirits was
kept in constant motion.[1] Galen had demonstrated that the
arteries and the veins communicated with each other at the
periphery. A small quantity of the blood went, he believed,
from the right side of the heart to the lungs, for their nourishment, and in this way passed to the left side of the heart; but the
chief communication between the two systems was through pores
in the ventricular septum, the thick muscular wall separating
the two chief chambers of the heart.

The literature may be searched in vain for any other than the
Galenic view up to 1553.[2] Even Vesalius, who could not understand from its structure how even the smallest quantity of blood
could pass through the septum dividing the ventricles, offered

[1] So firmly entrenched was the Galenic physiology that the new views of
Harvey made at first very slow progress. In Burton's *Anatomy of Melancholy*,
which is a sort of epitome of medical knowledge of the seventeenth century,
is the following description: 'The left creek (i.e. ventricle) has the form of
a cone, and is the seat of life, which, as a torch doth oil, draws blood unto
it begetting of it spirits and fire, and as a fire in a torch so are spirits in the
blood; and by that great artery called aorta, it sends vital spirits over the
body, and takes air from the lungs.'

[2] [In 1924 it was found that Ibn an-Nafis, a physician of Damascus, had
described the lesser circulation some 300 years before Servetus!—W. W. F.]

no other explanation. The more one knows of the Galenic physiology, the less one is surprised that it had so captivated the minds of men. The description by Servetus of the new way is found in the fifth book of the *Christianismi Restitutio*, in which he is discussing the nature of the Holy Spirit. After mentioning the threefold spirit of the body of man, natural, vital, and animal, he goes on to discuss the vital spirit, and in a few paragraphs describes the pulmonary circulation.

Rightly to understand the question here, the first thing to be considered is the substantial generation of the vital spirit—a compound of the inspired air with the most subtle portion of the blood. The vital spirit has, therefore, its source in the left ventricle of the heart, the lungs aiding most essentially in its production. It is a fine attenuated spirit, elaborated by the power of heat, of a crimson colour and fiery potency—the lucid vapour as it were of the blood, substantially composed of water, air, and fire; for it is engendered, as said, by the mingling of the inspired air with the more subtle portion of the blood which the right ventricle of the heart communicates to the left. This communication, however, does not take place through the septum, partition, or midwall of the heart, as commonly believed, but by another admirable contrivance, the blood being transmitted from the pulmonary artery to the pulmonary vein, by a lengthened passage through the lungs, in the course of which it is elaborated and becomes of a crimson colour. Mingled with the inspired air in this passage, and freed from fuliginous vapours by the act of expiration, the mixture being now complete in every respect, and the blood become fit dwelling-place of the vital spirit, it is finally attracted by the diastole, and reaches the left ventricle of the heart.

Now that the communication and elaboration take place in the lungs in the manner described, we are assured by the conjunctions and communications of the pulmonary artery with the pulmonary vein. The great size of the pulmonary artery seems of itself to declare how the matter stands; for this vessel would neither have been of such a size as it is, nor would such a force of the purest blood have been sent through it to the lungs for their nutrition only; neither would the heart have supplied the lungs in such fashion, seeing as we do that the lungs in the foetus are nourished from another source

—those membranes or valves of the heart not coming into play until the hour of birth, as Galen teaches. The blood must consequently be poured in such large measure at the moment of birth from the heart to the lungs for another purpose than the nourishment of those organs. Moreover, it is not simply air, but air mingled with blood that is returned from the lungs to the heart by the pulmonary veins.

It is in the lungs, consequently, that the mixture (of the inspired air with the blood) takes place, and it is in the lungs also, not in the heart, that the crimson colour of the blood is acquired. There is not indeed capacity or room enough in the left ventricle of the heart for so great and important an elaboration, neither does it seem competent to produce the crimson colour. To conclude, the septum or middle portion of the heart, seeing that it is without vessels and special properties, is not fitted to permit and accomplish the communication and elaboration in question, although it may be that some transudation takes place through it. It is by a mechanism similar to that by which the transfusion from the *vena portae* to the *vena cava* takes place in the liver, in respect of the blood, that the transfusion from the pulmonary artery to the pulmonary vein takes place in the lungs, in respect of the spirit. (Willis's translation.)

The important elements here are: first, the clear statement of the function of the pulmonary artery; secondly, the transmission of the impure or venous blood through the lungs from the right side of the heart to the left; thirdly, the recognition of an elaboration or transformation in the lungs, so that with the blood freed of 'fuliginous vapours', there was at the same time a change to the crimson colour of the arterial blood; fourthly, the direct denial of a communication of the two bloods, by means of orifices in the septum between the ventricles.

He had no idea of the general or systematic circulation, and so far as the left heart and the arteries were concerned he believed them to be the seat of the vital blood and spirits.

It is not hard to imagine how Servetus had become emancipated from the old views. A student at Paris at a most opportune period, when dissection had become popular, he had had as prosector to Guinther exceptional opportunities. But more important still, he had as fellow worker the anatomical arch-heretic,

Andreas Vesalius, already imbued with the conviction that his teachers were wrong in regarding Galen as inspired and infallible. It was at this very period that Vesalius had pointed out to his teacher Sylvius the error of Galen about the aortic valves; and when one considers the extraordinary rapidity with which Vesalius reformed human anatomy, before he had completed his twenty-eighth year, it is not surprising that his colleague and co-worker should have discovered one of the great truths of physiology.

The *Christianismi Restitutio* was never published, and the discovery of Servetus remained unrecognized until the attention of Wotton was called to it by Charles Bernard, a St. Bartholomew's Hospital surgeon.[1] Meanwhile it had been rediscovered, and among the many vagaries with which the history of the circulation of the blood is marked, not the least striking is the attempt to rob Servetus of his credit. In 1559 there was published a work by Realdo Colombo,[2] a student of Vesalius and his successor at Padua, in which the circulation of the blood from the right side of the heart to the left is clearly described. It is impossible to say that he had added anything to the account just given, and the far-fetched view has been maintained that Italian students at Paris had acquainted Servetus with the views of Colombo. It is claimed for Colombo also that he had a better idea of the function of respiration in the purification of the blood, by its mingling with the air, but Servetus distinctly states that the mixture takes place in the lungs, not, as was usually understood at the time, in the heart itself.

Caesalpinus (1569), for whom elaborate claims are made, also knew of the pulmonary circulation, but he thought part of the blood went through the median septum. A more important claim is made for him of the discovery of the general circulation, but it is remarkable that anyone knowing the history of the subject could read into his physiology anything more than the old Galenic views.

[1] William Wotton, *Reflections upon ancient and modern learning*, 1697, p. 229.
[2] *De Re Anatomica*, Venice, 1559.

The history of the circulation bristles with controversy and widely divergent opinions are held as to the merits of the different observers. That Servetus first advanced a step beyond Galen, that Colombo and Caesalpinus reached the same conclusion independently—all three recognizing the lesser circulation, is quite as certain as that it remained for Harvey to open an entirely new chapter in physiology, and to introduce modern experimental methods by which the complete circulation of the blood was first clearly demonstrated.[1]

A word about the book *Christianismi Restitutio, liber inter rariores longe rarissimus.* Only two complete copies are known, one in the Bibliothèque Nationale, Paris, and the other in the Imperial Library, Vienna, from which I was very kindly permitted to have photographs of the title-page and the pages describing the circulation of the blood reproduced. A third copy, imperfect, with the first sixteen pages in manuscript, is in the University Library, Edinburgh. The Paris copy is of special interest, as it belonged to Dr. Richard Mead, the distinguished physician and book collector, by whom it was exchanged with M. de Boze for a series of medals. In 1784 it was secured for the Royal Library. It may now be seen in a show case of the Bibliothèque Nationale, of which it is one of the rare treasures. An added interest is in the fact that on the title-page occurs the name 'Germain Colladon', the Geneva barrister who prosecuted Servetus; and it is in the highest degree probable that this was the identical copy used at the trial. In one place the book is stained, some suppose by moisture; others think it possible this was the very copy bound upon the victim himself, and snatched from the flames by someone who wished to preserve so interesting a record of the great heretic. The question has been examined carefully by the late Professor Laboulbène and M. Hahn, the distinguished librarian of the Paris Faculty of Medicine, both of whom are in favour of fire, not moisture, as the cause of the staining.

---

[1] John C. Dalton's *History of the Circulation*, 1884, gives by far the best and fullest account of the whole subject in English.

In 1790 the Vienne copy was reprinted at Nuremberg, page for page, but C. G. von Murr, who was responsible for the reprint, very wisely put the date 1790 at the bottom of the last page. Copies of this edition are not uncommon in the larger libraries. In 1723 Mead attempted to have a reprint made from his copy, but when it was nearly completed the Bishop of London had it suppressed, and (it is stated) the copies were burnt. A few, however, escaped, and Willis says that he saw one in the library of the London Medical Society. I regret to say that the librarian informs me that this no longer is to be found. A copy of the Mead partial reprint is in the Bibliothèque Nationale, and two copies are in the British Museum.

A last word on the attitude of John Calvin towards Servetus. Much scorn has been heaped upon the great reformer, and one cannot but regret that a man of such magnificent achievements should have been dragged into a miserable heresy hunt like a common inquisitor. Let us not estimate him by his century, as his friends plead, but frankly by his life, and as a man of like passions with ourselves. He had bitter provocation. Flouted for years by the persistent assaults of Servetus, and shocked out of all compassion by his blasphemies, is it to be wondered that the old Adam got the better of his Christian charity? Not only is it impossible to acquit Calvin of active complicity in this unhappy affair, but there was mixed up with it a personal hate, a vindictiveness unbecoming in so great a character, and we may say foreign to it. But let the long record of a self-denying life, devoted in an evil generation to the highest and the best, wipe out for all reasonable men this one blot. Let us, if we may judge him at all, do so as a man, not as a demi-god. We cannot defend him, let us not condemn him; let his one grievous fault, even though we may fear he never repented of it, be the shadow which throws into stronger relief the splendid outlines of a noble life. In his 'Defence',[1] the original edition of which I have here, and which is concerned largely with doctrinal questions, not only are there no expressions of regret for the part he played

[1] *Defensio Orthodoxae Fidei*, &c., 1554.

in the tragedy, but the work is filled with insults to his dead enemy, couched in the most vindictive language. On the spot where Servetus was burnt there stands to-day an expiatory monument which expresses the spirit of modern Protestantism. On one side is the record of his birth and death, on the other an inscription, of which the following is a translation: 'Duteous and grateful followers of Calvin our great Reformer, yet condemning an error which was that of his age, and strongly attached to liberty of conscience according to the true principles of the Reformation and the Gospel, we have erected this expiatory monument. Oct. 27, 1903.'

The erection next year at Vienne of a quatercentenary monument will complete the recognition by the modern world of the merits of one of the strangest figures on the rich canvas of the sixteenth century. The wandering Spanish scholar, the stormy disputant, the anatomical prosector, the mystic dreamer of a restored Christianity, the discoverer of one of the fundamental facts of physiology, has come at last to his own. There are those, I know, who feel that perhaps more than justice has been done; but in a tragic age Servetus played an unusually tragic part, and the pathos of his fate appeals strongly to us.

These, too, are days of retribution, of the restoration of all things, the days of the opening of the fifth seal, when the souls under the altar see their blood avenged, when we clothe in the white robes of charity those who were slain for the testimony which they held, little noting whether the martyr was Catholic or Protestant, caring only to honour one of that great company which no man can number, 'whose heroic sufferings', as Carlyle says, 'rise up melodiously together to heaven out of all lands and out of all time, as a sacred Miserere, their heroic actions also as a boundless everlasting Psalm of Triumph'.

Note.—The Servetus bibliography is fully given to 1890 in Professor A. van der Linde's *Michael Servetus*, Groningen, 1891. My personal interest dates many years back when Pastor Tollin's delightful sketches enlivened the numbers of Virchow's *Archives*. No one has ever had a more enthusiastic biographer, and to the writings of the

Madgeburg clergyman we owe the greater part of our modern knowledge of Servetus. The best account in English is by Willis—*Servetus and Calvin*, 1877. A German translation of the *Christianismi Restitutio* by Dr. Bernhard Spiess appeared in 1895 (2nd edition, Wiesbaden, Chr. Limbarth). I am indebted to Professor Harper of Princeton for an historical drama, *The Reformer of Geneva*, by Professor Shields (privately printed, Princeton University Press, 1897), which gives an admirable picture of Geneva at the time of the trial. From Chéreau's *Histoire d'un Livre*, 1879, I have 'cribbed' the idea of the introduction. The name of Mosheim must be mentioned, as his writings were for years the common tap from which all Servetus knowledge was derived.

8

WILLIAM BEAUMONT

A BACKWOOD PHYSIOLOGIST

COME with me for a few moments on a lovely June day in 1822, to what were then far-off northern wilds, to the Island of Michilimacinac, where the waters of Lake Michigan and Lake Huron unite and where stands Fort Mackinac, rich in the memories of Indian and voyageur, one of the four important posts on the upper lakes in the days when the rose and the fleur-de-lis strove for the mastery of the western world. Here the noble Marquette laboured for his Lord, and here beneath the chapel of St. Ignace they laid his bones to rest. Here the intrepid La Salle, the brave Tonty, and the resolute Du Luht had halted in their wild wanderings. Its palisades and block-houses had echoed the war-whoops of Ojibwas and Ottawas, of Hurons and Iroquois, and the old fort had been the scene of bloody massacres and hard-fought fights; but at the conclusion of the War of 1812, after two centuries of struggle, peace settled at last on the island. The fort was occupied by United States troops, who kept the Indians in check and did general police duty on the frontier, and the place had become a rendezvous for Indians and voyageurs in the employ of the American Fur Company. On this bright spring morning the village presented an animated scene. The annual return tide to the trading post was in full course, and the beach was thronged with canoes and bateaux laden with the pelts of the winter's hunt. Voyageurs and Indians, men, women, and children, with here and there a few soldiers, made up a motley crowd. Suddenly

An address before the St. Louis Medical Society, 4 October 1902. Published St. Louis, 1902. 29 pages. Printed in the *Journal of the American Medical Association*, 1902, xxxix, 1223–31. In *An Alabama Student* as 'A Backwood Physiologist'.

from the company's store there is a loud report of a gun, and amid the confusion and excitement the rumour spreads of an accident, and there is a hurrying of messengers to the barracks for a doctor. In a few minutes (Beaumont says twenty-five or thirty, an eyewitness says three) an alert-looking man in the uniform of a U.S. Army surgeon made his way through the crowd, and was at the side of a young French Canadian who had been wounded by the discharge of a gun, and with a composure bred of an exceptional experience of such injuries, prepared to make the examination. Though youthful in appearance, Surgeon Beaumont had seen much service, and at the capture of York and at the investment of Plattsburgh he had shown a coolness and bravery under fire which had won high praise from his superior officers. The man and the opportunity had met—the outcome is my story of this evening.

I. THE OPPORTUNITY—ALEXIS ST. MARTIN

On the morning of 6 June a young French Canadian, Alexis St. Martin, was standing in the company's store, 'where one of the party was holding a shotgun (not a musket), which was accidentally discharged, the whole charge entering St. Martin's body. The muzzle was not over three feet from him —I think not more than two. The wadding entered, as well as pieces of his clothing; his shirt took fire; he fell, as we supposed, dead.'

'Doctor Beaumont, the surgeon of the fort, was immediately sent for, and reached the wounded man in a very short time, probably three minutes. We had just gotten him on a cot, and were taking off some of his clothing. After the doctor had extracted part of the shot, together with pieces of clothing, and dressed his wound carefully, Robert Stuart and others assisting, he left him, remarking, "The man cannot live thirty-six hours; I will come and see him by and by." In two or three hours he visited him again, expressing surprise at finding him doing better than he had anticipated. The next day, after getting out more shot and clothing, and cutting off ragged edges of the wound, he informed Mr. Stuart, in my presence, that he thought he would recover.'[1]

The description of the wound has been so often quoted as reported in Beaumont's work, that I give here the interesting summary which I find in a 'Memorial' presented to the Senate and House of Representatives by Beaumont:

The wound was received just under the left breast, and supposed, at the time, to have been mortal. A large portion of the side was blown off, the ribs fractured, and openings made into the cavities of the chest and abdomen, through which protruded portions of the lungs and stomach, much lacerated and burnt, exhibiting altogether an appalling and hopeless case. The diaphragm was lacerated, and a perforation made directly into the cavity of the stomach, through which food was escaping at the time your memorialist was called to his relief. His life was at first wholly despaired of, but he very unexpectedly survived the immediate effects of the wound, and necessarily continued a long time under the constant professional care and treatment of your memorialist, and, by the blessing of God, finally recovered his health and strength.

At the end of about ten months the wound was partially healed, but he was still an object altogether miserable and helpless. In this situation he was declared 'a common pauper' by the civil authorities of the county, and it was resolved by them that they were not able, nor required, to provide for or support, and finally declined taking care of him, and, in pursuance of what they probably believed to be their public duty, authorized by the laws of the territory, were about to transport him, in this condition, to the place of his nativity in lower Canada, a distance of more than fifteen hundred miles.

Believing the life of St. Martin must inevitably be sacrificed if such attempt to remove him should be carried into execution at that time, your memorialist, after earnest, repeated, but unavailing, remonstrances against such a course of proceedings, resolved, as the only way to rescue St. Martin from impending misery and death, to arrest the process of transportation and prevent the consequent

---

[1] Statement of G. G. Hubbard, an officer of the company, who was present when St. Martin was shot, quoted by Dr. J. R. Baily, of Mackinac Island, in his address on the occasion of the Beaumont Memorial Exercises, Mackinac Island, 10 July 1900. *The Physician and Surgeon*, December 1900.

'PARTURIT OSLER, NASCITUR LIBER'
Writing the Text-book, Baltimore, 1891

A FAMILY SNAPSHOT AT OXFORD
BY DR. C. K. RUSSEL OF MONTREAL, JUNE 1905

suffering, by taking him into his own private family, where all the care and attention were bestowed that his condition required.

St. Martin was, at this time, as before intimated, altogether help-less and suffering under the debilitating effects of his wounds—naked and destitute of everything. In this situation your memorialist received, kept, nursed, medically and surgically treated and sustained him, at much inconvenience and expense, for nearly two years, dress-ing his wounds daily, and for considerable part of the time twice a day, nursed him, fed him, clothed him, lodged him and furnished him with such necessaries and comforts as his condition and suffering required.

At the end of these two years he had become able to walk and help himself a little, though unable to provide for his own necessities. In this situation your memorialist retained St. Martin in his family for the special purpose of making physiological experiments.

In the month of May 1825 Beaumont began the experiments. In June he was ordered to Fort Niagara, where, taking the man with him, he continued the experiments until August. He then took him to Burlington and to Plattsburgh. From the latter place St. Martin returned to Canada, without obtaining Dr. Beaumont's consent. He remained in Canada four years, worked as a voyageur, married and had two children. In 1829 Beaumont succeeded in getting track of St. Martin, and the American Fur Company engaged him and transported him to Fort Crawford on the upper Mississippi. The side and wound were in the same condition as in 1825. Experiments were continued uninterrup-tedly until March 1831, when circumstances made it expedient that he should return with his family to lower Canada. The 'circumstances', as we gather from letters, were the discontent and homesickness of his wife. As illustrating the mode of travel, Beaumont states that St. Martin took his family in an open canoe 'via the Mississippi, passing by St. Louis, ascended the Ohio river, then crossed the state of Ohio to the lakes, and descended the Erie and Ontario and the river St. Lawrence to Montreal, where they arrived in June'. Dr. Beaumont often lays stress on the physical vigour of St. Martin as showing how com-pletely he had recovered from the wound. In November 1832 he again engaged himself to submit to another series of experiments in Plattsburgh and Washington. The last recorded experiment is in November 1833.

Among the Beaumont papers, for an examination of which I am much indebted to his daughter, Mrs. Keim (Appendix A), there is a large mass of correspondence relating to St. Martin, extending from 1827, two years after he had left the doctor's employ, to October 1852. Alexis was in Dr. Beaumont's employ in the periods already specified. In 1833 he was enrolled in the United States Army at Washington as Sergeant Alexis St. Martin, of a detachment of orderlies stationed at the War Department. He was then twenty-eight years of age, and was five feet five inches in height.

Among the papers there are two articles of agreement, both signed by the contracting parties, one dated 19 October 1833, and the other 7 November of the same year. In the former he bound himself for a term of one year to

Serve, abide and continue with the said William Beaumont, wherever he shall go or travel or reside in any part of the world his covenant servant and diligently and faithfully, etc., . . . that he, the said Alexis, will at all times during said term when thereto directed or required by said William, submit to assist and promote by all means in his power such philosophical or medical experiments as the said William shall direct or cause to be made on or in the stomach of him, the said Alexis, either through and by means of the aperture or opening thereto in the side of him, the said Alexis, or otherwise, and will obey, suffer and comply with all reasonable and proper orders of or experiments of the said William in relation thereto and in relation to the exhibiting and showing of his said stomach and the powers and properties thereto and of the appurtenances and the powers, properties, and situation and state of the contents thereof.

The agreement was that he should be paid his board and lodging and $150 for the year. In the other agreement it is for two years, and the remuneration $400. He was paid a certain amount of the money down.

There are some letters from Alexis himself, all written for

him and signed with his mark. In June 1834 he writes that his wife was not willing to let him go, and thinks that he can do a great deal better to stay at home. From this time on Alexis was never again in Dr. Beaumont's employ.

There is a most interesting and protracted correspondence in the years 1836, 1837, 1838, 1839, 1840, 1842, 1846, 1851, and 1852, all relating to attempts to induce Alexis to come to St. Louis. For the greater part of this time he was in Berthier, in the district of Montreal, and the correspondence was chiefly conducted with a Mr. William Morrison, who had been in the north-west fur trade, and who took the greatest interest in Alexis, and tried to induce him to go to St. Louis. (See Appendix B.)

In 1846 Beaumont sent his son Israel for Alexis, and in a letter dated 9 August 1846, his son writes from Troy: 'I have just returned from Montreal, but without Alexis. Upon arriving at Berthier I found that he owned and lived on a farm about fifteen miles south-west of the village.' Nothing would induce him to go.

The correspondence with Mr. Morrison in 1851 and 1852 is most voluminous, and Dr. Beaumont offered Alexis $500 for the year, with comfortable support for his family. He agreed at one time to go, but it was too late in the winter and he could not get away.

The last letter of the series is dated 15 October 1852, and is from Dr. Beaumont to Alexis, whom he addresses as *Mon Ami*. Two sentences in this are worth quoting:

Without reference to past efforts and disappointments—or expectation of ever obtaining your services again for the purpose of experiments, etc., upon the proposals and conditions heretofore made and suggested, I now proffer to you in faith and sincerity, new, and I hope satisfactory, terms and conditions to ensure your prompt and faithful compliance with my most fervent desire to have you again with me—not only for my own individual gratification, and the benefits of medical science, but also for your own and family's present good and future welfare.' He concludes with, 'I can say no more, Alexis—you know what I *have* done for you many years since—what

I have been *trying*, and am still anxious and wishing to do with and for you—what efforts, anxieties, anticipations, and disappointments I have suffered from your non-fulfilment of my expectations. Don't disappoint me more nor forfeit the bounties and blessings reserved for you.

So much interest was excited by the report of the experiments that it was suggested to Beaumont that he should take Alexis to Europe and submit him there to a more extended series of observations by skilled physiologists. Writing 10 June 1833, he says: 'I shall engage him for five or six years if he will agree, of which I expect there is no doubt. He has always been pleased with the idea of going to France. I feel much gratified at the expression of Mr. Livingston's desire that we should visit Paris, and shall duly consider the interest he takes in the subject and make the best arrangements I can to meet his views and yours.' Mr. Livingston, the American minister, wrote from Paris, 18 March 1834, saying that he had submitted the work to Orfila and the Academy of Sciences, which had appointed a committee to determine if additional experiments were necessary, and whether it was advisable to send to America for Alexis. Nothing, I believe, ever came of this, nor, so far as I can find, did Alexis visit Paris. Other attempts were made to secure him for purposes of study. In 1840 a student of Dr. Beaumont's, George Johnson, then at the University of Pennsylvania, wrote saying that Dr. Jackson had told him of efforts made to get Alexis to London, and Dr. Gibson informed him that the Medical Society of London had raised £300 or £400 to induce St. Martin to come, and that he, Dr. Gibson, had been trying to find St. Martin for his London friends. There are letters in the same year from Dr. R. D. Thomson, of London, to Professor Silliman, urging him to arrange that Dr. Beaumont and Alexis should visit London. In 1856 St. Martin was under the observation of Dr. Francis Gurney Smith, in Philadelphia, who reported a brief series of experiments, so far as I know the only other report made on him.[1]

[1] *Medical Examiner*, 1856, and *Experiments on Digestion*, Philadelphia, 1856.

St. Martin had to stand a good deal of chaffing about the hole in his side. His comrades called him 'the man with a lid on his stomach'. In his memorial address, Mr. C. S. Osborn, of Sault Ste Marie, states that Miss Catherwood tells a story of Étienne St. Martin fighting with Charlie Charette because Charlie ridiculed his brother. Étienne stabbed him severely, and swore that he would kill the whole brigade if they did not stop deriding his brother's stomach.

At one time St. Martin travelled about exhibiting the wound to physicians, medical students, and before medical societies. In a copy of Beaumont's work, formerly belonging to Austin Flint, Jr., and now in the possession of a physician of St. Louis, there is a photograph of Alexis sent to Dr. Flint. There are statements made that he went to Europe, but of such a visit I can find no record.

My interest in St. Martin was of quite the general character of a teacher of physiology, who every session referred to his remarkable wound and showed Beaumont's book with the illustration. In the spring of 1880, while still a resident of Montreal, I saw a notice in the newspapers of his death at St. Thomas. I immediately wrote to a physician and to the parish priest, urging them to secure me the privilege of an autopsy, and offering to pay a fair sum for the stomach, which I agreed to place in the Army Medical Museum in Washington, but without avail. Subsequently, through the kindness of the Hon. Mr. Justice Baby, I obtained the following details of St. Martin's later life. Judge Baby writes to his friend, Prof. D. C. MacCallum of Montreal, as follows:

I have much pleasure to-day in placing in your hands such information about St. Martin as Revd. Mr. Chicoine, Curé of St. Thomas, has just handed over to me. Alexis Bidigan, *dit* St. Martin, died at St. Thomas de Joliette on the 24th of June, 1880, and was buried in the cemetery of the parish on the 28th of the same month. The last sacraments of the Catholic church were ministered to him by the Revd. Curé Chicoine, who also attended at his burial service. The body was then in such an advanced stage of decomposition that it could not be admitted into the church, but had to be left outside during the funeral service. The family resisted all requests—most pressing as they were—on the part of the members of the medical profession for an autopsy, and also kept the body at home much longer than usual and during a hot spell of weather, so as to allow decomposition to set in and baffle, as they thought, the doctors of the surrounding country and others. They had also the grave dug eight feet below the surface of the ground in order to prevent any attempt at a resurrection. When he died St. Martin was 83 years of age, and left a widow, whose maiden name was Marie Joly. She survived him by nearly seven years, dying at St. Thomas on the 20th of April, 1887, at the very old age of 90 years. They left four children, still alive—Alexis, Charles, Henriette, and Marie.

Now I may add the following details for myself. When I came to know St. Martin it must have been a few years before his death. A lawsuit brought him to my office here in Joliette. I was seized with his interests; he came to my office a good many times, during which visits he spoke to me at great length of his former life, how his wound had been caused, his peregrinations through Europe and the United States, etc. He showed me his wound. He complained bitterly of some doctors who had awfully misused him, and had kind words for others. He had made considerable money during his tours, but had expended and thrown it all away in a frolicsome way, especially in the old country. When I came across him he was rather poor, living on a small, scanty farm in St. Thomas, and very much addicted to drink, almost a drunkard one might say. He was a tall, lean man, with a very dark complexion, and appeared to me then of a morose disposition.

II. THE BOOK

In the four periods in which Alexis had been under the care and study of Beaumont a large series of observations had been recorded, amounting in all to 238. A preliminary account of the case, and of the first group of observations, appeared in the *Philadelphia Medical Recorder* in January 1825. During the stay in Washington in 1832 the great importance of the observations had become impressed on the Surgeon-General, Dr. Lovell, who seems to have acted in a most generous and kindly spirit.

Beaumont tried to induce him to undertake the arrangement of the observations, but Lovell insisted that he should do the work himself. In the spring of 1833 Alexis was taken to New York, and there shown to the prominent members of the profession, and careful drawings and coloured sketches were made of the wound by Mr. King. A prospectus of the work was issued and was distributed by the Surgeon-General, who speaks in a letter of sending them to Dr. Franklin Bache and to Dr. Stewart of Philadelphia, and in a letter from Dr. Bache to Dr. Beaumont, acknowledging the receipt of a bottle of gastric juice, Bache states that he has placed the prospectus in Mr. Judah Dobson's store and has asked for subscribers. Beaumont did not find New York a very congenial place. He complained of the difficulty of doing the work, owing to the vexatious social intercourse. He applied for permission to go to Plattsburgh, in order to complete the book. After having made inquiries in New York and Philadelphia about terms of publication, he decided, as the work had to be issued at his own expense, that it could be as well and much more cheaply printed at Plattsburgh, where he would also have the advice and help of his cousin, Dr. Samuel Beaumont. In a letter to the Surgeon-General, dated 10 June 1833, he acknowledges the permission to go to Plattsburgh, and says: 'I shall make my arrangements to leave here for Pl. in about a week to *rush* the execution of the Book as fast as possible. I am now having the drawings taken by Mr. King engraved here.'

The summer was occupied in making a fresh series of experiments and getting the work in type. On 3 December he writes to the Surgeon-General that the book will be ready for distribution in a few days, and that 1,000 copies will be printed.

The work is an octavo volume of 280 pages, entitled *Experiments and Observations on the Gastric Juice and the Physiology of Digestion*, by William Beaumont, M.D., Surgeon in the United States Army. Plattsburgh. Printed by F. P. Allen, 1833. While it is well and carefully printed, the paper and type are not of the best, and one cannot but regret that Beaumont did not take the advice of Dr. Franklin Bache, who urged him strongly not to have the work printed at Plattsburgh, but in Philadelphia, where it could be done in very much better style. The dedication of the work to Joseph Lovell, M.D., Surgeon-General of the United States Army, acknowledges in somewhat laudatory terms the debt which Beaumont felt he owed to his chief, who very gratefully acknowledges the compliment and the kindly feeling, but characterizes the dedication as 'somewhat apocryphal'.

The work is divided into two main portions; first, the preliminary observations on the general physiology of digestion in seven sections: Section I, Of Aliment; Section II, Of Hunger and Thirst; Section III, Of Satisfaction and Satiety; Section IV, Of Mastication, Insalivation, and Deglutition; Section V, Of Digestion by the Gastric Juice; Section VI, Of the Appearance of the Villous Coat, and of the Motions of the Stomach; Section VII, Of Chylification and Uses of the Bile and Pancreatic Juice. The greater part of the book is occupied by the larger section of the detailed account of the four series of experiments and observations. The work concludes with a series of fifty-one inferences from the foregoing experiments and observations.

The subsequent history of the book itself is of interest, and may be dealt with here. In 1834 copies of the Plattsburgh edition, printed by F. P. Allen, were issued by Lilly, Wait & Co., of Boston.

In the Beaumont correspondence there are many letters from a Dr. McCall, in Utica, N.Y., who was an intimate friend of a Mr. Wm. Combe, a brother of the well-known physiologist and popular writer, Dr. Andrew Combe of Edinburgh. Doubtless it was through this connexion that in 1838 Dr. Combe issued an edition in Scotland, with numerous notes and comments. (Appendix C.)

The second edition was issued from Burlington, Vt., in 1847, with the same title-page, but after *Second Edition* there are the words, *Corrected by Samuel Beaumont, M.D.*, who was Dr. William Beaumont's cousin. In the preface to this edition the statement is made that the first edition, though a large one of 3,000 copies, had been exhausted. This does not agree with the statement made in a letter of 3 December 1833, to the Surgeon-General, stating that the edition was to be 1,000 copies. Of course more may have been printed before the type was distributed. While it is stated to be a new and improved edition, so far as I can gather it is a verbatim reprint, with no additional observations, but with a good many minor corrections. In an appendix (D) I give an interesting letter from Dr. Samuel Beaumont with reference to the issue of this edition.

A German edition was issued in 1834, with the following title: *Neue Versuche und Beobachtungen über den Magensaft und die Physiologie der Verdauung, auf eine höchst merkwürdige Weise während einer Reihe von 7 Jahren an einem und demselben Subject angestellt.* Beaumont's earlier paper, already referred to, was abstracted in the *Magazin der ausländischen Litteratur der gesammten Heilkunde,* Hamburg, 1826, and also in the *Archives générales de Médecine,* Paris, 1828. I cannot find that there was a French edition of the work.

The *Experiments and Observations* attracted universal attention, both at home and abroad. The journals of the period contained very full accounts of the work, and within a few years the valuable additions to our knowledge filtered into the text-books of physiology, which to-day in certain descriptions of the gastric juice and of the phenomena of digestion copy even the very language of the work.

III. THE VALUE OF BEAUMONT'S OBSERVATIONS

There had been other instances of artificial gastric fistula in man which had been made the subject of experimental study, but the case of St. Martin stands out from all others on account of the ability and care with which the experiments were conducted. As Dr. Combe says, the value of these experiments consists partly in the admirable opportunities for observation which Beaumont enjoyed, and partly in the candid and truth-seeking spirit in which all his inquiries seem to have been conducted.

It would be difficult to point out any observer who excels him in devotion to truth, and freedom from the trammels of theory or prejudice. He tells plainly what he saw and leaves everyone to draw his own inferences, or where he lays down conclusions he does so with a degree of modesty and fairness of which few perhaps in his circumstances would have been capable.

To appreciate the value of Beaumont's studies it is necessary to refer for a few moments to our knowledge of the physiology of digestion in the year 1833, the date of the publication. Take, for example, the work on *Human Physiology* (published the year before the appearance of Beaumont's book), by Dunglison, a man of wide learning and thoroughly informed in the literature of the subject. The five or six old theories of stomach digestion, concoction, putrefaction, trituration, fermentation, and maceration, are all discussed, and William Hunter's pithy remark is quoted, 'some physiologists will have it, that the stomach is a mill, others, that it is a fermenting vat, others, again, that it is a stew-pan; but, in my view of the matter, it is neither a mill, a fermenting vat, nor a stew-pan; but a stomach, gentlemen, a stomach'.

The theory of chemical solution is accepted. This had been placed on a sound basis by the experiments of Réaumur, Spallanzani, and Stevens, while the studies of Tiedemann and Gmelin and of Prout had done much to solve the problems of the chemistry of the juice. But very much uncertainty existed as to the phenomena occurring during digestion in the stomach, the precise mode of action of the juice, the nature of the juice itself, and its action outside the body. On all these points the observations of Beaumont brought clearness and light where there had been previously the greatest obscurity.

The following may be regarded as the most important of the results of Beaumont's observations: First, the accuracy and completeness of description of the gastric juice itself. You will all recognize the following quotation, which has entered into the text-books and passes current to-day:

Pure gastric juice, when taken directly out of the stomach of a healthy adult, unmixed with any other fluid, save a portion of the mucus of the stomach with which it is most commonly and perhaps always combined, is a clear, transparent fluid; inodorous; a little saltish, and very perceptibly acid. Its taste, when applied to the tongue, is similar to thin mucilaginous water slightly acidulated with muriatic acid. It is readily diffusible in water, wine, or spirits; slightly effervesces with alkalis; and is an effectual solvent of the *materia alimentaria*. It possesses the property of coagulating albumen, in an eminent degree; is powerfully antiseptic, checking the putrefaction of meat; and effectually restorative of healthy action, when applied to old, fetid sores and foul, ulcerating surfaces.

Secondly, the confirmation of the observation of Prout that the important acid of the gastric juice was the muriatic or hydrochloric. An analysis of St. Martin's gastric juice was made by Dunglison, at that time a professor in the University of Virginia, and by Benjamin Silliman of Yale, both of whom determined the presence of free hydrochloric acid. A specimen was sent to the distinguished Swedish chemist, Berzelius, whose report did not arrive in time to be included in the work. In a letter dated 19 July 1834 he writes to Professor Silliman that he had not been able to make a satisfactory analysis of the juice. The letter is published in *Silliman's Journal*, vol. xxvii, July 1835.

Thirdly, the recognition of the fact that the essential elements of the gastric juice and the mucus were separate secretions.

Fourthly, the establishment by direct observation of the profound influence of mental disturbances on the secretion of the gastric juice and on digestion.

Fifthly, a more accurate and fuller comparative study of the digestion in the stomach with digestion outside the body, confirming in a most elaborate series of experiments the older observations of Spallanzani and Stevens.

Sixthly, the refutation of many erroneous opinions relating to gastric digestion, and the establishment of a number of minor points of great importance, such as, for instance, the rapid disappearance of water from the stomach through the pylorus, a point brought out by recent experiments, but insisted on and amply proved by Beaumont.

Seventhly, the first comprehensive and thorough study of the motions of the stomach, observations on which, indeed, is based the most of our present knowledge.

And lastly, a study of the digestibility of different articles of diet in the stomach, which remains to-day one of the most important contributions ever made to practical dietetics.

The greater rapidity with which solid food is digested, the injurious effects on the stomach of tea and coffee, when taken in excess, the pernicious influence of alcoholic drinks on the digestion, are constantly referred to. An all-important practical point insisted on by Beaumont needs emphatic reiteration to this generation:

The system requires much less than is generally supplied to it. The stomach disposes of a definite quantity. If more be taken than the actual wants of the economy require, the residue remains in the stomach and becomes a source of irritation and produces a consequent aberration of function, or passes into the lower bowel in an undigested state, and extends to them its deleterious influence. Dyspepsia is oftener the effect of over-eating and over-drinking than of any other cause.

One is much impressed, too, in going over the experiments, to note with what modesty Beaumont refers to his own work. He speaks of himself as a humble 'inquirer after truth and a simple experimenter'.

Honest objections, no doubt, are entertained against the doctrine of digestion by the gastric juice. That they are so entertained by these gentlemen I have no doubt. And I cheerfully concede to them the merit of great ingenuity, talents, and learning, in raising objections to the commonly received hypothesis, as well as ability in maintaining their peculiar opinions. But we ought not to allow ourselves to be seduced by the ingenuity of argument or the blandishments of style. Truth, like beauty, is 'when unadorned adorned the most'; and in prosecuting these experiments and inquiries, I believe I have been guided by its light. Facts are more persuasive than arguments, however ingeniously made, and by their eloquence I hope I have been able to plead for the support and maintenance of those doctrines which have had for their advocates such men as Sydenham, Hunter, Spallanzani, Richerand, Abernethy, Broussais, Philip, Paris,

Bostock, the Heidelberg and Paris professors, Dunglison, and a host of other luminaries in the science of physiology.

In reality Beaumont anticipated some of the most recent studies in the physiology of digestion. Doubtless many of you have heard of new work on the subject by Professor Pavlov of St. Petersburg. It has been translated into German, and I see that an English edition is advertised. He has studied the gastric juice in an isolated pouch, ingeniously made at the fundus of the stomach of the dog, from which the juice could be obtained in a pure state. One of his results is the very first announced by Beaumont, and confirmed by scores of observations on St. Martin, viz. that, as he says, 'the gastric juice never appears to be accumulated in the cavity of the stomach while fasting'. Pavlov has shown very clearly that there is a relation between the amount of food taken and the quantity of gastric juice secreted. Beaumont came to the same conclusion: 'when aliment is received the juice is given in exact proportion to its requirements for solution'. A third point on which Pavlov lays stress is the curve of secretion of the gastric juice, the manner in which it is poured out during digestion. The greatest secretion, he has shown, takes place in the earlier hours. On this point hear Beaumont: 'It (the gastric juice) then begins to exude from the proper vessels and increases in proportion to the quantity of aliment naturally required and received.' And again: 'When a due and moderate supply of food has been received it is probable that the whole quantity of gastric juice for its complete solution is secreted and mixed with it in a short time.' A fourth point, worked out beautifully by Pavlov, is the adaptation of the juice to the nature of the food; I do not see any reference to this by Beaumont, but there are no experiments more full than those in which he deals with the influence of exercise, weather, and the emotions on the quantity of the juice secreted.

IV. MAN AND DOCTOR

Sketches of Dr. Beaumont's life have appeared from time to time. There is a worthy memoir by Dr. T. Reyburn in the

St. Louis Medical and Surgical Journal, 1854, and Dr. A. J. Steele, at the first annual commencement of the Beaumont Medical College, 1887, told well and graphically the story of his life. A few years ago Dr. Frank J. Lutz, of this city, sketched his life for the memorial meeting of the Michigan State Medical Society on the occasion of the dedication of a Beaumont monument.

Among the papers kindly sent to me by his daughter, Mrs. Keim, are many autobiographical materials, particularly relating to his early studies and to his work as a surgeon in the War of 1812. There is an excellent paper in the handwriting, it is said, of his son, giving a summary of the earlier period of his life. So far as I know this has not been published, and I give it in full:

Dr. William Beaumont was born in the town of Lebanon, Conn., on the 21st day of November, A.D. 1785. His father was a thriving farmer and an active politician of the proud old Jeffersonian school, whose highest boast was his firm support and strict adherence to the honest principles he advocated. William was his third son, who, in the winter of 1806–7, in the 22nd year of his age, prompted by a spirit of independence and adventure, left the paternal roof to seek a fortune and a name. His outfit consisted of a horse and cutter, a barrel of cider, and one hundred dollars of hard-earned money. With this he started, laying his course northwardly, without any particular destination, Honour his rule of action, Truth his only landmark, and trust placed implicitly in Heaven. Traversing the western part of Massachusetts and Vermont in the spring of 1807 he arrived at the little village of Champlain, N.Y., on the Canada frontier—an utter stranger, friendless and alone. But honesty of purpose and true energy invariably work good results. He soon gained the people's confidence, and was entrusted with their village school, which he conducted about three years, devoting his leisure hours to the study of medical works from the library of Dr. Seth Pomeroy, his first patron. He then went over to St. Albans, Vt., where he entered the office of Dr. Benjamin Chandler and commenced a regular course of medical reading, which he followed for two years, gaining the utmost confidence and esteem of his kind preceptor and friends. About this time the war of 1812 commenced, and he applied for an appointment in the U.S. Army, successfully. He was appointed assistant-surgeon to the Sixth Infantry, and joined his regiment at Plattsburgh, N.Y., on the 13th of September, 1812. On the 19th of March, 1813, he marched from Plattsburgh with the First Brigade, for Sackett's Harbour, where they arrived on the 27th inst. Here he remained in camp till the 22nd of April, when he embarked with the troops on Lake Ontario. His journal will best tell this portion of his history:

'April 22, 1813—Embarked with Captain Humphreys, Walworth and Muhlenburg, and companies on board the schooner *Julia*. The rest of the brigade, and the Second, with Foresith's Rifle Regiment and the Eighth Artillery—on board a ship, brig, and schooner—remain in the harbour till next morning.

'23rd.—11 o'clock a.m.—Weighs anchor and put out under the impression we were going to Kingston. Got out 15 or 20 miles—encountered a storm—wind ahead and the fleet returned to harbour.

'24th.—6 o'clock a.m.—Put out with a fair wind—mild and pleasant—the fleet sailing in fine order.

'26th.—Wind pretty strong—increasing—waves run high, tossing our vessels roughly. At half-past four pass the mouth of Niagara river. This circumstance baffles imagination as to where we are going —first impressed with the idea of Kingston—then to Niagara—but now our destination must be 'Little York'. At sunset came in view of York Town and the Fort, where we lay off some 3 or 4 leagues for the night.

'27th.—Sailed into harbour and came to anchor a little below the British Garrison. Filled the boats and effected a landing, though not without difficulty and the loss of some men. The British marched their troops down the beach to cut us off as landing, and, though they had every advantage, they could not effect their design. A hot engagement ensued, in which the enemy lost nearly a third of their men, and were soon compelled to quit the field, leaving their dead and wounded strewn in every direction. They retired to the Garrison, but from the loss sustained in the engagement, the undaunted courage of our men, and the brisk firing from our fleet, with the 12 and 32-pounders, they were soon obliged to evacuate it and retreat with all possible speed. Driven to this alternative, they devised the inhuman project of blowing up their magazine, containing 300 pounds of powder, the explosion of which had wellnigh destroyed our army. Over 300 were wounded and about 60 killed on the spot, by stones of all dimensions falling, like a shower of hail, in the midst of our ranks. A most distressing scene ensues in the hospital. Nothing is heard but the agonizing groans and supplications of the wounded and the dying. The surgeons wade in blood, cutting off arms and legs and trepanning heads, while the poor sufferers cry, "O, my God! Doctor, relieve me from this misery! I cannot live!" 'Twas enough to touch the veriest heart of steel and move the most relentless savage. Imagine the shocking scene, where fellow beings lie mashed and mangled—legs and arms broken and sundered—heads and bodies bruised and mutilated to disfigurement! My deepest sympathies were roused—I cut and slashed for 36 hours without food or sleep.

'29th—Dressed upwards of 50 patients—from simple contusions to the worst of compound fractures—more than half the latter. Performed two cases of amputation and one of trepanning. At 12 p.m. retired to rest my fatigued body and mind.'

One month after the taking of York he witnessed the storming of Fort George. The troops were transported from York to 'Four-Mile Creek' (in the vicinity of Ft. George), where they encamped from the 10th of May to the 27th, when they advanced to the attack. His journal runs thus:

'May 27 (1813).—Embarked at break of day—Col. Scott with 800 men, for the advanced guard, supported by the First Brigade, commanded by General Boyd, moved in concert with the shipping to the enemy's shore and landed under their battery and in front of their fire with surprising success, not losing more than 30 men in the engagement, though the enemy's whole force was placed in the most advantageous situation possible. We routed them from their chosen spot—drove them from the country and took possession of the town and garrison.'

On the 11th of September, 1814, he was at the Battle of Plattsburgh, still serving as assistant-surgeon, though doing all the duty of a full surgeon. At the close of the war, in 1815, when the army was cut down, he was retained in service, but resigned soon after, deeming himself unjustly treated by the government in having others, younger and less experienced, promoted over him.

In 1816 he settled in Plattsburgh and remained there four years in successful practice. In the meantime his army friends had persuaded him to join the service again, and, having applied, he was reappointed, in 1820, and ordered to Ft. Mackinac as post-surgeon.

At the end of the first year he obtained leave of absence, returned to Plattsburgh, and married one of the most amiable and interesting ladies of that place. (She still survives her honoured husband, and in her green old age is loved devotedly by all who know her.) He returned to Mackinac the same year, and in 1822 came in possession of Alexis St. Martin, the subject of his *Experiments on the Gastric Juice*. By the accidental discharge of his gun, while hunting, St. Martin had dangerously wounded himself in the abdomen and came under the treatment of Dr. Beaumont, who healed the wound (in itself a triumph of skill almost unequalled) and in 1825 commenced a series of experiments, the results of which have a world-wide publication. These experiments were continued, with various interruptions, for eight years, during which time he was ordered from post to post—now at Niagara, N.Y., anon at Green Bay, Mich., and finally at Fort Crawford, on the Mississippi. In 1834 he was ordered to St. Louis, where he remained in service till 1839, when he resigned. He then commenced service with the citizens of St. Louis, and from that time till the period of his last illness, enjoyed an extensive and distinguished practice, interrupted only by the base attacks of a few disgraceful and malicious knaves (self-deemed members of the medical profession) who sought to destroy a reputation which they could not share. They gained nothing except some little unenviable notoriety, and they have skulked away like famished wolves, to die in their hiding-places.

The dates of Beaumont's commissions in the army are as follows: Surgeon's Mate, Sixth Regiment of Infantry, 2 December 1812; Cavalry, 27 March 1819; Post-Surgeon, 4 December 1819; Surgeon First Regiment and Surgeon, 6 November 1826.

From the biographical sketches of Reyburn, Steele, and Lutz, and from the personal reminiscences of his friends, Drs. J. B. Johnson, S. Pollak, and Wm. McPheeters, who fortunately remains with you, full of years and honours, we gather a clearly defined picture of the latter years of his life. It is that of a faithful, honest, hard-working practitioner, doing his duty to his patients, and working with zeal and ability for the best interests of the profession. The strong common sense which he exhibited in his experimental work made him a good physician and a trusty adviser in cases of surgery. Among his letters there are some interesting pictures of his life, particularly in his letters to his cousin, Dr. Samuel Beaumont. Writing to him 4 April 1846, he says:

I have a laborious, lucrative, and increasing practice, more than I can possibly attend to, though I have an assistant, Dr. Johnson, a young man who was a pupil of mine from 1835 to 1840. He then went to Philadelphia a year or two to attend lectures, and graduated, and returned here again in 1842, and has been very busy ever since, and is so now, but notwithstanding I decline more practice daily than half the doctors in the city get in a week. You thought when you were here before that there was too much competition for you ever to think of succeeding in business here—there is ten times as much now, and the better I succeed and prosper for it. You must come with a different feeling from your former—with a determination to follow in my wake and stem the current that I will break for you. I am now in the grand climacteric of life, three-score years and over, with equal or more zeal and ability to do good and contribute to professional service than at forty-five, and I now look forward with pleasing anticipation of success and greater usefulness—have ample competence for ourselves and children, and no doleful or dreaded aspect of the future—to be sure I have to wrestle with some adverse circumstances of life, and more particularly to defend myself against the envious, mean, and professional jealousies and the consequent prejudices of some men, but I triumph over them all and go ahead in defiance of them.[1]

His professional work increased enormously with the rapid growth of the city, but he felt, even in his old age, that delicious exhilaration which it is your pleasure and privilege to enjoy here in the west in a degree rarely experienced by your eastern confrères. Here is a cheery paragraph from a letter dated 20 October 1852:

Domestic affairs are easy, peaceable, and pleasant. Health of community good—no severe epidemic diseases prevalent—weather remark-

[1] He had evidently hopes that when his cousin and son arrived with Alexis they would arrange and plan for another series of experiments, and in another year or two make another book, better than the old one.

ably pleasant—business of all kinds increasing—product of the earth abundant—money plenty—railroads progressing with almost telegraphic speed—I expect to come to Plattsburgh next summer all the way by rail.

But work was becoming more burdensome to a man nearing threescore years and ten, and he expresses it in another letter when he says:

There is an immense professional practice in this city. I get tired of it, and have been trying hard to withdraw from it altogether, but the more I try the tighter I seem to be held to it by the people. I am actually persecuted, worried, and almost worn out with valetudinarian importunities and hypochondriacal groans, repinings, and lamentations—Amen.

He continued at work until March 1853, when he had an accident—a fall while descending some steps. A few weeks later a carbuncle appeared on the neck, and proved fatal, 25 April. One who knew him well wrote the following estimate (quoted by Dr. F. J. Lutz in his sketch of Beaumont):

He was gifted with strong natural powers, which, working upon an extensive experience in life, resulted in a species of natural sagacity, which, as I suppose, was something peculiar in him, and not to be attained by any course of study. His temperament was ardent, but never got the better of his instructed and disciplined judgement, and whenever or however employed, he ever adopted the most judicious means for attaining ends that were always honourable. In the sick room he was a model of patience and kindness; his intuitive perceptions, guiding a pure benevolence, never failed to inspire confidence, and thus he belonged to that class of physicians whose very presence affords Nature a sensible relief.

You do well, citizens of St. Louis and members of our profession, to cherish the memory of William Beaumont. Alive you honoured and rewarded him, and there is no reproach against you of neglected merit and talents unrecognized. The profession of the northern part of the state of Michigan has honoured itself in erecting a monument to his memory near the scene of his disinterested labours in the cause of humanity and science. His name is linked with one of your educational institutions, and joined with that of a distinguished labourer in another field of practice. But he has a far higher honour than any you can give him here—the honour that can only come when the man and the opportunity meet—and match. Beaumont is the pioneer physiologist of this country, the first to make an important and enduring contribution to this science. His work remains a model of patient, persevering investigation, experiment, and research, and the highest praise we can give him is to say that he lived up to and fulfilled the ideals with which he set out, and which he expressed when he said: 'Truth, like beauty, is "when unadorned, adorned the most", and, in prosecuting these experiments and inquiries, I believe I have been guided by its light.'

APPENDIX A

The Beaumont papers in the possession of his daughter, Mrs. Keim, of St. Louis, consist of (1) interesting certificates from his preceptors, Dr. Pomeroy and Dr. Chandler, the licence from the Third Medical Society of Vermont, the commissions in the U.S. Army, several certificates of honorary membership in societies, and the parchment of the M.D. degree conferred upon him, *honoris causa*, by the Columbian University of Washington, 1833; (2) a journal containing his experiences in the War of 1812, from which I have given an extract, a journal of his trip to Fort Mackinac, a journal containing the reports of many cases, among them that of St. Martin (in addition there is a protocol of the case in loose folio sheets), a journal of the experiments, and a commonplace book of receipts and jottings; (3) an extensive correspondence relating to St. Martin and the book, and many rough drafts of sections of the book; (4) a large mass of personal correspondence, much of it of interest as relating to conditions of practice in St. Louis.

The family has a miniature of him in his army uniform; the only picture which has been reproduced is of an older man from a daguerreotype. It is satisfactory to know that the ultimate destination of this most valuable collection of papers is the Surgeon-General's

Library of the United States Army, of which Dr. Beaumont was so distinguished an ornament.

APPENDIX B

On 20 October 1852 he writes to his cousin, Dr. Samuel Beaumont, on the subject of 'that old, fistulous Alexis', as he calls him. 'Alexis' answer to yours is the very facsimile or stereotype of all his Jesuitical letters to me for the last fifteen years. His object seems only to be to get a heavy bonus and undue advance from me and then disappoint and deceive me, or to palm and impose himself and whole family upon me for support for life.

'I have evaded his designs so far; but I verily fear that the strong and increasing impulse of conscious conviction of the great benefits and important usefulness of further and more accurate physiological investigation of the subject will compel me to still further efforts and sacrifices to obtain him. Physiological authors and most able writers on dietetics and gastric functions generally demand it of me in trumpet tones.

'I must have him at all hazards, and obtain the necessary assistance to my individual and private efforts or transfer him to some competent scientific institution for thorough investigation and report—I must retrieve my past ignorance, imbecility, and professional remissness of a quarter of a century, or more, by double diligence, intense study, and untiring application of soul and body to the subject before I die—

> Should posthumous Time retain my name,
> Let historic truths declare my fame.

'Simultaneous with this I write to Mr. Morrison and Alexis my last and final letters—perhaps, proposing to *him*, as bribe to his cupidity, to give him $500 to come to me *without* his family, for one year—$300 of them for his salary, and $200 for the support and contentment of his family to remain in Canada in the meantime—with the privilege of bringing them on here another year, upon my former proposition of $300 a year, at his own expense and responsibility, and support them himself after they get here out of his $300 salary—I think he will take the bait and come on this fall, and when I get him alone again into my keeping and engagement, I will take good care to control him as I please.'

APPENDIX C

Letter from Dr. Andrew Combe, 1 May 1838

'My Dear Sir—May I beg your acceptance of the accompanying volumes as a small expression of my respect for your character and scientific labours. I need not detain you by repeating in this note the high estimation in which I hold you. The volumes herewith sent will, I trust, convince you of the fact, and that it will not be my fault if you do not receive the credit justly due to your valuable and disinterested services.   I remain, My Dear Sir,

'Very respectfully yours,

'ANDW. COMBE.'

APPENDIX D

Letter from Dr. Samuel Beaumont, 16 March 1846

'Your letter of the 1st of February arrived here in the course of mail, and I have attended to the business which you authorized me to do. I am afraid, however, that you will be disappointed, and perhaps dissatisfied with the arrangement. Mr. Goodrich came here some five or six days after I received your letter, and made his proposal, which was to give you every tenth copy for the privilege of publishing an edition. The number he proposed to publish was fifteen hundred, which would give you 150 copies. I did not like to close the bargain on this condition, and he was not disposed to give any more. This was in the evening. I told him to give me time till the next morning, and I would make up my mind. In the morning, after consultation, I concluded to offer him the copyright for the unexpired time (only one year) for two hundred copies. After some demurring, we closed the bargain. I then thought and I still think it was not enough; but it was all I could get. In making up my mind the following considerations presented themselves: First, that the copyright would expire in one year, and he would then have the right to print it without consulting the author; second, that it would be somewhat mortifying to the author not to have his work republished, even if no great pecuniary benefit was to be obtained by such a republication; and it appeared to me to be quite certain that a new edition would not be soon printed, if I let this opportunity slip; third, I have been long anxious, as I presume you have been, to see the work gotten up in a better dress than it originally had, and in a way which will give it a general credit and more notoriety among all classes of the reading public than it has heretofore possessed—in fact, make it a standard work; fourth, it has given us a chance to give it a thorough correction, a thing which was very desirable. The work, you recollect, was got up in a great hurry, and a great many errors escaped our notice. You may also recollect that the Philadelphia reviewer spoke of the inaccuracies in the work. And he had reason enough for it. In looking over the work critically with a view of correction, I have been perfectly astonished at the errors that occur on almost every page. And although we understood perfectly what we meant to say, the reader would find it somewhat difficult to decipher our meaning. In the first 140 pages I made nearly 300 corrections. These are practically merely verbal alterations or change of phrases or sentences so as to make them more accurate or perspicuous. I have in no case so changed the text as to give it a different meaning. I flatter myself that it will now be more worthy the public patronage; and if for no other, this chance for correction I consider alone almost a sufficient remuneration for the brief limits of the copyright. I have also written a preface for the second edition, making quotations from American and European authorities in praise of the merits of the work. From delicacy I have written this as from the publisher. I think it is pretty well done. The work will probably be published in the course of about a month, and those designed for you will be delivered to me, when I shall send them to you. He guarantees not to sell in the state of Missouri, or the states south and west of that state. But that, of course, is all gammon. The book will be thrown into market, and he cannot control the direction in which it will go.'

9

THE YOUNG LAENNEC

THE story of Laennec, discoverer of auscultation, and founder of modern clinical medicine, has been told and retold, but not all told. We know of the struggle, the great achievement, and the early death, but much remained jealously guarded by the family—'a very precious mine containing all kinds of treasures, but principally letters— numberless letters, from Laennec, from his father, from his grandfather, from his uncle—then college exercises; verses and humorous works; political and religious pamphlets; inedited notes on different subjects, medical and miscellaneous; prize-lists, diplomas, all sorts of official papers, genealogical documents, and even souvenirs'. Some of these, so far as they relate to his life to 1806, are now laid before us in a charming brochure by Professor Alfred Rouxeau, of Nantes (*Laennec avant 1806,* Paris, Baillière & Fils).

Born in 1781, at Quimper, of strong Breton stock on both sides, neither the father nor the mother of Théophile appear to have shown any special ability; the former, indeed, had careless talents, but no persistency, while the mother died before the boy had reached his sixth year. The outlook would have been dark for her motherless children, had not their uncle William, a professor in the medical faculty at Nantes, and at the time rector of the university, offered them a home, and an ideal one it proved to be for the young Théophile.

Guillaume-François Laennec, a cultured, highly trained physician 'with a volcanic head, but a warm heart', quickly saw that his nephew was a boy of more than ordinary parts, and gave him the best training Nantes could afford. Keen at his books, but

---

This is Number XVII of the 'Men and Books' series from the *Canadian Medical Association Journal* (1913, iii. 137). See p. 62.

keen also at all games, the young student made rapid progress, and his studies were continued even during the horrors of the civil war. The ghastly guillotine was erected under the very windows of their house, to the basement and back rooms of which they had to flee to escape the shrieks of the victims and the noise of their falling heads! The uncle himself was a suspect, but doctors' heads had a value even in those terrible days. It is an extraordinary fact that the college (school) did not close, and the studies of 'le jeune citoyen Laennec' and of his brothers were not interrupted, but they had to participate in the famous Fête of the Supreme Being. Laennec became interested in Natural History, and made long excursions into the country to collect insects, plants, and birds. In 1795, at the early age of fourteen years and seven months, he began the study of medicine and was officially attached to one of the military hospitals as 'surgeon of the third class', a position corresponding to that of surgical dresser. The civil war had necessitated the creation of new military hospitals, and the work of the medical school at the Hôtel-Dieu (now the Temple of Humanity) had been interrupted, but dissections were continued at the Hôtel-Dieu in a room beneath and communicating with one of the wards. Physics and chemistry were taught at the 'École Centrale'.

The devoted uncle watched with pride the growing talents of the young student, though at times distressed by his irrepressible tendency to compose verses and to spend long hours in his natural history studies. In the letters to his father and stepmother a delightful picture is given of the inner life of the lad at this period, with its hopes and disappointments. Money was scarce, the times were perilous; it was difficult to get the necessaries of life, and such luxuries as dancing and flute playing did not appeal to the hard-pressed uncle. The young Laennec found it hard to get anything from his ne'er-do-well father, to whom, after an absence of nine years, he paid a visit at Quimper (1797). The stepmother wished him to take up some business, and it was only a strong appeal on the part of Dr. Laennec that frustrated her designs: 'For God's sake let him come back to me as

I sent him to you, good, gentle and studious; let him pursue in peace a course of study which is good for his health, sufficient for his fortune and honourable for his reputation'—and he had his way. The lad walked to and from Quimper to Nantes in four and a half days at the rate of about forty-one kilometres a day. There are sad letters telling of many trials and worries, lack of proper clothing, no money for books, or for his fees, and the uncle too hard-up to do anything, and the father too careless to answer letters. After following for five years the courses at the Hôtel-Dieu and the work at the military hospital, Laennec passed the examination for the grade of 'Officier de santé'.

In 1800 a widespread insurrection occurred in the west, and for a time he served with the regular army in the field. Then followed a period of great anxiety and depression. The desire of his life had been to finish at Paris, but there were no funds, and a sixth year of hope deferred had to be spent at Nantes. At last the fledgeling took flight, and in 1801, with a light heart and light pocket, with only eight hundred francs, the young Théophile set out to conquer Paris. In those terrible days Nantes had been a hard school, but he had laid a good foundation in practical work, he had picked up a fair education, and above all he had developed an intense love for his work. He had given play to a poetic temperament and Professor Rouxeau gives a number of small poems, some of which indicate that a certain 'Nisa' had stirred his Breton heart. With a group of old Nantes students and friends he was soon at home in Paris, and at once attached himself to the Charité Hospital, where Corvisart had already revolutionized the teaching of medicine. To-day Paris still follows this great master's method—the morning ward visit, and afterwards the amphitheatre lecture. We get a good idea of the state of medicine in Paris at this time from Joseph Frank's *Reise nach Paris und London* (Wien, 1805). Lectures on the doctrines of Hippocrates were still given three times a week, and one morning at the Hôtel-Dieu he saw thirty patients bled out of the one hundred and forty-two in the wards of Bosquillon; but Corvisart was effecting a revolution, and teaching men to observe and compare at bedside and in dead-house. Here, too, was working the man who was to influence Laennec strongly, Bayle; and for a short time he had the inestimable advantage of the instruction and example of Bichat. At the École Pratique he became associated with Dupuytren, and others of his teachers were Pinet and Cabanis. A good shorthand writer, he utilized this gift to make careful notes of lectures and reports on his cases.

In the *Journal de Médecine* in 1802 appeared his first important communication—'Histoires d'Inflammations du Péritoine', a clinical and pathological study on an affection at that time but little known.

In 1802, largely through the influence of Bayle, he became converted, and in 1803 joined the famous religious fraternity, the Congregation. In the letters to his father and uncle we can follow the progress of his scientific work, and papers appeared on the arachnoid, on a synovial membrane, &c.

In 1803, at the concours for the prizes at the School of Medicine, Laennec had a double triumph, taking those for medicine and surgery, and both in money—a welcome addition to his ever slender purse. One can imagine the delight of the uncle at Nantes—'He is a treasure, that boy!'—who predicted a professorship in a few years.

Leaving Nantes with a good knowledge of Latin, English, and German, Laennec worked hard at Greek, and in 1804 wrote his doctor's thesis on the doctrine of Hippocrates. A partially written 'Traité sur l'Anatomie Pathologique' of that period remained in manuscript until edited by Cornil in 1884. Working at clinical medicine and pathological anatomy, writing for the journals, an active participant in the medical societies, the young Breton of twenty-five had made a strong impression on his contemporaries; but life was still a struggle. He had begun to practice, and—have courage, young men!—had only taken one hundred and fifty francs in his first year and four hundred in the second. But he had much capital in his brain-pan, and how the promise of his youth was fulfilled Professor Rouxeau has reserved for another volume.

10

LETTERS TO MY HOUSE PHYSICIANS

LETTER I

FREIBURG, *May 17, 1890*

DEAR L[AFLEUR]: This is a charming town, beautifully situated at the south-western end of the Black Forest, and with a medical faculty which attracts students from all parts of Germany and not a few from abroad. During the past few years the number of men in attendance has risen rapidly and this semester has reached six hundred. I met here my friend Ramsay Wright, of Toronto University, and together we saw much of interest.

Bäumler, who has charge of the medical clinic, is a man of about forty-five, and we are very much indebted to him for making our short stay here agreeable and profitable. He was in London at the German Hospital, and subsequently practised there as a consultant for nine years, when he was called to the chair of medicine. The medical wards, containing about one hundred and twenty beds, are very conveniently arranged, and the plan of having a separate lecture-room for each department, which is almost universal at German universities, is very advantageous. There are three assistants, the first of whom, Dr. Reinhold, has been here three years, and, as is customary, is appointed for an indefinite term. The second and third assistants remain for one or two years. In addition, four men are named for periods of three months to act as clinical clerks in the wards.

To-day's routine was as follows: At 7 a.m. the professor gave a didactic lecture (of which five are delivered weekly) to about a

---

These letters were written during the course of the quinquennial brain-dusting in the summer of 1890. Five letters were published in the *New York Medical Journal*, 1890, lii. 81, 163, 191, 274, 333.

dozen students, the small number being due to a holiday yester-day and in part, no doubt, to the fact that attendance upon these systematic lectures is not compulsory. The subject was diseases of the oesophagus, and spontaneous rupture, perforation, and haemorrhage were discussed in a most exhaustive manner. Afterward, in his private room, Dr. Bäumler raised the question of the value of such teaching to the medical student and suggested that the same might be got in a shorter time from books. Pos-sibly; and, though I am strongly opposed to our present system of over-lecturing, I could not but feel that the men who had listened and taken notes had got their information in a much more inter-esting and instructive manner than if they had read the subjects in any text-book. Indeed, I do not know of any one *Practice* which contained all the information given in the three-quarters of an hour. The question must be discussed temperately, as it has two sides, one of which is ably presented in the May number of the *New Review* in a Lecture against Lecturing, by Professor Sedgwick.

One thing in the lecture-room pleased me greatly: around the walls were inscribed on each side—above the names of Hippo-crates, Galen, Vesalius, and Harvey, and beneath these in groups —those of the great clinicians of all countries; and it warmed my heart to see, as the representatives of America, the names of Flint and of dear old Dr. Bowditch. At eight o'clock the visit to the wards was made and new or specially interesting cases examined. In commenting upon a case of typhlitis, Bäumler spoke of the great frequency of recovery in this disease, which he thought, as is now almost universally accepted, was always at first an affection of the appendix. The tendency toward early operation was, in his opinion, at present too strong. I mentioned the case which we had in the wards a few months ago, and which was certainly a most encouraging one in support of early inter-ference; but who can say whether the small localized abscess found by Dr. Halsted at the point of the appendix might not have healed, or at any rate subsided, as the inflammation had done in a previous attack? Still, no one will deny that the lad is now better without his rudimentary appendage.

At nine o'clock the students assembled in the large ward, in the centre of which chairs were arranged on either side of a bed, a method which is followed in the case of fever patients, and other cases too ill to take to the auditorium. A *Practicant*, as a final student is called, was then asked to examine the patient before the class, and an hour was occupied in the thorough investigation of the case—one of typhoid fever. Comments were made on each interesting feature, and the symptoms summed up in a clear and orderly fashion, most instructive to the class, the members of which had an opportunity of afterward looking at the case. Typhoid patients are uniformly bathed whenever the temperature rises to 103° F., and no internal antipyretics are used. The good effects are not, it is thought, confined to the lowering of the fever. The mortality is here only about eight per cent. lower than in the ordinary symptomatic method; but you shall hear much more on this subject. A convenience which we do not always see in American hospitals is the stand in each ward for the examination of the urine, and a microscope with the necessary reagents. A clinic is held daily, and on Wednesday it lasts two hours; so we concluded that the Freiburg professor did a very full day's work before ten o'clock in the morning. In another ward we found waiting four candidates for the *Staats-Examen*—the test demanded by the State and which is a very formidable affair, lasting for several days in each subject. We then went to the post-mortem room to see a case of bullet-wound of the brain. Ziegler, the professor of pathology, came here last year from Tübingen, and lends additional strength to the faculty, as he is one of the most progressive of the younger generation of workers in his department. To English and American students he has become well known through McAlister's translation of his work on pathological anatomy, which has had an extraordinary success here, a sixth edition being in course of publication. He is a young-looking man, with a pleasing, frank manner, and he gave us a hearty welcome and asked us to come to the post-mortem room to see an examination of three students for the licence (*Staats-Examen*), and a most practical test it was.

The men drew lots for trunk, head, and position of scribe. The poor fellow who began the work had evidently not been a diligent attendant in the post-mortem room, for he bungled the inspection of the abdomen and thorax in a shocking manner. The examination of the heart—the *pons asinorum* of dissection—loosened his sweat centres, but Ziegler dealt with him most gently, considering the repeated aggravations. We could not wait to see the end, as it was a matter of several hours. In addition to this searching examination, there are others in pathological histology and general pathology. Von Kahlden, the Docent in pathology, showed us the laboratory, which is not large but very well equipped, particularly for histological work. We afterward spent a very pleasant evening with Ziegler and von Kahlden, both of whom are genial, sociable men. Ziegler must be most industrious, as, in addition to the teaching, which occupies, he said, at least three hours a day, the revision of his text-book has been continuously in hand, the editions having followed each other so rapidly; then he edits his *Beiträge*, which has become a most important pathological journal, and recently, in conjunction with von Kahlden, he has established the *Centralblatt für Pathologie*. By the way, I have sent out von Kahlden's new book on histological methods. Call the attention of S. to the section on Ehrlich's blood methods, which seems fuller than is usually given. To-day we saw Ziegler perform a most interesting autopsy before the class in a case of bullet-wound of the brain. Early in April the young lad had attempted suicide, and had discharged a revolver twice at his head. One bullet flattened against the frontal sinus, where it was found *post mortem*; the second passed through the left hemisphere to the occipital lobe, where it lay on the median surface close to the cuneus. There was a firm-walled tract in the course of the bullet. An operation for abscess had been performed yesterday, apparently only by enlargement of the original orifice and the insertion of a drainage-tube. There was extensive basic meningitis. The boy was hemiplegic and aphasic, but we did not learn whether an examination of his visual fields had been made, which would have been of great interest considering the position of the bullet in the occipital lobe.

One of the assistants showed us through the new surgical clinic, which is not yet completed. The operating theatre is very well arranged, with a composition stone floor and iron frames for the seats, so that the whole room can be flushed with the hose and thoroughly cleansed. Carbolic acid is the chief disinfectant, bichloride being rarely used, and the gauze for dressings is simply sterilized.

The Anatomical Institute is a fine new building, of about the size of one of the pay-wards, with a large lecture-room in the rear. Professor Wiedersheim is in charge, and, as is customary in German universities, is an anatomist in the wide and proper sense of the term, having to teach human and comparative anatomy and histology. One of his assistants takes the surgical anatomy, and this really meets the objection one often hears urged in America against a pure anatomist teaching medical students. In a well-equipped anatomical department how easy it would be to have one of the surgical assistants teach the senior students the surgical relations of the subject in special courses! The anatomical lecture-room is one of the best I have seen— high and spacious, with splendid light from the roof and sides. In the centre of the arena is a trap-door with hydraulic arrangement, by which, on turning a key in the floor, a table ascends from the preparation-room below. Wiedersheim is a beautiful draughtsman, and the blackboards were covered with elaborate diagrams, in coloured chalks, of the origin of the cranial nerves. In the schemata which he thus makes of the nervous system from day to day he always uses the same coloured chalk to indicate the same structure at different levels.

A man who has brought much renown to the university is Weismann, the professor of zoology, whose writings on heredity and Darwinism have attracted so much attention. In a recent pamphlet, *Über die Hypothese einer Vererbung von Verletzungen*, he makes a strong criticism of the recorded instances of the inheritance of peculiarities of structure acquired by accident or disease.

His collected essays have been issued in English by the Clarendon Press, at Oxford, and form, perhaps, the most notable contributions to the theory of evolution which have been made during the past decade.

We came to the conclusion that Freiburg had a most progressive university, and certainly, so far as medicine, pathology, and anatomy are concerned, the post-graduate student will find everything that he could desire.

LETTER II

BERN, *May 21, 1890*

DEAR T[OULMIN]: Within an hour after reaching Basel we were in the *Vesalianum*, as the anatomical institute is called, looking for the skeleton which Vesalius presented to the university when he was here in 1542–3 supervising the printing of his great work. Historically this is probably the most interesting museum specimen in existence, and to Professor Roth is due the credit of determining accurately the fact of its association with Vesalius. Several years ago he sent me his paper on the subject, an abstract of which you will find in the *Medical News* for 1887 (or 1888), in an editorial note. The plates of his work were drawn from this skeleton, which is treasured by the Basel faculty as a most precious relic. Above the glass case in which it is contained is the inscription: *Männliches Skelet das der Meister der Anatomie Andreas Vesal, aus Brüssel, der hiesigen Universität schenkte als er 1543 sich in Basel aufhielt um der Druck seines grossen anatomischen Werkes zu besorgen.* Well may he be called the Master of Anatomy, the great Reformer in Medicine, for his work loosened the chains of tradition in which the profession had been fast bound for centuries. His was a bold and venturesome spirit which could dare dispute the statements of Galen and Hippocrates, dogmas revered by the physicians of the sixteenth century as are to-day those of Calvin and of Luther by certain theologians. Professor Roth has recently published an interesting paper (*Quellen einer Vesalbiographie*, Basel, 1889), in which he has given the results of his researches among the archives of the University of Padua, and he has determined definitely for the first time the date and place of the graduation of Vesalius—Padua, December 5, 1537. Please note, too, that he was a young man when he published his great work, another illustration of the theory upon which I am always harping, that a man's productive years are in the third and fourth decades.

It is not a little remarkable that the skeleton should be in such a state of preservation; but above it lies another, prepared by Felix Platter, a renowned Basel professor of the sixteenth century, also in excellent condition.

The Basel Hospital is an old building but very conveniently arranged and with beautiful gardens, in the middle of which is a large summer ward for women and children. I am much indebted to Director Hoch for his kindness in showing me the different departments. In the operating room the table is constructed of zinc with a hot-water chamber, above which is a perforated plate so that irrigation can be carried out. The warming-pan—of which it is practically only a special example—is also perforated in the middle for the escape of the solutions. I am sure that for prolonged operations this is a great advantage in counteracting the depression so liable to occur both from the shock and from the anaesthetic. Not ten days ago I saw the same arrangement in use at the Physiological Laboratory of University College, London, in a prolonged experiment upon the brain of a monkey. Professor Schäfer told me that they had found the animals stood the operations very much better and revived more promptly if the body temperature was kept up in the artificial way. So important did he seem to think it that additional hot water was put in at the end of about an hour and a half.

We found Professor Socin in the operating-room with a class of about thirty men, a patient on the table, and a senior student in the arena, who, during the course of an hour, underwent a most searching examination on tuberculosis of joints and on the particular case before them. It was certainly a most instructive method of procedure, and it was fortunate the poor patient was deaf, as the questions of prognosis and of treatment were discussed

thoroughly. Amputation of the leg was then performed, as
the disease had progressed too far for resection. We could not
but feel, however, that it was hard to keep the poor man waiting
on the table. Certainly the ward would have been the more
appropriate place for the instruction. The Basel students have
an exceptionally clear and decisive teacher of surgery; here again
the coloured chalks on the blackboard were used at least half
a dozen times to illustrate special features of the disease and
steps of the operation.

Professor Immermann has charge of the medical clinic, and
has a conveniently arranged, though not large, clinical laboratory. The lecture-room is attached to the medical wards, and
we heard for half an hour a very practical talk on the treatment
of acute Bright's disease. A point specially insisted upon in the
later stages was the flushing of the tubes by a plentiful supply
of liquids. Then the class was taken into one of the men's
medical wards, and a student examined a case of typhlitis,
upon which the comments of Professor Immermann were very
interesting. The young man had been seized five days before
with pain in the right iliac region, not of an agonizing character,
and moderate fever, so that he had to give up work. He had not
been particularly constipated prior to the onset of the pain, but
he had had, several years ago, a somewhat similar attack. The
examination showed simply pain on deep pressure in the right
iliac fossa, no tumour, no signs of peritonitis. The case was
regarded as one of appendicitis, and, as the symptoms had pro-
gressively improved, the treatment was confined to the admini-
stration of opium and the use of local applications. Great stress
was laid on the absence of tumour as a differential point in the
diagnosis of appendicitis and typhlitis from faecal impaction.
I gathered that Professor Immermann believed in the existence
of a typhlitis apart from appendix disease; and the tumour,
which is more apt to be present in these cases, may be due either
to primary impaction or to faecal stasis in the caecum in consequence of the inflammation. Now, this was a case which illustrated the point I mention in my letter to L. I have not the

slightest doubt that, if a laparotomy had been performed, an inflamed and adherent, possibly a perforated, appendix would have been found, yet the lad was recovering under ordinary measures. Still, the risks are very great, balancing those of an operation even at this early stage, as perforation into the general peritoneum is always imminent, and then there is the liability to recurrence, as shown, indeed, in this case.

In the Vesalianum one of the Privat Docenten, von Lenhossék, showed us the method of preserving subjects, which is that of Laskowski, of Geneva.

In the pathological laboratory Professor Roth showed us a recent specimen of enormous epithelioma which had developed in an old leg ulcer, the result of a fracture many years before. The tumour had involved the bone and the leg had to be amputated. Under his direction, Dr. Dubler, the assistant, has been making an interesting research on suppuration, which has just been published. He comes to the conclusion, from a very large series of experiments, that the pus formation which follows the injection of chemical substances is the result of a delimiting inflammation about a primary necrotic area, and in the same way bacteria act by causing a necrosis, which the suppuration removes, so that there is no essential difference between the process in the two cases.

Here in Bern we found a model hospital on the pavilion plan, situated on a sloping hill on the outskirts of the town, and from the wards there is a magnificent view of the Bernese Oberland. The appearance of the pavilions, rising one above the other in the grounds, is very effective, and the new Royal Victoria Hospital in Montreal, which is also to be on the side of a hill, will, I think, resemble this very much. The Pathological Institute is a large, separate building, with every possible convenience for teaching and research. Professor Langhans was kind enough to show us all his treasures, not the least interesting of which was the skeleton of a bicapitate monster, presented to the university over a hundred years ago by the great Haller, who was a Swiss, and who lived near Bern, I believe, after his retirement from Göttingen. In the post-mortem theatre I was glad to see that to the students' desks towels were attached, a convenience rarely met with.

The medical clinic is in charge of Professor Sahli, a comparatively young man, appointed last year. There are two storeys in the chief medical pavilion, with four wards, and there is accommodation for about eighty patients. Connected with it by a covered passage is the lecture-room, with seats for about one hundred students. A very complete electrical equipment and tables for urinary and microscopical examination are on either side of the arena. There were eighty-four students at the clinic, eighteen of whom were women. After a careful analysis with a student of the chief points in the history and treatment of whooping-cough, a case of diabetes was brought in from the wards, and the next *Praktikant* on the list happened to be a woman, who went through the ordeal of questions in the various modes of testing for sugar in the urine. The saccharometer of Hermann and Pfister was shown, and then, after the clinic, those students who so desired had an opportunity of seeing the practical working of the apparatus. On either side of the amphitheatre is the clinical laboratory, with bacteriological, chemical, and microscopical rooms, large, admirably equipped, and very convenient to the wards. Bern is one of the Swiss schools most frequented by women, of whom about fifty are at present in attendance. I was told by one of the professors that they were good students; as a rule, very attentive and industrious, but not always sufficiently prepared in the preliminary subjects. Those at the lecture were all young, but I did not see one who looked likely to become the Trotula of the twentieth century.

LETTER III

MUNICH, *May 27, 1890*

DEAR R[EESE]: At Zurich we found Professor Eichhorst just about to go off for the day, but he very kindly took us through wards full of instructive cases, among which were very many of pneumonia, which he said was almost epidemic. There are special pavilions for contagious diseases, and we were very much interested to see, for the first time, the cases of phthisis isolated, a plan which had been carried out here for some years. Perhaps in old hospitals with insufficient ventilation this precaution may be necessary, but the experiments of Cornet show that the bacilli are not always present in the dust of wards in which there are patients with phthisis. The question is one attracting a great deal of attention in Germany, and I send you a paper by Professor Finkelnburg, of Bonn, in which he advocates strongly the erection of public sanatoria for consumptives. Another pamphlet on this subject by Cornet—*Wie schützt man sich gegen die Schwindsucht?*—will also interest you. The main point which he makes is the prevention of the desiccation of the sputa by the stringent use of spit-cups and the proper disinfection of the same. Professor Eichhorst's clinical laboratories are large, conveniently arranged rooms, two of which are especially equipped for bacteriological and chemical work. The latter is in charge of a young chemist, not a medical man who makes reports on regular forms. This seems to me a great advantage, particularly when there are elaborate and complicated analyses to be made. Here, too, we found the system of hydrotherapy in use in the treatment of typhoid fever, and the mortality had been reduced to the extremely low point of five per cent.

Professor Klebs was away, but one of his assistants showed us the pathological laboratory. We were also very disappointed not to have seen Professor Forel, who was at the Montpellier festival. We spent a delightful day with Professor Gaule, the physiologist. He first demonstrated some of his remarkable histological specimens, particularly a series of the frog's testis at different months of the year, prepared by his method, which you will find in any of the recent histological manuals. Not only in the testis, in which, in certain animals, we should expect marked seasonal changes, but in other organs, such as the liver, he holds there are variations in the constitution of the cell protoplasm throughout the year. Mrs. Gaule, an American lady and

a well-known histologist, is an active co-worker in the microscopical department of the laboratory.

I was still more interested in the brain of a dog which had had
a remarkable experimental history. The centre for the left fore-
leg was first destroyed, with the result of a paralysis, which
gradually disappeared. Then the corresponding centre in the
right side was destroyed, with the effect of producing paralysis
of the forelegs on both sides and loss of intelligence, so that the
dog lost knowledge of his tricks and was, in fact, like a puppy.
He regained power in the legs and was gradually re-educated,
with, however, great trouble, by one of the lady students of the
laboratory. Then a portion of the brain on the right hemisphere
behind the left-leg centre was removed, with the result of
paralysis of the leg, after which the animal was killed. The
experiment is chiefly of interest as showing substitution of function somewhat similar to that which took place in Barlow's
celebrated case of aphasia in which the patient, after recovery
from the effect of an embolus on the left middle cerebral,
gradually regained the power of speech, which was again lost in
a second attack, when an embolus plugged the artery of the
right side.

In lecturing, Professor Gaule uses the projection lantern very
frequently, and has it so arranged that the image is thrown from
behind the lecture-room upon a glass screen behind the movable
blackboard. I have never seen microscopic objects so beautifully
projected, and the technique was carried to such perfection that
even the movement of the ciliated epithelium could be seen
from all parts of the room.

Munich is the largest of the three Bavarian schools, and I was
particularly anxious to see the arrangements of the medical clinic,
which were reported to be unequalled in Europe. Unfortunately,
we came in the midst of the Whitsuntide holidays, when the
lectures had ceased and the laboratories were deserted. Professor
von Ziemssen (whose name is one of the most familiar to the
profession of English-speaking countries) was at home, and very
kindly showed us the clinical institute, which is attached as a

wing to one side of the main hospital building. It was erected in 1878, and when I tell you that the cost was over $50,000 you will have some idea of its extent. The ground floor is devoted largely to outdoor medical work—the ambulatorium, as it is called—and to rooms for the assistants and docents, with suitable arrangements for demonstrations and classes. The second floor has the professors' private rooms, the library, a room for the records, the auditorium, a large chemical laboratory, and a series of four rooms communicating with each other for microscopical, bacteriological, and electrical work. The institute is unusually rich in apparatus for experimental research, and going from room to room and listening to the description of treasures of all sorts for clinical investigation, I realized, as never before, what the Queen of Sheba felt when she said, after seeing the treasures of Solomon, 'that there was no more spirit in her'. The files of the *Deutsches Archiv für klinische Medicin* for the past twelve years show a record of good work of which the director of the institute may well feel proud. The hospital notes are very carefully kept and pigeon-holed, first by months, then at the end of the year bound loosely according to the disease. With an index of the names and another of the diseases, any case can in this way be referred to in a few minutes. Of models we were shown a number illustrating the alterations in position and size of the stomach—some in plaster, others in papier mâché. Dilatation of this organ is very much more common here than with us, owing to the enormous quantities of beer consumed. Some of the men connected with the breweries are said to drink from twelve to twenty litres daily. Voit makes the statement that the average consumption of beer in Munich is two litres and a half *per capita* daily. It is cheap and good, a litre costing only twenty-four or twenty-six pfennigs; and when one sees the crowded state of the beer-houses at all hours of the day, Voit's estimate appears very moderate. The influence of the beer is shown in another way—viz. in inducing hypertrophy of the heart, upon the frequency of which in Munich and on its association with beer drinking Professor Bollinger has recently written.

Von Ziemssen thought that it was the combination of hard work with heavy drinking that rapidly raised the aortic blood-pressure and was so dangerous. The cases were met with chiefly in those whose occupations necessitated great muscular exertion, such as draymen and porters. Though less common, these cases are by no means rare in our large cities among men who work hard and who at the same time drink heavily.

Within the past ten years Munich has gradually acquired a thorough drainage system, and we were shown a set of charts in course of preparation for the Berlin Congress, illustrating the remarkable reduction in the number of cases of typhoid fever. In certain sections of the city, formerly much affected, the disease is now almost unknown. The chart showing the hospital experience during this period follows the same falling curve. Munich is now one of the healthiest of the continental cities, whereas it formerly had an exceptionally high death-rate, particularly from zymotic diseases. The medical wards are in the part of the hospital adjoining the clinical institute, but, as the building is very old, the arrangement of the rooms is not very satisfactory. A new surgical department is nearly completed. Professor von Ziemssen lives in a separate house within the hospital grounds, so that he is not far from his work and can readily, as he expressed it, stand like a colossus with one foot in the wards and the other in the laboratory. It is a pleasure to think that one who has done so much for the profession is so well provided for and has everything that a teacher or investigator could desire or deserve.

We took advantage of the vacation and went to Ober-Ammergau to see the Passion Play. The crucifixion scene is frightfully realistic, every detail represented, even to the piercing of the side, from which the blood—an aniline fluid, I suppose—flows freely. A problem, much discussed of old, why Christ should have died after so comparatively short a time upon the cross seemed to my mind to receive its solution in the mental and physical exhaustion consequent upon the trials of the preceding twenty-four hours. There is a remarkable book dealing with this subject by Dr. Stroud, *Theory of the Physical Cause of the Death of Christ*, in which he argues that it was due to rupture of the heart; but this would be highly improbable in a vigorous, healthy man of thirty-three.

In looking over the Passion Play literature, we find a long account of the performance in 1830 by Oken, the anatomist, and it was extremely interesting to find that his description of the play as given sixty years ago might have been written of this year's representation.

II

THE STUDENT LIFE

Take therefore no thought for the morrow: for the morrow
shall take thought for the things of itself.

SERMON ON THE MOUNT.

I

EXCEPT it be a lover, no one is more interesting as an
object of study than a student. Shakespeare might have
made him a fourth in his immortal group. The lunatic
with his fixed idea, the poet with his fine frenzy, the
lover with his frantic idolatry, and the student aflame with the
desire for knowledge are of 'imagination all compact'. To an
absorbing passion, a whole-souled devotion, must be joined an
enduring energy, if the student is to become a devotee of the
grey-eyed goddess to whose law his services are bound. Like the
quest of the Holy Grail, the quest of Minerva is not for all. For
the one, the pure life; for the other, what Milton calls 'a strong
propensity of nature'. Here again the student often resembles
the poet—he is born, not made. While the resultant of two
moulding forces, the accidental, external conditions, and the
hidden, germinal energies, which produce in each one of us
national, family, and individual traits, the true student possesses
in some measure a divine spark which sets at naught their laws.
Like the Snark, he defies definition, but there are three un-
mistakable signs by which you may recognize the genuine article
from a Boojum—an absorbing desire to know the truth, an
unswerving steadfastness in its pursuit, and an open, honest
heart, free from suspicion, guile, and jealousy.

Valedictory address given to students at McGill University, 14 April 1905.
Reprinted in *Aequanimitas*. Published by the Oxford University Press, 1905.
Included, in part, in Christopher Morley's *Modern Essays*, New York, 1921,
128–44; and in *The Student Life and Other Essays*, with an introduction by
H. H. Bashford, London, 1928, 1–46.

At the outset do not be worried about this big question—Truth. It is a very simple matter if each one of you starts with the desire to get as much as possible. No human being is constituted to know the truth, the whole truth, and nothing but the truth; and even the best of men must be content with fragments, with partial glimpses, never the full fruition. In this unsatisfied quest the attitude of mind, the desire, the thirst—a thirst that from the soul must rise!—the fervent longing, are the be-all and the end-all. What is the student but a lover courting a fickle mistress who ever eludes his grasp? In this very elusiveness is brought out his second great characteristic—steadfastness of purpose. Unless from the start the limitations incident to our frail human faculties are frankly accepted, nothing but disappointment awaits you. The truth is the best you can get with your best endeavour, the best that the best men accept—with this you must learn to be satisfied, retaining at the same time with due humility an earnest desire for an ever larger portion. Only by keeping the mind plastic and receptive does the student escape perdition. It is not, as Charles Lamb remarks, that some people do not know what to do with truth when it is offered to them, but the tragic fate is to reach, after years of patient search, a condition of mind-blindness in which the truth is not recognized, though it stares you in the face. This can never happen to a man who has followed step by step the growth of a truth, and who knows the painful phases of its evolution. It is one of the great tragedies of life that every truth has to struggle to acceptance against honest but mind-blind students. Harvey knew his contemporaries well, and for twelve successive years demonstrated the circulation of the blood before daring to publish the facts on which the truth was based.[1] Only steadfastness of purpose and humility enable the student to shift his position to meet the new conditions in which new truths are born, or old ones modified beyond recognition. And, thirdly, the honest

[1] 'These views, as usual, pleased some more, others less; some chid and calumniated me, and laid it to me as a crime that I had dared to depart from the precepts and opinions of all Anatomists.'—*De Motu Cordis*, chap. i.

heart will keep him in touch with his fellow students, and furnish that sense of comradeship without which he travels an arid waste alone. I say advisedly an honest *heart*—the honest head is prone to be cold and stern, given to judgement, not mercy, and not always able to entertain that true charity which, while it thinketh no evil, is anxious to put the best possible interpretation upon the motives of a fellow worker. It will foster, too, an attitude of generous, friendly rivalry, untinged by the green peril, jealousy, that is the best preventive of the growth of a bastard scientific spirit, loving seclusion and working in a lock-and-key laboratory, as timorous of light as is a thief.

You have all become brothers in a great society, not apprentices, since that implies a master, and nothing should be farther from the attitude of the teacher than much that is meant in that word, used though it be in another sense, particularly by our French brethren in a most delightful way, signifying a bond of intellectual filiation. A fraternal attitude is not easy to cultivate —the chasm between the chair and the bench is difficult to bridge. Two things have helped to put up a cantilever across the gulf. The successful teacher is no longer on a height, pumping knowledge at high pressure into passive receptacles. The new methods have changed all this. He is no longer *Sir Oracle*, perhaps unconsciously by his very manner antagonizing minds to whose level he cannot possibly descend, but he is a senior student anxious to help his juniors. When a simple, earnest spirit animates a college, there is no appreciable interval between the teacher and the taught—both are in the same class, the one a little more advanced than the other. So animated, the student feels that he has joined a family whose honour is his honour, whose welfare is his own, and whose interests should be his first consideration.

The hardest conviction to get into the mind of a beginner is that the education upon which he is engaged is not a college course, not a medical course, but a life course, for which the work of a few years under teachers is but a preparation. Whether you will falter and fail in the race or whether you will be faithful to the end depends on the training before the start, and on your staying powers, points upon which I need not enlarge. You can all become good students, a few may become great students, and now and again one of you will be found who does easily and well what others cannot do at all, or very badly, which is John Ferriar's excellent definition of a genius.

In the hurry and bustle of a business world, which is the life of this continent, it is not easy to train first-class students. Under present conditions it is hard to get the needful seclusion, on which account it is that our educational market is so full of wayside fruit. I have always been much impressed by the advice of St. Chrysostom: 'Depart from the highway and transplant thyself in some enclosed ground, for it is hard for a tree which stands by the wayside to keep her fruit till it be ripe.' The dilettante is abroad in the land, the man who is always venturing on tasks for which he is imperfectly equipped, a habit of mind fostered by the multiplicity of subjects of the curriculum; and while many things are studied, few are studied thoroughly. Men will not take time to get to the heart of a matter. After all, concentration is the price the modern student pays for success. Thoroughness is the most difficult habit to acquire, but it is the pearl of great price, worth all the worry and trouble of the search. The dilettante lives an easy, butterfly life, knowing nothing of the toil and labour with which the treasures of knowledge are dug out of the past, or wrung by patient research in the laboratories. Take, for example, the early history of this country—how easy for the student of the one type to get a smattering, even a fairly full acquaintance with the events of the French and Spanish settlements. Put an original document before him, and it might as well be Arabic. What we need is the other type, the man who knows the records, who, with a broad outlook and drilled in what may be called the embryology of history, has yet a powerful vision for the minutiae of life. It is these kitchen and backstair men who are to be encouraged, the men who know the subject in hand in all possible relation-ships. Concentration has its drawbacks. It is possible to become so absorbed in the problem of the 'enclitic δε', or the structure of the flagella of the *Trichomonas*, or of the toes of the prehistoric horse, that the student loses the sense of proportion in his work, and even wastes a lifetime in researches which are valueless because not in touch with current knowledge. You remember poor Casaubon, in *Middlemarch*, whose painful scholarship was lost on this account. The best preventive to this is to get denationalized early. The true student is a citizen of the world, the allegiance of whose soul, at any rate, is too precious to be restricted to a single country. The great minds, the great works transcend all limitations of time, of language, and of race, and the scholar can never feel initiated into the company of the elect until he can approach all of life's problems from the cosmopolitan standpoint. I care not in what subject he may work, the full knowledge cannot be reached without drawing on supplies from lands other than his own—French, English, German, American, Japanese, Russian, Italian—there must be no discrimination by the loyal student, who should willingly draw from any and every source with an open mind and a stern resolve to render unto all their dues. I care not on what stream of knowledge he may embark, follow up its course, and the rivulets that feed it flow from many lands. If the work is to be effective he must keep in touch with scholars in other countries. How often has it happened that years of precious time have been given to a problem already solved or shown to be insoluble, because of the ignorance of what had been done elsewhere. And it is not only book knowledge and journal knowledge, but a knowledge of men that is needed. The student will, if possible, see the men in other lands. Travel not only widens the vision and gives certainties in place of vague surmises, but the personal contact with foreign workers enables him to appreciate better the failings or successes in his own line of work, perhaps to look with more charitable eyes on the work of some brother whose limitations and opportunities have been more restricted than his own. Or, in contact with a mastermind, he may take fire, and the glow of the enthusiasm may be the inspiration of his life. Concentration must then be associated with large views on the relation of the problem, and a knowledge of its status elsewhere; otherwise it may land him in the slough of a specialism so narrow that it has depth and no breadth, or he may be led to make what he believes to be important discoveries, but which have long been current coin in other lands. It is sad to think that the day of the great polymathic student is at an end; that we may, perhaps, never again see a Scaliger, a Haller, or a Humboldt—men who took the whole field of knowledge for their domain and viewed it as from a pinnacle. And yet a great specializing generalist may arise, who can tell? Some twentieth-century Aristotle may be now tugging at his bottle, as little dreaming as are his parents or his friends of a conquest of the mind, beside which the wonderful victories of the Stagirite will look pale. The value of a really great student to the country is equal to half a dozen grain elevators or a new transcontinental railway. He is a commodity singularly fickle and variable, and not to be grown to order. So far as his advent is concerned there is no telling when or where he may arise. The conditions seem to be present even under the most unlikely externals. Some of the greatest students this country has produced have come from small villages and country places. It is impossible to predict from a study of the environment, which a 'strong propensity of nature', to quote Milton's phrase again, will easily bend or break.

The student must be allowed full freedom in his work, undisturbed by the utilitarian spirit of the Philistine, who cries, *Cui bono?* and distrusts pure science. The present remarkable position in applied science and in industrial trades of all sorts has been made possible by men who did pioneer work in chemistry, in physics, in biology, and in physiology, without a thought in their researches of any practical application. The members of this higher group of productive students are rarely understood by the common spirits, who appreciate as little their unselfish devotion as their unworldly neglect of the practical side of the problems.

Everywhere now the medical student is welcomed as an

honoured member of the guild. There was a time, I confess, and
it is within the memory of some of us, when, like Falstaff, he
was given to 'taverns and sack and wine and metheglins, and to
drinkings and swearings and starings, pribbles and prabbles';
but all that has changed with the curriculum, and the 'Meds'
now roar you as gently as the 'Theologs'. On account of the
peculiar character of the subject-matter of your studies, what
I have said upon the general life and mental attitude of the
student applies with tenfold force to you. Man, with all his
mental and bodily anomalies and diseases—the machine in
order, the machine in disorder, and the business yours to put it
to rights. Through all the phases of its career this most complicated mechanism of this wonderful world will be the subject of
our study and of your care—the naked, new-born infant, the
artless child, the lad and the lassie just aware of the tree of
knowledge overhead, the strong man in the pride of life, the
woman with the benediction of maternity on her brow, and the
aged, peaceful in the contemplation of the past. Almost everything has been renewed in the science and in the art of medicine,
but all through the long centuries there has been no variableness
or shadow of change in the essential features of the life which
is our contemplation and our care. The sick love-child of Israel's
sweet singer, the plague-stricken hopes of the great Athenian
statesman, Elpenor bereft of his beloved Artemidora, and
'Tully's daughter mourned so tenderly', are not of any age or
any race—they are here with us to-day, with the Hamlets, the
Ophelias, and the Lears. Amid an eternal heritage of sorrow and
suffering our work is laid, and this eternal note of sadness
would be insupportable if the daily tragedies were not relieved
by the spectacle of the heroism and devotion displayed by the
actors. Nothing will sustain you more potently than the power
to recognize in your humdrum routine, as perhaps it may be
thought, the true poetry of life—the poetry of the commonplace,
of the ordinary man, of the plain, toil-worn woman, with their
loves and their joys, their sorrows and their griefs. The comedy,
too, of life will be spread before you, and nobody laughs more

often than the doctor at the pranks Puck plays upon the Titanias and the Bottoms among his patients. The humorous side is really almost as frequently turned towards him as the tragic. Lift up one hand to heaven and thank your stars if they have given you the proper sense to enable you to appreciate the inconceivably droll situations in which we catch our fellow creatures. Unhappily, this is one of the free gifts of the gods, unevenly distributed, not bestowed on all, or on all in equal portions. In undue measure it is not without risk, and in any case in the doctor it is better appreciated by the eye than expressed on the tongue. Hilarity and good humour, a breezy cheerfulness, a nature 'sloping toward the southern side', as Lowell has it, help enormously both in the study and in the practice of medicine. To many of a sombre and sour disposition it is hard to maintain good spirits amid the trials and tribulations of the day, and yet it is an unpardonable mistake to go about among patients with a long face.

Divide your attentions equally between books and men. The strength of the student of books is to sit still—two or three hours at a stretch—eating the heart out of a subject with pencil and note-book in hand, determined to master the details and intricacies, focusing all your energies on its difficulties. Get accustomed to test all sorts of book problems and statements for yourself, and take as little as possible on trust. The Hunterian 'Do not think, but try' attitude of mind is the important one to cultivate. The question came up one day, when discussing the grooves left on the nails after fever, how long it took for the nail to grow out, from root to edge. A majority of the class had no further interest; a few looked it up in books; two men marked their nails at the root with nitrate of silver, and a few months later had positive knowledge on the subject. They showed the proper spirit. The little points that come up in your reading try to test for yourselves. With one fundamental difficulty many of you will have to contend from the outset—a lack of proper preparation for really hard study. No one can have watched successive groups of young men pass through the special schools without profoundly regretting the haphazard, fragmentary character of their preliminary education. It does seem too bad that we cannot have a student in his eighteenth year sufficiently grounded in the humanities and in the sciences preliminary to medicine—but this is an educational problem upon which only a Milton or a Locke could discourse with profit. With pertinacity you can overcome the preliminary defects and once thoroughly interested, the work in books becomes a pastime. A serious drawback in the student life is the selfconsciousness, bred of too close devotion to books. A man gets shy, 'dysopic', as old Timothy Bright calls it, and shuns the looks of men, and blushes like a girl.

The strength of a student of men is to travel—to study men, their habits, character, mode of life, their behaviour under varied conditions, their vices, virtues, and peculiarities. Begin with a careful observation of your fellow students and of your teachers; then, every patient you see is a lesson in much more than the malady from which he suffers. Mix as much as you possibly can with the outside world, and learn its ways. Cultivated systematically, the student societies, the students' union, the gymnasium, and the outside social circle will enable you to conquer the diffidence so apt to go with bookishness and which may prove a very serious drawback in after-life. I cannot too strongly impress upon the earnest and attentive men among you the necessity of overcoming this unfortunate failing in your student days. It is not easy for everyone to reach a happy medium, and the distinction between a proper self-confidence and 'cheek', particularly in junior students, is not always to be made. The latter is met with chiefly among the student pilgrims who, in travelling down the Delectable Mountains, have gone astray and have passed to the left hand, where lieth the country of Conceit, the country in which you remember the brisk lad Ignorance met Christian.

I wish we could encourage on this continent among our best students the habit of wandering. I do not know that we are quite prepared for it, as there is still great diversity in the curricula, even among the leading schools, but it is undoubtedly a great

advantage to study under different teachers, as the mental horizon is widened and the sympathies enlarged. The practice would
do much to lessen that narrow 'I am of Paul and I am of Apollos'
spirit which is hostile to the best interests of the profession.

There is much that I would like to say on the question of
work, but I can spare only a few moments for a word or two.
Who will venture to settle upon so simple a matter as the best
time for work? One will tell us there is no best time; all are
equally good; and truly, all times are the same to a man whose
soul is absorbed in some great problem. The other day I asked
Edward Martin, the well-known story-writer, what time he
found best for work. 'Not in the evening, and never between
meals!' was his answer, which may appeal to some of my hearers.
One works best at night; another, in the morning; a majority
of the students of the past favour the latter. Erasmus, the great
exemplar, says, 'Never work at night; it dulls the brain and hurts
the health'. One day, going with George Ross through Bedlam,
Dr. Savage, at that time the physician in charge, remarked upon
two great groups of patients—those who were depressed in the
morning and those who were cheerful, and he suggested that
the spirits rose and fell with the bodily temperature—those with
very low morning temperatures were depressed, and vice versa.
This, I believe, expresses a truth which may explain the extraordinary difference in the habits of students in this matter of
the time at which the best work can be done. Outside of the
asylum there are also the two great types, the student-lark who
loves to see the sun rise, who comes to breakfast with a cheerful
morning face, never so 'fit' as at 6 a.m. We all know the type.
What a contrast to the student-owl with his saturnine morning
face, thoroughly unhappy, cheated by the wretched breakfast
bell of the two best hours of the day for sleep, no appetite, and
permeated with an unspeakable hostility to his vis-à-vis, whose
morning garrulity and good humour are equally offensive. Only
gradually, as the day wears on and his temperature rises, does he
become endurable to himself and to others. But see him really
awake at 10 p.m. while our blithe lark is in hopeless coma over

his books, from which it is hard to rouse him sufficiently to get his boots off for bed, our lean owl-friend, Saturn no longer in the ascendant, with bright eyes and cheery face, is ready for four hours of anything you wish—deep study, or

Heart-affluence in discursive talk,

and by 2 a.m. he will undertake to unsphere the spirit of Plato. In neither a virtue, in neither a fault, we must recognize these two types of students, differently constituted, owing possibly— though I have but little evidence for the belief—to thermal peculiarities.

II

In the days of probation the student's life may be lived by each one of you in its fullness and in its joys, but the difficulties arise in the break which follows departure from college and the entrance upon new duties. Much will now depend on the attitude of mind which has been encouraged. If the work has been for your degree, if the diploma has been its sole aim and object, you will rejoice in a freedom from exacting and possibly unpleasant studies, and with your books you will throw away all thoughts of further systematic work. On the other hand, with good habits of observation you may have got deep enough into the subject to feel that there is still much to be learned, and if you have had ground into you the lesson that the collegiate period is only the beginning of the student life, there is a hope that you may enter upon the useful career of the *student-practitioner*. Five years, at least, of trial await the man after parting from his teachers, and entering upon an independent course—years upon which his future depends, and from which his horoscope may be cast with certainty. It is all the same whether he settles in a country village or goes on with hospital and laboratory work; whether he takes a prolonged trip abroad; or whether he settles down in practice with a father or a friend—these five waiting years fix his fate so far as the student life is concerned. Without any strong natural propensity to study, he may feel such a relief after graduation that the effort to take to books is beyond his mental strength, and a weekly journal with an occasional text-book furnish pabulum enough, at least to keep his mind hibernating. But ten years later he is dead mentally, past any possible hope of galvanizing into life as a student, fit to do a routine practice, often a capable, resourceful man, but without any deep convictions, and probably more interested in stocks or in horses than in diagnosis or therapeutics. But this is not always the fate of the student who finishes his work on Commencement Day. There are men full of zeal in practice who give good service to their fellow creatures, who have not the capacity or the energy to keep up with the times. While they have lost interest in science, they are loyal members of the profession, and appreciate their responsibilities as such. That fateful first lustrum ruins some of our most likely material. Nothing is more trying to the soldier than inaction, to mark time while the battle is raging all about him; and waiting for practice is a serious strain under which many yield. In the cities it is not so hard to keep up: there is work in the dispensaries and colleges, and the stimulus of the medical societies; but in smaller towns and in the country it takes a strong man to live through the years of waiting without some deterioration. I wish the custom of taking junior men as partners and assistants would grow on this continent. It has become a necessity, and no man in large general practice can do his work efficiently without skilled help. How incalculably better for the seniors, how beneficial to the patients, how helpful in every way if each one of you, for the first five or ten years, was associated with an older practitioner, doing his night work, his laboratory work, his chores of all sorts. You would, in this way, escape the chilling and killing isolation of the early years, and amid congenial surroundings you could, in time, develop into that flower of our calling—the cultivated general practitioner. May this be the destiny of a large majority of you! Have no higher ambition! You cannot reach any better position in a community; the family doctor is the man behind the gun, who does our effective work. That his life is hard and exacting; that he is underpaid and overworked; that he has but little time for study and less for recreation—these are the blows that may give finer temper to his steel, and bring out the nobler elements in his character. What lot or portion has the general practitioner in the student life? Not, perhaps, the fruitful heritage of Judah or Benjamin, but he may make of it the goodly portion of Ephraim. A man with powers of observation, well trained in the wards, and with the strong natural propensity to which I have so often referred, may live the ideal student life, and even reach the higher levels of scholarship. Adams, of Banchory (a little Aberdeenshire village), was not only a good practitioner and a skilful operator, but he was an excellent naturalist. This is by no means an unusual or remarkable combination, but Adams became, in addition, one of the great scholars of the profession. He had a perfect passion for the classics, and amid a very exacting practice found time to read 'almost every Greek work which has come down to us from antiquity, except the ecclesiastical writers'. He translated the works of Paulus Aegineta, the works of Hippocrates, and the works of Aretaeus, all of which are in the Sydenham Society's publications, monuments of the patient skill and erudition of a Scottish village doctor, an incentive to every one of us to make better use of our precious time.

Given the sacred hunger and proper preliminary training, the student-practitioner requires at least three things with which to stimulate and maintain his education, a note-book, a library, and a quinquennial brain-dusting. I wish I had time to speak of the value of note-taking. You can do nothing as a student in practice without it. Carry a small note-book which will fit into your waistcoat pocket, and never ask a new patient a question without note-book and pencil in hand. After the examination of a pneumonia case two minutes will suffice to record the essentials in the daily progress. Routine and system when once made a habit, facilitate work, and the busier you are the more time you will have to make observations after examining a patient. Jot a comment at the end of the notes: 'clear case', 'case illustrating obscurity of symptoms', 'error in diagnosis', &c.

The making of observations may become the exercise of a jack-daw trick, like the craze which so many of us have to collect articles of all sorts. The study of the cases, the relation they bear to each other and to the cases in literature—here comes in the difficulty. Begin early to make a threefold category—clear cases, doubtful cases, mistakes. And learn to play the game fair, no self-deception, no shrinking from the truth; mercy and consideration for the other man, but none for yourself, upon whom you have to keep an incessant watch. You remember Lincoln's famous *mot* about the impossibility of fooling all of the people all the time. It does not hold good for the individual who can fool himself to his heart's content all of the time. If necessary, be cruel; use the knife and the cautery to cure the intumescence and moral necrosis which you will feel in the posterior parietal region, in Gall and Spurzheim's centre of self-esteem, where you will find a sore spot after you have made a mistake in diagnosis. It is only by getting your cases grouped in this way that you can make any real progress in your post-collegiate education; only in this way can you gain wisdom with experience. It is a common error to think that the more a doctor sees the greater his experience and the more he knows. No one ever drew a more skilful distinction than Cowper in his oft-quoted lines, which I am never tired of repeating in a medical audience:

> Knowledge and wisdom, far from being one,
> Have oft-times no connexion. Knowledge dwells
> In heads replete with thoughts of other men;
> Wisdom in minds attentive to their own.
> Knowledge is proud that he has learned so much;
> Wisdom is humble that he knows no more.

What we call sense or wisdom is knowledge, ready for use, made effective, and bears the same relation to knowledge itself that bread does to wheat. The full knowledge of the parts of a steam-engine and the theory of its action may be possessed by a man who could not be trusted to pull the lever to its throttle. It is only by collecting data and using them that you can get sense. One of the most delightful sayings of antiquity is the remark of Heraclitus upon his predecessors—that they had much knowledge but no sense—which indicates that the noble old Ephesian had a keen appreciation of their difference; and the distinction, too, is well drawn by Tennyson in the oft-quoted line:

Knowledge comes but wisdom lingers.

Of the three well-stocked rooms which it should be the ambition of every young doctor to have in his house, the library, the laboratory, and the nursery—books, balances, and bairns—as he may not achieve all three, I would urge him to start at any rate with the books and the balances. A good weekly and a good monthly journal to begin with, and read them. Then, for a systematic course of study, supplement your college text-books with the larger systems—Allbutt or Nothnagel—a system of surgery, and, as your practice increases, make a habit of buying a few special monographs every year. Read with two objects: first, to acquaint yourself with the current knowledge on the subject and the steps by which it has been reached; and secondly, and more important, read to understand and analyse your cases. To this line of work we should direct the attention of the student before he leaves the medical school, pointing in specific cases just where the best articles are to be found, sending him to the Index Catalogue—that marvellous storehouse, every page of which is interesting and the very titles instructive. Early learn to appreciate the differences between the descriptions of disease and the manifestations of that disease in an individual—the difference between the composite portrait and one of the component pictures. By exercise of a little judgement you can collect at moderate cost a good working library. Try, in the waiting years, to get a clear idea of the history of medicine. Read Foster's *Lectures on the History of Physiology* and Baas's *History of Medicine*. Get the 'Masters of Medicine' Series, and subscribe to the *Library and Historical Journal.*[1]

Every day do some reading or work apart from your profession.

---

[1] [A contemporary journal now dead.—ED.]

I fully realize, no one more so, how absorbing is the profession of medicine; how applicable to it is what Michelangelo says: 'There are sciences which demand the whole of a man, without leaving the least portion of his spirit free for other distractions'; but you will be a better man and not a worse practitioner for an avocation. I care not what it may be; gardening or farming, literature or history or bibliography, any one of which will bring you into contact with books. (I wish that time permitted me to speak of the other two rooms which are really of equal importance with the library, but which are more difficult to equip, though of co-ordinate value in the education of the head, the heart, and the hand.) The third essential for the practitioner as a student is the quinquennial brain-dusting, and this will often seem to him the hardest task to carry out. Every fifth year, back to the hospital, back to the laboratory, for renovation, rehabilitation, rejuvenation, reintegration, resuscitation, &c. Do not forget to take the note-books with you, or the sheets, in three separate bundles, to work over. From the very start begin to save for the trip. Deny yourself all luxuries for it; shut up the room you meant for the nursery—have the definite determination to get your education thoroughly well started; if you are successful you may, perhaps, have enough saved at the end of three years to spend six weeks in special study; or in five years you may be able to spend six months. Hearken not to the voice of old 'Dr. Hayseed', who tells you it will ruin your prospects, and that he 'never heard of such a thing' as a young man, not yet five years in practice, taking three months' holiday. To him it seems preposterous. Watch him wince when you say it is a speculation in the only gold mine in which the physician should invest—Grey Cortex! What about the wife and babies, if you have them? Leave them! Heavy as are your responsibilities to those nearest and dearest, they are outweighed by the responsibilities to yourself, to the profession, and to the public. Like Isaphaena, the story of whose husband—ardent, earnest soul, peace to his ashes! —I have told in the little sketch of An Alabama Student, your wife will be glad to bear her share in the sacrifice you make.

With good health and good habits the end of the second lustrum should find you thoroughly established—all three rooms well furnished, a good stable, a good garden, no mining stock, but a life insurance, and, perhaps, a mortgage or two on neighbouring farms. Year by year you have dealt honestly with yourself; you have put faithfully the notes of each case into their proper places, and you will be gratified to find that, though the doubtful cases and mistakes still make a rather formidable pile, it has grown relatively smaller. You literally 'own' the countryside, as the expression is. All the serious and dubious cases come to you, and you have been so honest in the frank acknowledgement of your own mistakes, and so charitable in the contemplation of theirs, that neighbouring doctors, old and young, are glad to seek your advice. The work, which has been very heavy, is now lightened by a good assistant, one of your own students, who becomes in a year or so your partner. This is not an overdrawn picture, and it is one which may be seen in many places except, I am sorry to say, in the particular as to the partner. This is the type of man we need in the country districts and the smaller towns. He is not a whit too good to look after the sick, not a whit too highly educated—impossible! And with an optimistic temperament and a good digestion he is the very best product of our profession, and may do more to stop quackery and humbuggery, inside and outside of the ranks, than could a dozen prosecuting county attorneys. Nay, more! such a doctor may be a daily benediction in the community—a strong, sensible, whole-souled man, often living a life of great self-denial, and always of tender sympathy, worried neither by the vagaries of the well nor by the testy waywardness of the sick, and to him, if to any, may come (even when he knows it not) the true spiritual blessing—that 'blessing which maketh rich and addeth no sorrow'.

The danger in such a man's life comes with prosperity. He is safe in the hard-working day, when he is climbing the hill, but once success is reached, with it come the temptations to which many succumb. Politics has been the ruin of many country doctors, and often of the very best, of just such a good fellow as he of whom I have been speaking. He is popular; he has a little money; and he, if anybody, can save the seat for the party! When the committee leaves you, take the offer under consideration, and if in the ten or twelve years you have kept on intimate terms with those friends of your student days, Montaigne and Plutarch, you will know what answer to return. If you live in a large town, resist the temptation to open a sanatorium. It is not the work for a general practitioner, and there are risks that you may sacrifice your independence and much else besides. And, thirdly, resist the temptation to move into a larger place. In a good agricultural district, or in a small town, if you handle your resources aright, taking good care of your education, of your habits, and of your money, and devoting part of your energies to the support of the societies, &c., you may reach a position in the community of which any man may be proud. There are country practitioners among my friends with whom I would rather change places than with any in our ranks, men whose stability of character and devotion to duty make one proud of the profession.

Curiously enough, the student-practitioner may find studiousness to be a stumbling-block in his career. A bookish man may never succeed; deep-versed in books, he may not be able to use his knowledge to practical effect; or, more likely, his failure is not because he has studied books much, but because he has not studied men more. He has never got over that shyness, that diffidence, against which I have warned you. I have known instances in which this malady was incurable; in others I have known a cure effected not by the public, but by the man's professional brethren, who, appreciating his work, have insisted upon utilizing his mental treasures. It is very hard to carry student habits into a large city practice; only zeal, a fiery passion, keeps the flame alive, smothered as it is so apt to be by the dust and ashes of the daily routine. A man may be a good student who reads only the book of nature. Such a one[1] I remember in the

[1] The late John Bell.

early days of my residence in Montreal—a man whose devotion to patients and whose kindness and skill quickly brought him an enormous practice. Reading in his carriage and by lamplight at Lucina's bedside, he was able to keep well informed; but he had an insatiable desire to know the true inwardness of a disease, and it was in this way I came into contact with him. Hard pushed day and night, yet he was never too busy to spend a couple of hours with me searching for data which had not been forthcoming during life, or helping to unravel the mysteries of a new disease, such as pernicious anaemia.

III

The *student-specialist* has to walk warily, as with two advantages there are two great dangers against which he has constantly to be on guard. In the bewildering complexity of modern medicine it is a relief to limit the work of a life to a comparatively narrow field which can be thoroughly tilled. To many men there is a feeling of great satisfaction in the mastery of a small department, particularly one in which technical skill is required. How much we have benefited from this concentration of effort in dermatology, laryngology, ophthalmology, and in gynaecology! Then, as a rule, the specialist is a free man, with leisure or, at any rate, with some leisure; not the slave of the public, with the incessant demands upon him of the general practitioner. He may live a more rational life, and has time to cultivate his mind, and he is able to devote himself to public interests and to the welfare of his professional brethren, on whose suffrages he so largely depends. How much we are indebted in the larger cities to the disinterested labours of this favoured class the records of our libraries and medical societies bear witness. The dangers do not come to the strong man in a speciality, but to the weak brother who seeks in it an easier field in which specious garrulity and mechanical dexterity may take the place of solid knowledge. All goes well when the man is larger than his speciality and controls it, but when the speciality runs away with the man there is disaster, and a topsy-turvy condition which, in every branch, has done incalculable injury. Next to the danger from small men is the serious risk of the loss of perspective in prolonged and concentrated effort in a narrow field. Against this there is but one safeguard—the cultivation of the sciences upon which the speciality is based. The student-specialist may have a wide vision—no student wider—if he gets away from the mechanical side of the art, and keeps in touch with the physiology and pathology upon which his art depends. More than any other of us, he needs the lessons of the laboratory, and wide contact with men in other departments may serve to correct the inevitable tendency to a narrow and perverted vision, in which the life of the ant-hill is mistaken for the world at large.

Of the *student-teacher* every faculty affords examples in varying degrees. It goes without saying that no man can teach successfully who is not at the same time a student. Routine, killing routine, saps the vitality of many who start with high aims, and who, for years, strive with all their energies against the degeneration which it is so prone to entail. In the smaller schools isolation, the absence of congenial spirits working at the same subject, favours stagnation, and after a few years the fires of early enthusiasm no longer glow in the perfunctory lectures. In many teachers the ever-increasing demands of practice leave less and less time for study, and a first-class man may lose touch with his subject through no fault of his own, but through an entanglement in outside affairs which he deeply regrets yet cannot control. To his five natural senses the student-teacher must add two more—the sense of responsibility and the sense of proportion. Most of us start with a highly developed sense of the importance of the work, and with a desire to live up to the responsibilities entrusted to us. Punctuality, the class first, always and at all times; the best that a man has in him, nothing less; the best the profession has on the subject, nothing less; fresh energies and enthusiasm in dealing with dry details; animated, unselfish devotion to all alike; tender consideration for his assistants— these are some of the fruits of a keen sense of responsibility in a good teacher. The sense of proportion is not so easy to acquire, and much depends on the training and on the natural disposition. There are men who never possess it; to others it seems to come naturally. In the most careful ones it needs constant cultivation —*nothing over-much* should be the motto of every teacher. In my early days I came under the influence of an ideal student-teacher, the late Palmer Howard, of Montreal. If you ask what manner of man he was, read Matthew Arnold's noble tribute to his father in his well-known poem, *Rugby Chapel*. When young, Dr. Howard had chosen a path—'path to a clear-purposed goal', and he pursued it with unswerving devotion. With him the study and the teaching of medicine were an absorbing passion, the ardour of which neither the incessant and ever-increasing demands upon his time nor the growing years could quench. When I first, as a senior student, came into intimate contact with him in the summer of 1871, the problem of tuberculosis was under discussion, stirred up by the epoch-making work of Villemin and the radical views of Niemeyer. Every lung lesion at the Montreal General Hospital had to be shown to him, and I got my first-hand introduction to Laennec, to Graves, and to Stokes, and became familiar with their works. No matter what the hour, and it usually was after 10 p.m., I was welcome with my bag, and if Wilks and Moxon, Virchow, or Rokitanski gave us no help, there were the *Transactions* of the Pathological Society and the big *Dictionnaire* of Dechambre. An ideal teacher because a student, ever alert to the new problems, an indomitable energy enabled him in the midst of an exacting practice to maintain an ardent enthusiasm, still to keep bright the fires which he had lighted in his youth. Since those days I have seen many teachers, and I have had many colleagues, but I have never known one in whom was more happily combined a stern sense of duty with the mental freshness of youth.

But as I speak, from out the memory of the past there rises before me a shadowy group, a long line of students whom I have taught and loved, and who have died prematurely—mentally, morally, or bodily. To the successful we are willing and anxious to bring the tribute of praise, but none so poor to give recognition to the failures. From one cause or another, perhaps because when not absorbed in the present, my thoughts are chiefly in the past, I have cherished the memory of many young men whom I have loved and lost. *Io victis*: let us sometimes sing of the vanquished. Let us sometimes think of those who have fallen in the battle of life, who have striven and failed, who have failed even without the strife. How many have I lost from the student band by mental death, and from so many causes—some stillborn from college, others dead within the first year of infantile marasmus, while mental rickets, teething, tabes, and fits have carried off many of the most promising minds! Due to improper feeding within the first five fateful years, scurvy and rickets head the mental mortality bills of students. To the teacher-nurse it is a sore disappointment to find at the end of ten years so few minds with the full stature, of which the early days gave promise. Still, so widespread is mental death that we scarcely comment upon it in our friends. The real tragedy is the moral death which, in different forms, overtakes so many good fellows who fall away from the pure, honourable, and righteous service of Minerva into the idolatry of Bacchus, of Venus, or of Circe. Against the background of the past these tragedies stand out, lurid and dark, and as the names and faces of my old boys recur (some of them my special pride), I shudder to think of the blighted hopes and wrecked lives, and I force my memory back to those happy days when they were as you are now, joyous and free from care, and I think of them on the benches, in the laboratories, and in the wards—and there I leave them. Less painful to dwell upon, though associated with a more poignant grief, is the fate of those whom physical death has snatched away in the bud or blossom of the student life. These are among the tender memories of the teacher's life, of which he does not often care to speak, feeling with Longfellow that the surest pledge of their remembrance is 'the silent homage of thoughts unspoken'. As I look back it seems now as if the best of us had died, that the brightest and the keenest had been taken and the more commonplace among us had been spared. An old mother, a devoted sister, a loving brother, in some cases a broken-hearted wife, still pay the tribute of tears for the untimely ending of their high hopes, and in loving remembrance I would mingle mine with theirs. What a loss to our profession have been the deaths of such true disciples as Zimmerman, of Toronto; of Jack Cline and of R. L. MacDonnell, of Montreal; of Fred Packard and of Kirkbride, of Philadelphia; of Livingood, of Lazear, of Oppenheimer, and of Oechsner, in Baltimore—cut off with their leaves still in the green, to the inconsolable grief of their friends!

To each one of you the practice of medicine will be very much as you make it—to one a worry, a care, a perpetual annoyance; to another, a daily joy and a life of as much happiness and usefulness as can well fall to the lot of man. In the student spirit you can best fulfil the high mission of our noble calling—in his *humility*, conscious of weakness, while seeking strength; in his *confidence*, knowing the power, while recognizing the limitations of his art; in his *pride* in the glorious heritage from which the greatest gifts to man have been derived; and in his sure and certain hope that the future holds for us richer blessings than the past.

12

TEACHING AND THINKING

THE TWO FUNCTIONS OF A MEDICAL SCHOOL

> Let us then blush, in this so ample and so wonderful field
> of nature (where performance still exceeds what is promised),
> to credit other men's traditions only, and thence come un-
> certain problems to spin out thorny and captious questions.
> *Nature* her selfe must be our adviser; the path she chalks
> must be our walk: for so while we confer with our own eies,
> and take our rise from meaner things to higher, we shall at
> length be received into her Closet-secrets.
>
> WILLIAM HARVEY: Preface to *Anatomical Exercitations*
> *concerning the Generation of Living Creatures*, 1653.

I

MANY things have been urged against our nineteenth-century civilization—that political enfranchise-ment only ends in anarchy, that the widespread unrest in spiritual matters leads only to unbelief, and that the best commentary on our boasted enlightenment is the picture of Europe in arms and the nations everywhere gnarring at each other's heels. Of practical progress in one direction, however, there can be no doubt; no one can dispute the enormous increase in the comfort of each individual life. Collectively the human race, or portions of it at any rate, may in the past have enjoyed periods of greater repose, and longer intervals of freedom from strife and anxiety; but the day has never been when the unit has been of such value, when the man, and the man alone, has been so much the measure, when the individual as a living organism has seemed so sacred, when the obligations to regard his rights have seemed so imperative. But

Remarks at the opening of the new building of the Medical Faculty, McGill College, 8 January 1895. *Montreal Medical Journal*, 1894–5, xxiii. 561–72. Reprinted in *Aequanimitas*.

even these changes are as nothing in comparison with the remarkable increase in his physical well-being. The bitter cry of Isaiah
that with the multiplication of the nations their joys have not
been increased, still echoes in our ears. The sorrows and troubles
of men, it is true, may not have been materially diminished,
but bodily pain and suffering, though not abolished, have been
assuaged as never before, and the share of each in the *Weltschmerz*
has been enormously lessened.

Sorrows and griefs are companions sure sooner or later to join
us on our pilgrimage, and we have become perhaps more sensitive
to them, and perhaps less amenable to the old-time remedies of
the physicians of the soul; but the pains and woes of the body,
to which we doctors minister, are decreasing at an extraordinary rate, and in a way that makes one fairly gasp in hopeful
anticipation.

In his *Grammar of Assent*, in a notable passage on suffering,
John Henry Newman asks, 'Who can weigh and measure the
aggregate of pain which this one generation has endured, and
will endure, from birth to death? Then add to this all the pain
which has fallen and will fall upon our race through centuries
past and to come.' But take the other view of it—think of the
Nemesis which has overtaken pain during the past fifty years!
Anaesthetics and antiseptic surgery have almost manacled the
demon, and since their introduction the aggregate of pain which
has been prevented far outweighs in civilized communities that
which has been suffered. Even the curse of travail has been lifted
from the soul of women.

The greatest art is in the concealment of art, and I may say
that we of the medical profession excel in this respect. You of
the public who hear me, go about the duties of the day profoundly indifferent to the facts I have just mentioned. You do
not know, many of you do not care, that for the cross-legged
Juno who presided over the arrival of your grandparents, there
now sits a benign and straight-legged goddess. You take it for
granted that if a shoulder is dislocated there is chloroform and
a delicious Nepenthe instead of the agony of the pulleys and

paraphernalia of fifty years ago. You accept with a selfish complacency, as if you were yourselves to be thanked for it, that the arrows of destruction fly not so thickly, and that the pestilence now rarely walketh in the darkness; still less do you realize that you may now pray the prayer of Hezekiah with a reasonable prospect of its fulfilment, since modern science has made to almost every one of you the present of a few years.

I say you do not know these things. You hear of them, and the more intelligent among you perhaps ponder them in your hearts, but they are among the things which you take for granted, like the sunshine, and the flowers and the glorious heavens.

'Tis no idle challenge which we physicians throw out to the world when we claim that our mission is of the highest and of the noblest kind, not alone in curing disease but in educating the people in the laws of health, and in preventing the spread of plagues and pestilences; nor can it be gainsaid that of late years our record as a body has been more encouraging in its practical results than those of the other learned professions. Not that we all live up to the highest ideals, far from it—we are only men. But we have ideals, which mean much, and they are realizable, which means more. Of course there are Gehazis among us who serve for shekels, whose ears hear only the lowing of the oxen and the jingling of the guineas, but these are exceptions. The rank and file labour earnestly for your good, and self-sacrificing devotion to your interests animates our best work.

The exercises in which we are to-day engaged form an incident in this beneficent work which is in progress everywhere; an incident which will enable me to dwell upon certain aspects of the university as a factor in the promotion of the physical well-being of the race.

II

A great university has a dual function, to teach and to think. The educational aspects at first absorb all its energies, and in equipping various departments and providing salaries, it finds itself hard pressed to fulfil even the first of the duties. The story of the progress of the medical school of this institution illustrates the struggles and difficulties, the worries and vexations attendant upon the effort to place it in the first rank as a teaching body. I know them well, since I was in the thick of them for ten years, and see to-day the realization of many of my day-dreams. Indeed in my wildest flights I never thought to see such a splendid group of buildings as I have just inspected. We were modest in those days, and I remember when Dr. Howard showed me in great confidence the letter of the Chancellor, in which he conveyed his first generous bequest to the Faculty, it seemed so great that in my joy I was almost ready to sing my *Nunc dimittis.* The great advances here, at the Montreal General Hospital, and at the Royal Victoria (both of which institutions form most essential parts of the medical schools of this city) mean increased teaching facilities, and of necessity better equipped doctors! Here is the kernel of the whole matter, and it is for this that we ask the aid necessary to build large laboratories and large hospitals in which the student may learn the science and art of medicine. Chemistry, anatomy, and physiology give that perspective which enables him to place man and his diseases in their proper position in the scheme of life, and afford at the same time that essential basis upon which alone a trustworthy experience may be built. Each one of these is a science in itself, complicated and difficult, demanding much time and labour for its acquisition, so that in the few years which are given to their study the student can only master the principles and certain of the facts upon which they are founded. Only so far as they bear upon a due understanding of the phenomena of disease do these subjects form part of the medical curriculum, and for us they are but means—essential means it is true—to this end. A man cannot become a competent surgeon without a full knowledge of human anatomy and physiology, and the physician without physiology and chemistry flounders along in an aimless fashion, never able to gain any accurate conception of disease, practising a sort of popgun pharmacy, hitting now the malady and again the patient, he himself not knowing which.

The primary function of this department of the university is to instruct men about disease, what it is, what are its manifestations, how it may be prevented, and how it may be cured; and to learn these things the four hundred young men who sit on these benches have come from all parts of the land. But it is no light responsibility which a faculty assumes in this matter. The task is beset with difficulties, some inherent in the subject and others in the men themselves, while not a few are caused by the lack of common sense in medical matters of the people among whom we doctors work.

The processes of disease are so complex that it is excessively difficult to search out the laws which control them, and, although we have seen a complete revolution in our ideas, what has been accomplished by the new school of medicine is only an earnest of what the future has in store. The three great advances of the century have been a knowledge of the mode of controlling epidemic diseases, the introduction of anaesthetics, and the adoption of antiseptic methods in surgery. Beside them all others sink into insignificance, as these three contribute so enormously to the personal comfort of the individual. The study of the causes of so-called infectious disorders has led directly to the discovery of the methods for their control, for example, such a scourge as typhoid fever becomes almost unknown in the presence of perfect drainage and an uncontaminated water-supply. The outlook, too, for specific methods of treatment in these affections is most hopeful. The public must not be discouraged by a few, or even by many failures. The thinkers who are doing the work for you are on the right path, and it is no vain fancy that before the twentieth century is very old there may be effective vaccines against many of the contagious diseases.

But a shrewd old fellow remarked to me the other day, 'Yes, many diseases are less frequent, others have disappeared, but new ones are always cropping up, and I notice that with it all there is not only no decrease, but a very great increase in the number of doctors'.

The total abolition of the infectious group we cannot expect, and for many years to come there will remain hosts of bodily ills, even among preventable maladies, to occupy our labours; but there are two reasons which explain the relative numerical increase in the profession in spite of the great decrease in the number of certain diseases. The development of specialties has given employment to many extra men who now do much of the work of the old family practitioner, and again people employ doctors more frequently and so give occupation to many more than formerly.

It cannot be denied that we have learned more rapidly how to prevent than how to cure diseases, but with a definite outline of our ignorance we no longer live now in a fool's paradise, and fondly imagine that in all cases we control the issues of life and death with our pills and potions. It took the profession many generations to learn that fevers ran their course, influenced very little, if at all, by drugs, and the £60 which old Dover complained were spent in drugs in a case of ordinary fever about the middle of the last century are now better expended on a trained nurse, with infinitely less risk, and with infinitely greater comfort to the patient. Of the difficulties inherent in the art not one is so serious as this which relates to the cure of disease by drugs. There is so much uncertainty and discord even among the best authorities (upon non-essentials, it is true) that I always feel the force of a well-known stanza in *Rabbi Ben Ezra*:

> Now, who shall arbitrate?
> Ten men love what I hate,
> Shun what I follow, slight what I receive;
> Ten, who in ears and eyes
> Match me: we all surmise,
> They this thing, and I that: whom shall my soul believe?

One of the chief reasons for this uncertainty is the increasing variability in the manifestations of any one disease. As no two faces, so no two cases are alike in all respects, and unfortunately it is not only the disease itself which is so varied, but the subjects themselves have peculiarities which modify its action.

With the diminished reliance upon drugs, there has been a return with profit to the older measures of diet, exercise, baths, and frictions, the remedies with which the Bithynian Asclepiades doctored the Romans so successfully in the first century. Though used less frequently, medicines are now given with infinitely greater skill; we know better their indications and contradictions, and we may safely say (reversing the proportion of fifty years ago) that for one damaged by dosing, one hundred are saved.

Many of the difficulties which surround the subject relate to the men who practise the art. The commonest as well as the saddest mistake is to mistake one's profession, and this we doctors do often enough, some of us, without knowing it. There are men who have never had the preliminary education which would enable them to grasp the fundamental truths of the science on which medicine is based. Others have poor teachers, and never receive that bent of mind which is the all-important factor in education; others again fall early into the error of thinking that they know it all, and benefiting neither by their mistakes nor their successes, miss the very essence of all experience, and die bigger fools, if possible, than when they started. There are only two sorts of doctors; those who practise with their brains, and those who practise with their tongues. The studious, hard-working man who wishes to know his profession thoroughly, who lives in the hospitals and dispensaries, and who strives to obtain a wide and philosophical conception of disease and its processes, often has a hard struggle, and it may take years of waiting before he becomes successful; but such form the bulwarks of our ranks, and outweigh scores of the voluble Cassios who talk themselves into, and often out of, practice.

Now of the difficulties bound up with the public in which we doctors work, I hesitate to speak in a mixed audience. Common sense in matters medical is rare, and is usually in inverse ratio to the degree of education. I suppose as a body, clergymen are better educated than any other, yet they are notorious supporters of all the nostrums and humbuggery with which the daily and religious papers abound, and I find that the farther away they have wandered from the decrees of the Council of Trent, the more apt are they to be steeped in thaumaturgic and Galenical superstition. But know also, man has an inborn craving for medicine. Heroic dosing for several generations has given his tissues a thirst for drugs. As I once before remarked, the desire to take medicine is one feature which distinguishes man, the animal, from his fellow creatures. It is really one of the most serious difficulties with which we have to contend. Even in minor ailments, which would yield to dieting or to simple home remedies, the doctor's visit is not thought to be complete without the prescription. And now that the pharmacists have cloaked even the most nauseous remedies, the temptation is to use medicine on every occasion, and I fear we may return to that state of polypharmacy, the emancipation from which has been the sole gift of Hahnemann and his followers to the race. As the public becomes more enlightened, and as we get more sense, dosing will be recognized as a very minor function in the practice of medicine in comparison with the old measures of Asclepiades.

After all, these difficulties—in the subject itself, in us, and in you—are lessening gradually, and we have the consolation of knowing that year by year the total amount of unnecessary suffering is decreasing at a rapid rate.

In teaching men what disease is, how it may be prevented, and how it may be cured, a university is fulfilling one of its very noblest functions. The wise instruction and the splendid example of such men as Holmes, Sutherland, Campbell, Howard, Ross, Macdonnell, and others have carried comfort into thousands of homes throughout this land. The benefits derived from the increased facilities for the teaching of medicine which have come with the great changes made here and at the hospitals during the past few years will not be confined to the citizens of this town, but will be widely diffused and felt in every locality to which the graduates of this school may go; and every gift which promotes higher medical education, and which enables the medical faculties throughout the country to turn out better doctors, means fewer mistakes in diagnosis, greater skill in dealing

202 SELECTED WRITINGS OF SIR WILLIAM OSLER

with emergencies, and the saving of pain and anxiety to countless sufferers and their friends.

The physician needs a clear head and a kind heart; his work is arduous and complex, requiring the exercise of the very highest faculties of the mind, while constantly appealing to the emotions and finer feelings. At no time has his influence been more potent than at present, at no time has he been so powerful a factor for good, and as it is one of the highest possible duties of a great university to fit men for this calling, so it will be your highest mission, students of medicine, to carry on the never-ending warfare against disease and death, better equipped, abler men than your predecessors, but animated with their spirit and sustained by their hopes, 'for the hope of every creature is the banner that we bear'.

III

The other function of a university is to think. Teaching current knowledge in all departments, teaching the steps by which the *status praesens* has been reached, and teaching how to teach, form the routine work of the various college faculties. All this may be done in a perfunctory manner by men who have never gone deeply enough into the subjects to know that really thinking about them is in any way necessary or important. What I mean by the thinking function of a university, is that duty which the professional corps owes to enlarge the boundaries of human knowledge. Work of this sort makes a university great, and alone enables it to exercise a wide influence on the minds of men.

We stand to-day at a critical point in the history of this faculty. The equipment for teaching, to supply which has taken years of hard struggle, is approaching completion, and with the co-operation of the General and the Royal Victoria Hospitals students can obtain in all branches a thorough training. We have now reached a position in which the higher university work may at any rate be discussed, and towards it progress in the future must trend. It may seem to be discouraging, after so much has been done and so much has been so generously given, to say that there remains a most important function to foster and sustain, but this aspect of the question must be considered when a school has reached a certain stage of development. In a progressive institution the changes come slowly, the pace may not be perceived by those most concerned, except on such occasions as the present, which serve as land-marks in its evolution. The men and methods of the old Coté Street school were better than those with which the faculty started; we and our ways at the new building on University Street were better than those of Coté Street; and now you of the present faculty teach and work much better than we did ten years ago. Everywhere the old order changeth, and happy those who can change with it. Like the defeated gods in Keats's *Hyperion*, too many unable to receive the balm of the truth, resent the wise words of Oceanus (which I quoted here with very different feelings some eighteen years ago in an introductory lecture).

> So on our heels a fresh perfection treads,
> . . . born of us
> And fated to excel us.

Now the fresh perfection which will tread on our heels will come with the opportunities for higher university work. Let me indicate in a few words its scope and aims. Teachers who teach current knowledge are not necessarily investigators; many have not had the needful training; others have not the needful time. The very best instructor for students may have no conception of the higher lines of work in his branch, and contrariwise, how many brilliant investigators have been wretched teachers? In a school which has reached this stage and wishes to do thinking as well as teaching, men must be selected who are not only thoroughly *au courant* with the best work in their department the world over, but who also have ideas, with ambition and energy to put them into force—men who can add, each one in his sphere, to the store of the world's knowledge. Men of this stamp alone confer greatness upon a university. They should be sought for far and wide; an institution which wraps itself in Strabo's cloak and does not look beyond the college gates in selecting professors may get good teachers, but rarely good thinkers.

One of the chief difficulties in the way of advanced work is the stress of routine class and laboratory duties, which often sap the energies of men capable of higher things. To meet this difficulty it is essential, first, to give the professors plenty of assistance, so that they will not be worn out with teaching; and, secondly, to give encouragement to graduates and others to carry on researches under their direction. With a system of fellowships and research scholarships a university may have a body of able young men, who on the outposts of knowledge are exploring, surveying, defining, and correcting. Their work is the outward and visible sign that a university is thinking. Surrounded by a group of bright young minds, well trained in advanced methods, not only is the professor himself stimulated to do his best work, but he has to keep far afield and to know what is stirring in every part of his own domain.

With the wise co-operation of the university and the hospital authorities Montreal may become the Edinburgh of America, a great medical centre to which men will flock for sound learning, whose laboratories will attract the ablest students, and whose teaching will go out into all lands, universally recognized as of the highest and of the best type.

Nowhere is the outlook more encouraging than at McGill. What a guarantee for the future does the progress of the past decade afford! No city on this continent has endowed higher education so liberally. There remains now to foster that undefinable something which, for want of a better term, we call the university spirit, a something which a rich institution may not have, and with which a poor one may be saturated, a something which is associated with men and not with money, which cannot be purchased in the market or grown to order, but which comes insensibly with loyal devotion to duty and to high ideals, and without which *Nehushtan* is written on the portals of any school of medicine, however famous.

13

THE GROWTH OF TRUTH

AS ILLUSTRATED IN THE DISCOVERY OF THE CIRCULATION OF THE BLOOD

I

ONLY those of us, Mr. President and Fellows, who have had the good fortune to hold the distinguished position which by your kind grace, Sir, I hold to-day, only those of us who have delivered the Harveian Oration, can appreciate the extraordinary difficulties besetting a subject, every aspect of which has been considered, very often too, by men who have brought to the task a combination of learning and literary skill at once the envy and the despair of their successors. But I take it, Sir, that in this Ambarvalia or commemorative festival for blessing the fruits of our great men, ordained definitely as such by him whose memory is chiefly in our minds to-day, our presence here in due order and array confers distinction upon an occasion of which the oration is but an incident. But, honour worthy of such a theme should be associated with full knowledge of the conditions under which these great men lived and moved; and here comes in the real difficulty, because it is rarely possible to bring the fruits of independent critical investigation into their lives and works. Particularly hard is it for those of us who have had to live the life of the arena: our best efforts bear the stamp of the student, not of the scholar. In my own case, a deep reverence for the mighty minds of old, and a keen appreciation of the importance

Being the Harveian Oration delivered at the Royal College of Physicians, London, 18 October 1906. Published London, 1907. Printed in the *British Medical Journal*, 1906, ii. 1077–84; *Lancet*, 1906, ii. 1113–20; *Boston Medical and Surgical Journal*, 1906, clv. 491–502; in *An Alabama Student* as 'Harvey and His Discovery'.

to our profession of a study of history, may be put in the scales against defects as to the appreciation of which I have still remaining sufficient self-detachment. The lesson of the day is the lesson of their lives. But because of the ever-increasing mental strain in this age of hurry, few of us have the leisure, fewer still, I fear, the inclination, to read it thoroughly. Only with a knowledge of the persistency with which they waged the battle for Truth, and the greatness of their victory, does the memory of the illustrious dead become duly precious to us.

History is simply the biography of the mind of man; and our interest in history, and its educational value to us, is directly proportionate to the completeness of our study of the individuals through whom this mind has been manifested. To understand clearly our position in any science to-day, we must go back to its beginnings, and trace its gradual development, following certain laws, difficult to interpret and often obscured in the brilliancy of achievements—laws which everywhere illustrate this biography, this human endeavour, working through the long ages; and particularly is this the case with that history of the organized experience of the race which we call science.

In the first place, like a living organism, Truth grows, and its gradual evolution may be traced from the tiny germ to the mature product. Never springing, Minerva-like, to full stature at once, Truth may suffer all the hazards incident to generation and gestation. Much of history is a record of the mishaps of truths which have struggled to the birth, only to die or else to wither in premature decay. Or the germ may be dormant for centuries, awaiting the fullness of time.

Secondly, all scientific truth is conditioned by the state of knowledge at the time of its announcement. Thus, at the beginning of the seventeenth century, the science of optics and mechanical appliances had not made possible (so far as the human mind was concerned) the existence of blood capillaries and blood corpuscles. Jenner could not have added to his *Inquiry* a discourse on immunity; Sir William Perkin and the chemists made Koch possible; Pasteur gave the conditions that produced Lister; Davy and others furnished the preliminaries necessary for anaesthesia. Everywhere we find this invariable filiation, one event following the other in orderly sequence—'Mind begets mind', as Harvey says; 'opinion is the source of opinion. Democritus with his atoms, and Eudoxus with his chief good, which he placed in pleasure, impregnated Epicurus; the four elements of Empedocles, Aristotle; the doctrine of the ancient Thebans, Pythagoras and Plato; geometry, Euclid' (*De Generatione*).

And, thirdly, to scientific truth alone may the *homo mensura* principle be applied, since of all mental treasures of the race it alone compels general acquiescence. That this general acquiescence, this aspect of certainty, is not reached *per saltum*, but is of slow, often of difficult, growth—marked by failures and frailties, but crowned at last with an acceptance accorded to no other product of mental activity—is illustrated by every important discovery from Copernicus to Darwin.

The growth of Truth corresponds to the states of knowledge described by Plato in the *Theaetetus*—acquisition, latent possession, conscious possession. Scarcely a discovery can be named which does not present these phases in its evolution. Take, for example, one of the most recent: Long years of labour gave us a full knowledge of syphilis; centuries of acquisition added one fact to another, until we had a body of clinical and pathological knowledge of remarkable fullness. For the last quarter of a century we have had latent possession of the cause of the disease, as no one could doubt the legitimate inference from discoveries in other acute infections. The conscious possession has just been given to us. After scores of investigators had struggled in vain with the problem, came Schaudinn with an instinct for truth, with a capacity to pass beyond the routine of his day, and with a vision for the whole where others had seen but in part. It is one of the tragedies of science that this brilliant investigator, with capabilities for work so phenomenal, should have been cut off at the very threshold of his career. The cancer problem, still in the stage of latent possession, awaits the advent of a man of the same type. In a hundred other less important problems, acquisition has by slow stages become latent possession; and there needs but the final touch—the crystal in the saturated solution—to give us conscious possession of the truth. But when these stages are ended, there remains the final struggle for general acceptance. Locke's remark that 'Truth scarce ever yet carried it by vote anywhere at its first appearance' is borne out by the history of all discoveries of the first rank. The times, however, are changing; and it is interesting to compare the cordial welcome of the pallid spirochaete with the chilly reception of the tubercle bacillus. Villemin had done his great work, Cohnheim and Salmonson had finally solved the problem of infectivity, when Koch published his memorable studies. Others before him had seen the bacillus, but the conscious possession of the truth only came with his marvellous technique. Think of the struggle to secure acceptance! The seniors among us who lived through that instructive period remember well that only those who were awake when the dawn appeared assented at once to the brilliant demonstration. We are better prepared to-day; and a great discovery like that of Schaudinn is immediately put to the test by experts in many lands, and a verdict is given in a few months. We may have become more plastic and receptive, but I doubt it; even our generation—that great generation of the last quarter of the nineteenth century, had a practical demonstration of the slowness of the acceptation of an obvious truth in the long fight for the aseptic treatment of wounds. There may be present some who listened, as I did in October, 1873, to an introductory lecture at one of the largest of the metropolitan schools, the burden of which was the finality of surgery. The distinguished author and teacher, dwelling on the remarkable achievements of the past, concluded that the art had all but reached its limit, little recking that within a mile from where he spoke, the truth for which he and thousands had been striving—now a conscious possession in the hands of Joseph Lister—would revolutionize it. With scores of surgeons here and there throughout the world this truth had been a latent possession. Wounds had healed *per primam* since Machaon's day; and there were men before Joseph

Lister who had striven for cleanliness in surgical technique; but not until he appeared could a great truth become so manifest that it everywhere compelled acquiescence. Yet not without a battle—a long and grievous battle, as many of us well knew who had to contend in hospitals with the opposition of men who could not—not who would not—see the truth.

Sooner or later—insensibly, unconsciously—the iron yoke of conformity is upon our necks; and in our minds, as in our bodies, the force of habit becomes irresistible. From our teachers and associates, from our reading, from the social atmosphere about us we catch the beliefs of the day, and they become ingrained —part of our nature. For most of us this happens in the hap-hazard process we call education, and it goes on just as long as we retain any mental receptivity. It was never better expressed than in the famous lines that occurred to Henry Sidgwick in his sleep:

> We think so because all other people think so;
> Or because—or because—after all, we do think so;
> Or because we were told so, and think we must think so;
> Or because we once thought so, and think we still think so;
> Or because, having thought so, we think we will think so.

In departing from any settled opinion or belief, the variation, the change, the break with custom may come gradually; and the way is usually prepared; but the final break is made, as a rule, by some one individual, the masterless man of Kipling's splendid allegory, who sees with his own eyes, and with an instinct or genius for truth, escapes from the routine in which his fellows live. But he often pays dearly for his boldness. Walter Bagehot tells us that the pain of a new idea is one of the greatest pains to human nature.

It is, as people say, so upsetting; it makes you think that, after all, your favourite notions may be wrong, your firmest beliefs ill-founded; it is certain that till now there was no place allotted in your mind to the new and startling inhabitant; and now that it has conquered an entrance, you do not at once see which of your old ideas it will not turn out, with which of them it can be reconciled, and with which it is at essential enmity.

It is on this account that the man who expresses a new idea is very apt to be abused and ill-treated. All this is common among common men, but there is something much worse which has been illustrated over and over again in history. How eminent soever a man may become in science, he is very apt to carry with him errors which were in vogue when he was young—errors that darken his understanding, and make him incapable of accepting even the most obvious truths. It is a great consolation to know that even Harvey came within the range of this law—in the matter of the lymphatic system—it is the most human touch in his career.

By no single event in the history of science is the growth of truth, through the slow stages of acquisition, the briefer period of latent possession, and the, for us, glorious period of conscious possession, better shown than in the discovery of the circulation of the blood. You will all agree with me that a Fellow of this college must take his courage in both hands who would, in this place and before this audience, attempt to discuss any aspect of this problem. After nearly three centuries of orations the very pictures and books in this hall might be expected to cry out upon him. But I have so taken my courage, confident that in using it to illustrate certain aspects of the growth of truth I am but obeying the command of Plato, who insists that principles such as these cannot be too often or too strongly enforced. There is a younger generation, too, the members of which are never the worse for the repetition of a good story, stale though it may be in all its aspects to their elders; and then there is that larger audience to be considered to which the season is never inappropriate to speak a word.

II

The sixteenth century, drawing to a close, had been a period of acquisition unequalled in history. Brooding over the face of the waters of medievalism, the spirit of the Renaissance brought forth a science of the world and of man which practically created a new heaven and a new earth, and the truths announced by Copernicus and Galileo far transcended

> the searching schoolmen's view
> And half had staggered that stout Stagyrite.

Among other things, it had given to medicine a new spirit, a new anatomy, and a new chemistry. In the latter part of the fifteenth century Hippocrates and Galen came to their own again. A wave of enthusiasm for the fathers in medicine swept over the profession; and for at least two generations the best energies of its best minds were devoted to the study of their writings. How numerous and important is that remarkable group of men, the medical humanists of the Renaissance, we may judge by a glance at Bayle's *Biographie Médicale*, in which the lives are arranged in chronological order. From Garbo of Bologna, surnamed the expositor, to Rabelais, more than 150 biographies and bibliographies are given, and at least one-half of these men had either translated or edited works of the Greek physicians. Of our founder, one of the most distinguished of the group, and of his influence in reviving the study of Galen and so indirectly of his influence upon Harvey, Dr. Payne's story still lingers in our memories. Leonicenus, Linacre, Gonthier, Monti, Koch, Camerarius, Caius, Fuchs, Zerbi, Cornarus, and men of their stamp not only swept away Arabian impurities from the medicine of the day, but they revived Greek ideals and introduced scientific methods.

The great practical acquisition of the century was a new anatomy. Vesalius and his followers gave for the first time an accurate account of the structure of the human body, and while thus enlarging and correcting the work of Galen, contributed to weaken the almost divine authority with which he dominated the schools. Nearly another century passed before chemistry, in the hands of Boyle and others, reached its modern phase, but the work of Paracelsus, based on that of the 'pious Spagyrist', Basil Valentine, by showing its possibilities, had directed men's minds strongly to the new science. Of the three, the new spirit alone was essential, since it established the intellectual and moral freedom by which the fetters of dogma, authority, and scholasticism were for ever loosened from the minds of men.

Into this world, we may say, stepped a young Folkestone lad, when, on the last day of May, 1593, he matriculated at Cambridge. Harvey's education may be traced without difficulty, because the influences which shaped his studies were those which had for a century prevailed in the profession of this country. We do not know the reason for selection of Caius College, which, so far as I can gather, had no special connexion with the Canterbury school. Perhaps it was chosen because of the advice of the family physician, or of a friend, or of his rector; or else his father may have known Caius; or the foundation may already have become famous as a resort for those about to 'enter on the physic line'. Or, quite as likely, as we so often find in our experience, some trivial incident may have turned his thoughts towards medicine. When he came up in 1593, there were those of middle age who could tell racy stories of Caius, the co-founder of the college, against whose iron rule they had rebelled. 'Charged not only with a show of a perverse stomach to the professors of the Gospel, but with Atheism', the last days of Caius's noble life were embittered by strife and misunderstanding. Doubtless the generous souls among them had long since learned to realize the greatness of his character, and were content to leave 'the heat of his faith to God's sole judgement, and the light of his good works to men's imitation', with which words, half a century later, the inimitable Fuller concludes a short sketch of his life. I like to think that, perhaps, one of these very rebels, noting the studious and inquisitive nature of Harvey, had put into the lad's hand the little tractate, *De libris propriis*, from which to glean a knowledge of the life and works of their great benefactor.

The contemplation of such a career as that of Caius could not but inspire with enthusiasm any young man. No one in the profession in England had before that time reached a position which I may describe as European. An enthusiastic student and the friend of all the great scholars of the day; a learned commentator on the works of the Fathers; the first English student in clinical medicine; a successful teacher and practitioner; a keen naturalist; a liberal patron of learning and letters; a tender and sympathetic friend—Johannes Caius is one of the great figures in our history. Nor need I dwell, before this audience, on his devotion to our interests, other than to say that the memory of no Fellow on our roll should be more precious to us. Four years hence, on 6 October, will occur the quater-centenary of his birth. As well in love as in gratitude, we could celebrate it in no more appropriate manner, and in none that would touch his spirit more closely, than by the issue of a fine edition of his principal works (including the manuscript annals of the College). For the preparation of this there are those among us well fitted, not less by veneration for his memory than by the possession of that critical scholarship which he valued so highly.

When Harvey set out on the grand tour, Italy was still the *mater gloriosa studiorum*; to which one hundred years earlier, so tradition says, Linacre on leaving had erected an altar. The glamour of the ideals of the Renaissance had faded somewhat since the days when John Free, an Oxford man, had made the ancient learning his own; and had so far bettered the instruction of his masters that he was welcomed as a teacher in Padua, Ferrara, and Florence. In a measure, too, the national glory had departed, dimmed amid the strife and warfare which had cost the old republics their independence. Many years earlier Fracastorius, one of our medical poets, had sung of her decadence:

> To what estate, O wretched Italy,
> Has civil strife reduc'd and moulder'd Thee!
> Where now are all thy ancient glories hurl'd?
> Where is thy boasted Empire of the world?
> What nook in Thee from barbarous Rage is freed
> And has not seen thy captive children bleed?[1]

And matters had not improved but had grown worse. In the sixteenth century Italian influence had sunk deeply into the social, professional, and commercial life of England, more

[1] *Syphilis.* Englished by N. Tate, 1686.

deeply, indeed, than we appreciate;[1] and it was not for a generation or two later that the candlesticks were removed from the
Cisalpine towns to Montpellier, Paris, and Leyden. In 1593 a
well-to-do young Englishman who wished to study medicine
thoroughly went to north Italy, and most naturally to Padua—
'fair Padua, nursery of the arts'—whose close affiliations with us
may be gathered from the fact that, of universities next to
Oxford and Cambridge, she has given us more Presidents than
any other. In the years that had passed since Vesalius had retired
in disgust, the fame of its anatomical school had been well
maintained by Fallopius, Columbus, and Fabricius, worthy successors of the great master. Of each may be said what Douglas
says of the first named: 'In docendo maxime methodicus, in
medendo felicissimus, in secando expertissimus.' While the
story of Harvey's student life can never be told as we could wish,
we know enough to enable us to understand the influences
which moulded his career. In Fabricius he found a man to make
his life-model. To the enthusiastic teacher and investigator were
added those other qualities so attractive to the youthful mind,
generous sympathies and a keen sense of the wider responsibilities
of his position, as shown in building, at his own expense, a new
anatomical theatre for the university. Wide as was the range of
his master's studies, embracing not alone anatomy but medicine
and surgery, the contributions by which he is most distinguished
are upon subjects in which Harvey himself subsequently made
an undying reputation. The activity of his literary life did not
begin until he had been teaching nearly forty years, and it is a
fact of the highest significance that, corresponding to the very
period of Harvey's stay in Padua, Fabricius must have been
deep in the study of embryology and of the anatomy of the
vascular system. His great work on generation was the model
on which Harvey based his own, in some ways, more accurate
studies—studies in which, as my colleague Professor Brooks of
the Johns Hopkins University has pointed out, he has forestalled
Wolf and von Baer.

[1] *Italian Renaissance in England*, Einstein. Macmillan, 1902.

The work of Fabricius which really concerns us here is the *de Venarum Ostiolis*. Others before him had seen and described the valves of the veins, Carolus, one of the great Stephani, Sylvius and Paul Sarpi. But an abler hand in this work has dealt with the subject, and has left us a monograph which for completeness and for accuracy and beauty of illustration has scarcely its equal in anatomical literature. Compare Plate VII, for example, with the illustrations of the same structures in the Bidloo or the Cowper *Anatomy*, published nearly one hundred years later; and we can appreciate the advantages which Harvey must have enjoyed in working with such a master. Indeed, it is not too far-fetched to imagine him, scalpel in hand, making some of the very dissections from which these wonderful drawings were taken. But here comes in the mystery. How Fabricius, a man who did such work—how a teacher of such wide learning and such remarkable powers of observation, could have been so blinded as to overlook the truth which was tumbling out, so to speak, at his feet, is to us incomprehensible. But his eyes were sealed, and to him, as to his greater predecessors in the chair, clear vision was denied. The dead hand of the great Pergamite lay heavy on all thought, and Descartes had not yet changed the beginning of philosophy from wonder to doubt. Not without a feeling of pity do we read of the hopeless struggle of these great men to escape from slavish submission to authority. But it is not for us in these light days to gauge the depth of the sacred veneration with which they regarded the Fathers. Their mental attitude is expressed in a well-known poem of Browning's:

> those divine men of old time
> Have reached, thou sayest well, each at one point
> The outside verge that rounds our faculty,
> And where they reached who can do more than reach?

Willing to correct observations or to extend anatomy by careful dissection, it was too much to expect from them either a new interpretation of the old facts or a knowledge of the new method by which those facts could be correctly interpreted.

The ingenious explanation which Fabricius gave of the use of the valves of the veins—to serve as dams or checks to the flow of the blood, so that it would not irrigate too rapidly and over-flow the peripheral vessels to the deprivation of the upper parts of the limbs—shows how the old physiology dominated the most distinguished teacher of the time in the most distinguished school of Europe. This may have been the very suggestion to his pupil of the more excellent way. Was it while listening to this ingenious explanation of his master that, in a moment of abstrac-tion—dimly dreaming, perhaps, of an English home far away and long forsaken—that there came to Harvey a heaven-sent moment, a sudden inspiration, a passing doubt nursed for long in silence, which ultimately grew into the great truth of 1616?[1]

The works of Vesalius, of Fallopius, and of Fabricius effected a revolution in anatomy, but there was not at the close of the sixteenth century a new physiology. Though he had lost an anatomical throne, Galen ruled absolutely in all conceptions of the functions of the body, and in no department more serenely than in that relating to the heart, the blood and its movements. Upon his views I need not dwell further than to remind you that he regarded the liver as the source of the blood, of which there were two kinds, the one in the veins, the other in the arteries, both kinds in ceaseless ebb and flow, the only communication between these closed systems being through pores in the ventricular sep-tum. He knew the lesser circulation, but thought it only for the nutrition of the lungs. The heart was a lamp which is furnished with oil by the blood and with air from the lungs. Practically until the middle of the seventeenth century Galen's physiology ruled the schools, and yet for years the profession had been in latent possession of a knowledge of the circulation. Indeed, a good case has been made out for Hippocrates, in whose works occur some remarkably suggestive sentences.[2] In the sixteenth century the lesser circulation was described with admirable full-

---

[1] Boyle states that in the only conversation he ever had with him, Harvey acknowledged that a study of the valves of the veins had led him to the dis-covery of the circulation of the blood.   [2] Willis's *William Harvey*, pp. 21–2.

ness by Servetus and by Columbus, and both Sarpi and Caesalpinus had Hippocratic glimmerings of the greater circulation.
These men, with others doubtless, were in latent possession of
the truth. But every one of them saw darkly through Galenical
glasses, and theirs was the hard but the common lot never to
reach such conscious possession as everywhere to make men
acquiesce. One must have the disinterestedness of the dead to
deal with a problem about which controversy has raged, and in
which national issues have been allowed to blur the brightness
of an image which would be clear as day to those with eyes to
see. Nor would I refer to a matter long since settled by those
best competent to judge, had not the well-known work of
Luciani, the distinguished Professor of Physiology at Rome,
appeared recently in German dress, edited by Professor Ver-
worn, and spread broadcast views to which, with a chauvinism
unworthy of their history, our Italian brethren still adhere. It
has been well said 'that he alone discovers who proves', and in
the matter of the circulation of the blood, this was reserved for
the pupil of Fabricius. Skipping many arduous years we next
meet him as Lumleian Lecturer to the College.

III

The really notable years in the annals of medicine are not very
numerous. We have a calendar filled with glorious names, but
among the saints of science, if we know an era it is as much as
can be expected—perhaps because such men are less identified
with achievements than representative of the times in which
they lived. With many of our greatest names we cannot associate
any fixed dates. The Grecians who made Hippocrates possible
live in memory with some theory, or a small point in anatomy,
or in regard to the place of their birth; while the 'floruit' cannot
always be fixed with accuracy.

Hippocrates himself, Erasistratus, Galen, and Aretaeus have
no days in our calendar. We keep no festival in their honour as
the churches do those of St. Jerome and St. Chrysostom. It is
not until after the Renaissance that certain years (*anni mirabiles*)

stand out in bold relief as connected with memorable discoveries, or with the publication of revolutionary works. Nevertheless, only a few in each century; even the sixteenth, so rich in discoveries, has not more than five or six such years, and not one of them is connected with work done in this country. As to the seventeenth century, it is hard to name four made memorable by the announcement of great discoveries or the publication of famous works; in the eighteenth century not three, while in the century just completed, though it is replete with extraordinary discoveries, one is hard pressed to name half a dozen years which flash into memory as made ever memorable by great achievements. Of the three most important, anaesthesia, sanitation, and antiseptic surgery, only of the first can the date be fixed, 1846, and that for its practical application. For the other two discoveries, who will settle upon the year in which the greatest advance was made, or one which could be selected for an anniversary in our calendar?

There is one *dies mirabilis* in the history of the College—in the history, indeed, of the medical profession of this country, and the circumstances which made it memorable are well known to us. At ten o'clock on a bright spring morning, 17 April 1616, an unusually large company was attracted to the New Anatomical Theatre of the Physicians' College, Amen Street. The second Lumleian Lecture of the annual course, given that year by a new man, had drawn a larger gathering than usual, due in part to the brilliancy of the demonstration on the previous day, but also it may be because rumours had spread abroad about strange views to be propounded by the lecturer. I do not know if at the College the same stringent rules as to compulsory attendance prevailed as at the Barber Surgeons' Hall. Doubtless not,[1] but the President, and Censors, and Fellows would be there in due array; and with the help of the picture of 'The Anatomy Lecture by Banister', which is in the Hunterian collection, Glasgow, and

---

[1] Mr. William Fleming, the College Bedell, calls my attention to the Statutes of that period. Under penalty of a fine all Fellows and candidates were commanded to attend for at least five years.

a photograph of which Dr. Payne has recently put in our library, we can bring to mind this memorable occasion. We see the 'Anatomy', one of the six annually handed over to the College, on the table, the prosector standing by the skeleton near at hand, and very probably on the wall the very *Tabulae* of dissection of the arteries, veins, and nerves that hang above us to-day. But the centre of attention is the lecturer—a small dark man, wand in hand, with black piercing eyes, a quick vivacious manner, and with an ease and grace in demonstrating, which bespeaks the mastery of a subject studied for twenty years with a devotion that we can describe as Hunterian. A Fellow of nine years' standing, there was still the salt of youth in William Harvey when, not, as we may suppose, without some trepidation, he faced his auditors on this second day—a not uncritical audience, including many men well versed in the knowledge of the time and many who had heard all the best lecturers of Europe.

The President, Henry Atkins, after whose name in our Register stands the mysterious word 'Corb', had already had his full share of official lectures, less burdensome three hundred years ago than now. Let us hope the lecture of the previous day had whetted his somewhat jaded appetite. The Censors of the year formed an interesting group: John Argent, a Cambridge man, a 'great prop of the college', and often President, of whom but little seems known; Richard Palmer, also of Cambridge, and remembered now only for his connexion with Prince Henry's typhoid fever, as Dr. Norman Moore has told us; Mathew Gwinne of Oxford, first Professor of Physic at Gresham College and a playwright of some note in his day; and Theodore Goulston of Merton College, one of our great benefactors, and for 267 years past and gone purveyor-in-chief of reputation to the younger Fellows of the College. Mayerne would be there, not yet a Fellow, but happy in his escape from the Paris Faculty; still dusty with conflict, he would scent the battle afar in the revolutionary statements which he heard. Meverell, fresh from incorporation at Cambridge, also not yet a Fellow; Moundeford, often President, whose little book *Vir Bonus* sets forth his life.

Paddy, a noteworthy benefactor, a keen student, still gratefully remembered at Oxford, would have strolled in with his old friend Gwinne; Baldwin Hamey the elder, also a benefactor, would be there, and perhaps he had brought his more interesting son, then preparing to enter Leyden, whose memory should be ever green among us. Let us hope Thomas Winston, probably an old fellow-student at Padua, and later appointed Professor of Physic at Gresham College, was absent, as we can then be more charitable towards the sins of omission in his work on anatomy, published after his death, which, so far as I can read, contrary to the statement of Munk (*Roll of the College*), contains no word of the new doctrine. As an old Paduan, and fresh from its anatomical school, the younger Craige would not be absent. Fludd, the Rosicrucian, of course, was present; attracted, perhaps, by rumours of anti-Galenical doctrines which had served to keep him out of the College; nor would he be likely to be absent at the festival of one whom he calls his 'physicall and theosophicall patron'. And certainly on such an occasion that able Aberdonian, Alexander Reid, would be there, whose Σωματογραφία had just appeared,[1] with an extraordinarily full account of the vascular system. Reid was a good anatomist, one of our most distinguished Medico-Chirurgical Fellows, and a liberal benefactor. If, as has been stated, he was not a convert on account of his age, it was on account of his youth, for the Harveian doctrine, if in meagre form, is to be found in the later editions (5th) of his *Manual*. But we would miss Lodge, the poet, 'cried up to the last for physic', as he had recently started for the Continent. And we may be sure that Harvey's old fellow-students at Padua—Fortescue, Fox, Willoughby, Mounsell, and Darcy—would honour their friend and colleague with their presence; and Edward Lister, also a fellow-Paduan, the first of his name in a family which has given three other members to our profession—two distinguished and one immortal.[2] It was

[1] Copy in Bodleian Library.
[2] I followed Munk's *Roll*, but Lord Lister tells me that he does not know of a relationship. I am sorry, as Martin Lister deserves the honour.

not a large gathering, as the Fellows, members, licentiates, and candidates numbered only about forty; but as the lecture was a great event in the community, there would be present many interested and intelligent laymen, of the type of Digby, and Ashmole, and Pepys—the 'curious', as they were called, for whom throughout the seventeenth century the anatomy lecture equalled in attraction the play. Delivered in Latin, and interspersed here and there with English words and illustrations, there were probably more who saw than who comprehended, as Sir Thomas Browne indicated to his son Edward when he lectured at Chirurgeons' Hall.

It is a fortunate, and perhaps a unique, circumstance in bibliography that the manuscript of this course of lectures should have been preserved, and that we should be able to follow step by step the demonstration—a long and formidable procedure, as the whole anatomy of the thoracic organs was discussed. I dare say there was a prolonged break between the morning and the afternoon lecture 'for a fine dinner', such as Pepys described, when, on 27 February 1663, he went with Harvey's pupil, Scarborough, to Chirurgeons' Hall and was used with 'extraordinary great respect'. Towards the close, after discussing, in novel and modern terms, the structure and action of the heart, Harvey summed up in a few sentences the conclusion of the matter. They stand as follows in the *Praelectiones* (published by the College in 1886):

> W. H. constat per fabricam cordis sanguinem
> per pulmones in Aortam perpetuo
> transferri, as by two clacks of a
> water bellows to rayse water
> constat per ligaturam transitum sanguinis
> ab arteriis ad venas
> unde perpetuum sanguinis motum
> in circulo fieri pulsu cordis.

Probably few in the lecture hall appreciated the full meaning of these words, which to some must have seemed a blot on the whole performance; while others, perhaps, all with the feelings of the fishes after St. Anthony's well-known sermon,

> Much delighted were they,
> But preferred the old way,

returned to their homes wondering what he would say on the morrow when the 'divine banquet of the brain' was to be spread before them.

One thing was certain—the lecture gave evidence of a skilled anatomist of remarkably wide experience and well versed in literature from Aristotle to Fabricius. While Harvey could agree with John Hunter, who states in a manuscript introductory lecture in the College library—'I deliver nothing I have not seen and observed myself'—he could not add with him, 'I am not a reader of books'. Nearly one hundred references to some twenty authors occur in the manuscript of the thorax, or, as he calls it, the 'parlour' lecture.

It is a great pity that we have no contemporary account of the impression on such men as Mayerne or Reid of the new doctrines, for which we have the author's statement that they were taught annually and elaborated. So far as I know there is no reference to show that the lectures had any immediate influence in the profession, or indeed that the subject-matter ever got beyond the circle of the College. We are not without a first-hand account by the author of his reception: 'These views as usual pleased some more, others less; some chid and calumniated me, and laid it to me as a crime that I had dared to depart from the precepts and opinions of all anatomists; others desired further explanation of the novelties.'

It is difficult for us to realize the mental attitude of the men who listened year by year as the turn of the 'Parlour Lecture' came. Their opinions, no less firmly held than is our positive knowledge, did not get much beyond: 'The great dictator Hippocrates puts us in mind of it, Galen has a thousand times inculcated the same, the prince of the Arabian tribe, Avicen, has set his seal unto it.' This expresses their mental state, and such a heresy as a general circulation could scarcely be appreciated; and in a man of such good parts as Harvey would in pity be condoned, just as we overlook the mild intellectual vagaries of our friends.

Bootless to ask, impossible to answer, is the question why Harvey delayed for twelve years the publication of his views. He seems to have belonged to that interesting type of man, not uncommon in every age, who knows too much to write. It is not a little remarkable that this reticence of learning has been a strong mental feature in some of the greatest of discoverers. Perhaps it was the motive of Copernicus, who so dreaded the prejudices of mankind that for thirty years he is said to have detained in his closet the *Treatise of Revolutions*. From what Harvey says, very much the same reasons restrained the publication of his work. To the lesser circulation, with the authority of Galen and Columbus to support it, men 'will give their adhesion', but the general circulation 'is of so novel and unheard-of character that I not only fear injury to myself from the envy of a few, but I tremble lest I have mankind at large for my enemies, so much doth wont and custom, that has become as another nature, and doctrine once sown and that hath struck deep root and rested from antiquity, influence all men'. He felt, as he says to Riolan, that it was in some sort criminal to call in question doctrines that had descended through a long succession of ages and carry the authority of the ancients; but he appealed unto Nature that bowed to no antiquity and was of still higher authority than the ancients. Men have been for years in conscious possession of some of the greatest of truths before venturing to publish them. Napier spent twenty years developing the theory of Logarithms; and Bacon kept the *Novum Organum* by him for twelve years, and year by year touched it up—indeed, Rowley states that he saw twelve copies. Two other famous discoveries by Englishmen have the same curious history—the two which can alone be said to be greater than the demonstration of the circulation of the blood. Zachariah Wood speaks of Harvey as the surmiser of the little world, to distinguish him from another Englishman who first went about the greater world. But a greater than both—Isaac Newton—had grasped the secret of a cosmic circulation, and brooded in silence over the motion of the spheres for more than twenty years before publishing the *Principia*. Between the writing of the rough sketch in 1842 and the appearance of the *Origin of Species* seventeen years elapsed; and from the date of the journal notes, 1836, in which we have the first intimation of Darwin's theory, more than twenty years. In Harvey's case this intellectual reticence, this hesitation 'to quit the peaceful haven', as he says, has cost us dear. Only a happy accident gave us the *De Generatione*, and the College can never be too grateful to Sir George Ent for that Christmas visit, 1650, so graphically described, and to which we owe one of the masterpieces of English medicine. How many seventeenth-century treatises we could have spared to have had the *Practice of Medicine conformable to his Thesis of the Circulation of the Blood*! How instructive his prospective *Medical Observations* would have been we can gather from the remarkable series of cases scattered through the manuscript notes and his published writings. His 'treatise apart' on *Eventilation* or *Respiration*; the *Medical Anatomy*, or *Anatomy in its Application to Medicine*, as he says, 'I also intend putting to press'; the work 'from observations in my possession' on *Organs of Motion in Animals*—all of these, with the work on *Generation in Insects*, and others mentioned by Dr. Merrett,[1] the then library keeper, 1667, were probably dispersed when those sons of Belial ransacked his chambers at Whitehall.

'Still the die is cast, and my trust is in the love of truth and the candour that inheres in cultivated minds.' With these words he consoles himself, knowing from experience that the publication of even a portion of the work, as in one place he calls the little book, would raise a tempest. Zachariah Wood in the preface to the English edition, 1673, expresses what many of his contemporaries must have felt, 'Truly a bold man indeed, O disturber of the quiet of physicians! O seditious citizen of the Physical Commonwealth! who first of all durst oppose an opinion

[1] Munk, *Roll of the College*, vol. i, p. 132.

conformed for so many ages by the consent of all.' De Back of Amsterdam describes the dilemma in which teachers found themselves:

This new thing I did examine, which the first entrance did seem very easily to be refuted, but being weighed in a just balance, and having added to reason my own ey-sight it was found inexpugnable, nay (the very prick of truth enforcing) to be embraced with both arms. What should I doe? Must Hippocrates be left, Galen slighted? No, if we follow the truth senced with reason and our sense, we are still Hippocrates his, we are still Galens. (English edition, 1653.)

The history of the next thirty years illustrates the truth of Locke's dictum in the struggle for acceptance. Not the least interesting part of the story, it should be told at greater length and with more detail than it has yet received—more than I am able to give it. That the repeated demonstrations, aided by the strong personal influence of the man, brought the College, as a body, to the new views is witnessed rather by the esteem and affection the Fellows bore to Harvey than by any direct evidence. The appearance of the book in 1628 made no great stir; it was not a literary sensation—a not uncommon fate of epoch-making works, the authors of which are too far ahead of their contemporaries to be appreciated. The same event happened to Newton's *Principia*; as Sir William Petty remarks, 'I have not met with one man that put an extraordinary value on the book'.

Among Englishmen, Primrose alone, brought up among the strictest sect of the Galenists, and at the time not a Fellow—wrote a criticism from the old standpoint (1632), and remained unconvinced twelve years later, as his controversy with Regius shows. And only one special treatise in favour of the circulation was written in England—that of Sir George Ent, a pupil and friend of Harvey, who wrote (1641) specially against Parisanus, a Venetian, a foeman quite unworthy of his quill. In the universities the new doctrine rapidly gained acceptance—in Cambridge through the influence of Glisson, while in part to Harvey's work and influence may be attributed that only too brief but golden renaissance of science at Oxford. A little incident mentioned in the autobiographical notes of the celebrated Wallis shows how the subject was taken up quite early in the universities: 'And I took into it the speculative part of physick and anatomy as parts of natural philosophy, and, as Dr. Glisson has since told me, I was the first of his sons who (in a public disputation) maintained the circulation of the blood, which was then a new doctrine, though I had no design of practising physick.' This was in the early 'thirties'. But the older views were very hard to displace, and as late as 1651 we find such intelligent members of the 'invisible college' as Boyle and Petty carrying out experiments together in Ireland to satisfy themselves as to the truth of the circulation of the blood.

It took much longer for the new views to reach the text-books of the day. From no work of the period does one get a better idea of the current anatomical and physiological teaching in London than from Crooke's *Body of Man* (1615 and 1631). Collected out of Vesalius, Plantinus, Platerius, Laurentius, Valverda, Bauhinus, and others, it is an epitome of their opinions, with the comments of the professor who read the anatomy lecture to the Company of the Barber-Surgeons. In the preface to the first edition he speaks of the contentment and profit he had received from Dr. Davies's Lumleian Lectures at the College of Physicians. There is no indication in the second edition that he had benefited by the instruction of Dr. Davies's successor. Galen is followed implicitly, with here and there minor deviations. The views of Columbus on the lesser circulation are mentioned only to be dismissed as superfluous and erroneous. The Gresham Professor of the day, Dr. Winston, makes no mention of the new doctrine in his Anatomy Lectures which were published after his death, 1651, and are of special interest as showing that at so late a date a work could be issued with the Galenical physiology unchanged. In Alexander Reid's *Manual*, the popular text-book of the day, the Harveian views are given in part in the fifth edition, in which, as he says in the preface, 'the book of the breast' is altogether new—an item of no little interest, since he was a man advanced in years, and, as he says, 'the hourglass hasteneth, and but a few sands remain unrun'. Highmore, the distinguished Dorsetshire anatomist, and a pupil of Harvey, in his well-known *Anatomy* published in 1651, gives the ablest exposition of his master's views that had appeared in any systematic work of the period, and he urges his readers to study the *De Motu Cordis* as 'fontem ipsum' from which to get clearer knowledge. He quotes an appropriate motto for the period— *laudamus veteres: sed nostris utimur annis*. But even so late as 1671 the old views were maintained in the English edition of Riolan. And yet the knowledge of Harvey's views must have spread broadcast, not only in the profession, but in that large outside circle of distinguished men who felt the new spirit of science working in their veins. From converse or from the Lumleian Lectures, which no doubt he often attended, Kenelm Digby must have had the information about Harvey's views on generation, as at the date of the issue of his *Two Treatises*, 1644, they had not been published anywhere. While he knew well the motion of the blood as expounded by Harvey, and having, in making his great antidote, studied the action of the viper's heart, Digby, like Descartes, could not emancipate himself from the old views, as shown in the following passage:

But if you desire to follow the blood all along every steppe, in its progresse from the hart round about the body, till it returne back againe to its center, Doctor Harvey, who most acutely teacheth this doctrine, must be your guide. He will show you how it issueth from the hart by the arteries; from whence it goeth on warming the flesh, untill it arrive to some of the extremities of the body: and by then it is grown so coole (by long absence from the fountaine of its heate; and by evaporating its owne stocke of spirits, without any new supply) that it hath need of being warmed anew; it findeth itself returned backe againe to the hart, and is there heated againe, which returne is made by the veines, as its going forwardes, is performed only by the arteries.

Sir William Temple well expresses the attitude of mind of the intellectual Philistine of the time, who looked for immediate results. Speaking of the work of Harvey and of Copernicus he says:

Whether either of these be modern discoveries or derived from old foundations is disputed; nay, it is so too, whether they are true or no; for though reason may seem to favour them more than the contrary opinions, yet sense can hardly allow them, and to satisfy mankind both these must concur. But if they are true, yet these two great discoveries have made no change in the conclusions of Astronomy nor in the practice of Physic, and so have been but little use to the world, though, perhaps, of much honour to the authors.[1]

It is pleasant to notice that our old friend, Sir Thomas Browne, with his love of paradox, declared that he preferred the circulation of the blood to the discovery of America.

Of the reception of Harvey's views in Holland and Germany there is nothing to add to the admirable account given by Willis. The early and strenuous advocacy of Descartes must have influenced the Dutch physicians; but in this, as in so many other things, the infection of his early years proved too powerful, and he could not get rid of the 'ancient spirits'. Of the discovery of the circulation he says[2] it is 'la plus belle et la plus utile que l'on pût faire en médecine'. 'Tout à fait contraire au sein (sic) touchant le mouvement du cœur', which he held to be due to an ebullition of the spirits—a sort of ferment (espèce de levain) existing in it. Much more actively discussed in Holland than elsewhere, the writings of Drake, Walaeus, Regius, Plempius, Sylvius, de Back, Conringius, T. Bartholin (the Dane), and others threshed out the whole question very thoroughly, and their views, with those of Hoffman, Slegel, and others, are referred to by Willis and given in greater detail by Riolan.[3]

In the oft-quoted statement that Harvey, 'conquering envy, hath established a new doctrine in his lifetime', Hobbes was right so far as England and Holland are concerned. But it was far otherwise in France, where it met with a bitter and protracted hostility. The Medical School of the University of Paris, at the time one of the best organized and most important in Europe, declined to accept the circulation of the blood during his lifetime

[1] *Works*, 1814, vol. iii, p. 293.   [2] Cousins's edition, vol. ix, p. 159.
[3] *Opuscula Anatomica*. London, 1649.

and for some years after his death. The history of the period is pictured for us in vivid colours in that *journal intime* which Gui Patin kept up with his friends, Spon and Falconet of Lyons and the Belins (*père et fils*). With all his faults, particularly his scandalous lack of charity, one cannot but feel the keenest sympathy with this dear old man. Devoted to his saints, Hippocrates and Galen, Fernel and Duret, and to his teachers, Piêtre and Riolan, to him the circulation of the blood was never more than an ingenious paradox. To such a lover of books and of good literature everything can be forgiven, and in his letters we follow with deepest interest his vigorous campaign against his dear enemies, the *Cuisiniers arabesques*, who had enslaved people and physicians alike, the haemophobes, the chemists, the astrologers and the *stibiate*, or as he calls it, the *Stygiate* group. To him the Koran was less dangerous than the works of Paracelsus, the appearance of the new Geneva edition of which he deeply deplores. Reverence for Galen and friendship with Riolan, rather than any deep interest in the question, inspired his opposition. To him the new doctrine was ridiculous, and it was he who called the partisans of it *circulateurs* in allusion to the Latin word, *circulator*, meaning charlatan. In 1652 he writes to Spon that the question is still open whether the blood passes through the septum of the heart or through the lungs. In 1659 he promises to send him a work of Vinean against the circulation.[1] More extraordinary still is the fact that as late as 1670, twelve years after Harvey's death, the thesis of one Cordelle, a bachelor of medicine, publicly discussed the circulation of the blood, and Gui Patin, who presided, decided in the negative. The fiction of an ingenious narrator, *le doux songe* of Harvey, are the terms in which he speaks of it. The whole passage is worth quoting as possibly the last public denouncement of what seemed a rank heresy to the old Galenists:

Supposer que le sang se meut toujours circulairement, que de la veine cave ascendante il tombe dans l'oreillette droite du cœur, que de là il aille traverser toute la substance du poumon pour retomber

[1] *Lettres*, vol. i, p. 324, édition 1694.

de là dans l'oreillette gauche en passant par la veine pulmonaire, et qu'enfin de là il soit projeté dans l'aorte et toutes les artères qui le feront passer dans les veines et dans le cœur, lui faisant par ce moyen suivre un circuit, voilà le doux songe de Harvey, la fiction d'un narrateur ingénieux, mais nullement prouvée par l'évidence. La circulation du sang, son transport circulaire par les vaisseaux, c'est l'enfantement d'un esprit oisif, un vrai nuage qu'embrassent les Ixions pour procréer les Centaurs et les monstres.[1]

As I said, we can forgive a great deal to the man who has left us such a picture of seventeenth-century life, drawn, all unconsciously, with a master hand; and through the mists of prejudice and hate we can recognize the good sense which had the courage to protest against the *forfanterie arabesque et bézoardesque* in much of the therapeutics of the day.

Though a professor in the Paris Faculty and a brilliant lecturer, Patin at that time did not occupy such a distinguished position, nor was his opposition of such importance as that of Riolan— 'John Riolan, the Son, the most experienced Physician in the Universitie of Paris, the Prince of Dissection of Bodies, and the King's professor, and Dean of Anatomie and of the knowledge of simples, chief physician to the queen-mother of Louis XIII' —as he is quaintly, but very truly, described by Harvey.[2] Brought up by his father to regard Hippocrates and Galen as the sources of all wisdom, the intensity of his zeal increased with his years until at last 'to see the physic of Galen kept in good repair' became the passion of his life. The deep pity of it all is that such mental blindness should have stricken a really great man, for he was a brilliant anatomist and teacher, the author of the best anatomical text-book of its day, a man of affairs, profoundly versed in literature, a successful practitioner, and for years the head of the profession in France.

The opposition of such a man was serious, and naturally had a profound influence. Not content with the comparatively brief statement in the *Encheiridion*, 1648, Riolan published in England

---

[1] *Gui Patin*, Félix Larrieu. Paris, 1889.
[2] Title-page of English edition of the Letter.

the following year his *Opuscula anatomica nova*, one very large
section of which is taken up with the problem of circulation.
It was this probably as much as a present of the *Encheiridion*
that induced Harvey to break his long silence and to reply.
After a report of a discussion upon a thesis in 1645 and a statement of objections, a most interesting discussion follows of the
literature, in which the opinions of various writers are examined,
particularly those of Cartesius, Conringius, Walaeus, and
Plempius.

It is quite possible that the second *Disquisition* of Harvey to
Riolan, published with the first in duodecimo form at Cambridge in 1649, was brought out by Riolan's later publication,
though it is not directly referred to. Little did Harvey appreciate
that his old friend was both blind and deaf—incapable of seeing
obvious facts. It was not a question of being conversant with
anatomy or of having had experience, on both of which points
Harvey dwells at length. Riolan knew his anatomy as well as,
or better than, any man of his generation. It was not that he
would not—but that he could not—see the truth which was
staring him in the face. As Raynaud[1] mentions, an occasional
thesis (Fagon, 1663; Mattot, 1665) supporting the circulation
did slip through the Faculty: but the official recognition in
France did not come until 1673, when Louis XIV founded a
special Chair of Anatomy at the Jardin des Plantes for the
propagation of the new discoveries.

The satire of Molière and the *Arrêt burlesque* of Boileau completed the discomfiture of the 'anticirculateurs', but it had taken
nearly half a century to overcome the opposition of those who
saw in the new doctrines the complete destruction of the ancient
system of medicine.

IV

Even when full grown in the conscious stage Truth may
remain sterile without influence or progress on any aspects of
human activity. One of the most remarkable of phenomena in

[1] *Les Médecins au temps de Molière*, 1863.

mental biography is the failure of the Greeks to succeed after giving the world such a glorious start. They had every essential for permanent success: scientific imagination, keen powers of observation; and if in the days of Hippocrates the mathematical method of interrogating Nature prevailed rather than the experimental, Galen carried the latter to a degree of perfection never again reached until the time of Harvey. Only when placed in its true position in relation to Greek religion and philosophy, as has been done so skilfully by Gomperz,[1] do we realize the immensity of the debt we owe to those 'our young light-hearted masters'. And Gomperz makes clear the nature of the debt of Greek thought to the practical sense of the physicians. But alas! upon the fires they kindled were poured the dust and ashes of contending philosophies, and neither the men of the Alexandrian school nor the brilliant labours of the most encyclopaedic mind that has ever been given to medicine sufficed to replenish them. Fortunately, here and there amid the embers of the Middle Ages glowed the coals from which we have lighted the fires of modern progress. The special distinction which divides modern from ancient science is its fruitful application to human needs —not that this was unknown to the Greeks; but the practical recognition of the laws of life and matter has in the past century remade the world. In making knowledge effective we have succeeded where our masters failed. But this last and final stage, always of slow and painful consummation, is evolved directly from truths which cannot be translated into terms intelligible to ordinary minds. Newton's great work influenced neither the morals nor the manners of his age, nor was there any immediate tangible benefit that could be explained to the edification or appreciation of the 'ordinary man' of his day; yet it set forward at a bound the human mind, as did such truths as were proclaimed by Copernicus, by Kepler, by Darwin, and others. In a

[1] The three volumes of his *Greek Thinkers*, now in English dress, should be studied by every young man who wishes to get at the foundations of philosophy. The picturesque style of Professor Gomperz and his strong sympathy with science add greatly to the interest of the work.

less conspicuous manner Harvey's triumph was on the same high plane. There was nothing in it which could be converted immediately into practical benefit, nothing that even the Sydenhams of his day could take hold of and use. Not so much really in the demonstration of the fact of the circulation as in the demonstration of the method—the *Inventum mirabile* sought for by Descartes, the *Novum Organum* of Bacon—lies the true merit of Harvey's work. While Bacon was thinking, Harvey was acting; and before Descartes had left his happy school at La Flèche Harvey was using *la nouvelle méthode*; and it is in this way that the *De Motu Cordis* marks the break of the modern spirit with the old traditions. No longer were men to rest content with careful observation and with accurate description; no longer were men to be content with finely-spun theories and dreams, which 'serve as a common subterfuge of ignorance'; but here for the first time a great physiological problem was approached from the experimental side by a man with a modern scientific mind, who could weigh evidence and not go beyond it, and who had the sense to let the conclusions emerge naturally but firmly from the observations. To the age of the hearer, in which men had heard, and heard only, had succeeded the age of the eye, in which men had seen and had been content only to see. But at last came the age of the hand—the thinking, devising, planning hand; the hand as an instrument of the mind, now reintroduced into the world in a modest little monograph of seventy-two pages, from which we may date the beginning of experimental medicine.

No great discovery in science is ever without a corresponding influence on medical thought, not always evident at first, and apt to be characterized by the usual vagaries associated with human effort. Very marked in each generation has been the change wrought in the conceptions of disease and in its treatment by epoch-making discoveries as to the functions of the body. We ourselves are deeply involved to-day in toxins and antitoxins, in opsonins, tulases, and extracts as a direct result of the researches in bacteriology and in internal secretion. There

were sanguine souls in Harvey's day, who lamented with Floyer
that the discovery had not brought great and general innovations
into the whole practice of physic. But had the old Lichfield
physician lived he would have seen the rise of a school based
directly upon the studies of Harvey and Sanctorius, the brilliant
reasonings of Descartes and the works of Bellini and Borelli.
The mechanical school rose in its pride on solid foundations
which appealed to practical men with singular force. Very soon
that 'beatific epitome of creation', man, was 'marked out like a
spot of earth or a piece of timber with rules and compasses',
and the medical terminology of the day became unintelligible
to the older practitioners who could make nothing of the 'wheels
and pulley, wedges, levers, screws, cords, canals and cisterns,
sieves and strainers', and they cracked their jokes on 'angles,
cylinders, celerity, percussion, resistance, and such-like terms
which they said had no more to do with physic or the human
body than a carpenter has in making Venice treacle or curing a
fever'. Once accepted, men had a feeling that so important a
discovery must change all the usual conceptions of disease. As
has been said before, Harvey tells that he had in preparation a
*Practice of Medicine conformable to his Thesis of the Circulation of the
Blood*, and it soon became customary to put in the title-pages of
works some reference to the new doctrine. Even Riolan's
Opuscula anatomica makes an allusion to it. Walaeus, a keen
defender of Harvey, published in 1660 a little compendium of
practice *ad circulationem sanguinis adornata*, but there is nothing
in it to suggest any radical change in treatment. Rolfinck's
Dissertationes Anatomicae, 1650, embracing the older and more
recent views in medicine, are *ad circulationem accommodatae*, and
even as late as 1690 the well-known anatomy of Dionis was
suivant la circulation. With the loss of his work on the *Practice
of Medicine* it is impossible to say whether Harvey's own practice was modified in any way. To part from the spirits and
humours must have left his attitude of mind very sceptical, and
that his 'therapeutic way' was not admired (as Aubrey tells us)
speaks for a change which may have set many against him. More

important than any influence upon treatment was the irresistible change in the conceptions of disease caused by destruction of the doctrine of spirits and humours, which had prevailed from the days of Hippocrates. While Harvey, as he says, had in places to use the language of physiology, that is, the language of the day, he makes it very clear, particularly in the second letter to Riolan, that he will have none of the old doctrine to which the *De Motu Cordis* dealt the death-blow.

But the moving hand reminds your orator, Mr. President, of a bounden duty laid upon him by our great Dictator to commemorate on this occasion by name all of our benefactors; to urge others to follow their example; to exhort the Fellows and Members to study out the secrets of Nature by way of experiment; and, lastly, for the honour of the profession, to continue in love and affection among ourselves. No greater tribute to Harvey exists than in these simple sentences in which he established this lectureship, breathing as they do the very spirit of the man, and revealing to us his heart of hearts. Doubtless no one more than he rejoices that our benefactors have now become so numerous as to nullify the first injunction; and the best one can do is to give a general expression of our thanks, and to mention here and there, as I have done, the more notable among them. But this is not enough. While we are praising famous men, honoured in their day and still the glory of this College, the touching words of the son of Sirach remind us: 'Some there be that have no memorial, who are perished as though they had never been, and are become as though they had never been born.' Such renown as they had, time has blotted out; and on them the iniquity of oblivion has blindly scattered her poppy. A few are embalmed in the biographical dictionaries; a few are dragged to light every year at Sotheby's, or the memory is stirred to reminiscence as one takes down an old volume from one's shelves. But for the immense majority on the long roll of our Fellows—names! names! names!—nothing more; a catalogue as dry and meaningless as that of the ships in Homer, or as the genealogy of David in the Book of Chronicles. Even the dignity of the Presidential chair does not suffice to float a man down the few centuries that have passed since the foundation of the College. Who was Richard Forster? Who was Henry Atkins? Perhaps two or three among us could tell at once. And yet by these men the continuity and organic life of the College has been carried on, and in maintaining its honour and furthering its welfare, each one in his day was a benefactor, whose memory it is our duty, as well as our pleasure, to recall. Much of the nobility of the profession depends upon this great cloud of witnesses, who pass into the silent land—pass, and leave no sign, becoming as though they had never been born. And it was the pathos of this fate, not less pathetic because common to all but a few, that wrung from the poet that sadly true comparison of the race of man to the race of leaves!

The story of Harvey's life, and a knowledge of the method of his work, should be the best stimulus to the Fellows and Members to carry out the second and third of his commands; and the final one, to continue in love and affection among ourselves, should not be difficult to realize. Sorely tried as he must have been, and naturally testy, only once in his writings, so far as I have read, does the old Adam break out. With his temperament, and with such provocation, this is an unexampled record, and one can appreciate how much was resisted in those days when tongue and pen were free. Over and over again he must have restrained himself as he did in the controversy with Riolan, of whom, for the sake of old friendship, he could not find it in his heart to say anything severe. To-day his commands are easier to follow, when the deepened courtesies of life have made us all more tolerant of those small weaknesses, inherent in our nature, which give diversity to character without necessarily marring it. To no man does the right spirit in these matters come by nature, and I would urge upon our younger Fellows and Members, weighing well these winged words, to emulate our great exemplar, whose work shed such lustre upon British Medicine, and whom we honour in this College not less for the scientific method which he inculcated than for the admirable virtues of his character.

14

A WAY OF LIFE

What each day needs that shalt thou ask,
Each day will set its proper task.
GOETHE.

FELLOW STUDENTS—Every man has a philosophy of
life in thought, in word, or in deed, worked out in
himself unconsciously. In possession of the very best,
he may not know of its existence; with the very worst
he may pride himself as a paragon. As it grows with the growth
it cannot be taught to the young in formal lectures. What have
bright eyes, red blood, quick breath, and taut muscles to do
with philosophy? Did not the great Stagirite say that young men
were unfit students of it?—they will hear as though they heard
not, and to no profit. Why then should I trouble you? Because
I have a message that may be helpful. It is not philosophical, nor
is it strictly moral or religious, one or other of which I was told
my address should be, and yet in a way it is all three. It is the
oldest and the freshest, the simplest and the most useful, so
simple indeed is it that some of you may turn away disappointed
as was Naaman the Syrian when told to go wash in Jordan and
be clean. You know those composite tools, to be bought for
50 cents, with one handle to fit a score or more of instruments.
The workmanship is usually bad, so bad, as a rule, that you will
not find an example in any good carpenter's shop; but the boy
has one, the chauffeur slips one into his box, and the sailor into
his kit, and there is one in the odds-and-ends drawer of the
pantry of every well-regulated family. It is simply a handy thing
about the house, to help over the many little difficulties of the

An address given to Yale students 20 April 1913. Published by Constable
& Co., London, 1913: Hoeber, New York, 1914; and in *The Student Life and
Other Essays*, London, 1928, 75–99.

day. Of this sort of philosophy I wish to make you a present—a handle to fit your life tools. Whether the workmanship is Sheffield or shoddy, this helve will fit anything from a hatchet to a corkscrew.

My message is but a word, *a Way*, an easy expression of the experience of a plain man whose life has never been worried by any philosophy higher than that of the shepherd in *As You Like It*. I wish to point out a path in which the wayfaring man, though a fool, cannot err; not a system to be worked out painfully only to be discarded, not a formal scheme, simply a habit as easy—or as hard!—to adopt as any other habit, good or bad.

I

A few years ago a Xmas card went the rounds, with the legend 'Life is just one "derned" thing after another', which, in more refined language, is the same as saying 'Life is a habit', a succession of actions that become more or less automatic. This great truth, which lies at the basis of all actions, muscular or psychic, is the keystone of the teaching of Aristotle, to whom the formation of habits was the basis of moral excellence. 'In a word, habits of any kind are the result of actions of the same kind; and so what we have to do, is to give a certain character to these particular actions.' (*Ethics.*) Lift a seven months old baby to his feet—see him tumble on his nose. Do the same at twelve months —he walks. At two years he runs. The muscles and the nervous system have acquired the habit. One trial after another, one failure after another, has given him power. Put your finger in a baby's mouth, and he sucks away in blissful anticipation of a response to a mammalian habit millions of years old. And we can deliberately train parts of our body to perform complicated actions with unerring accuracy. Watch that musician playing a difficult piece. Batteries, commutators, multipliers, switches, wires innumerable control those nimble fingers, the machinery of which may be set in motion as automatically as in a pianola, the player all the time chatting as if he had nothing to do in controlling the apparatus—habit again, the gradual acquisition of power by long practice and at the expense of many mistakes. The same great law reaches through mental and moral states. 'Character', which partakes of both, in Plutarch's words, is 'long-standing habit'.

Now the way of life that I preach is a habit to be acquired gradually by long and steady repetition. It is the practice of living for the day only, and for the day's work, *Life in day-tight compartments.* 'Ah,' I hear you say, 'that is an easy matter, simple as Elisha's advice!' Not as I shall urge it, in words which fail to express the depth of my feelings as to its value. I started life in the best of all environments—in a parsonage, one of nine children. A man who has filled Chairs in four universities, has written a successful book, and has been asked to lecture at Yale, is supposed popularly to have brains of a special quality. A few of my intimate friends really know the truth about me, as I know it! Mine, in good faith I say it, are of the most mediocre character. But what about those professorships, &c.? Just habit, a way of life, an outcome of the day's work, the vital importance of which I wish to impress upon you with all the force at my command.

Dr. Johnson remarked upon the trifling circumstances by which men's lives are influenced, 'not by an ascendant planet, a predominating humour, but by the first book which they read, some early conversation which they have heard, or some accident which excited ardour and enthusiasm'. This was my case in two particulars. I was diverted to the Trinity College School, then at Weston, Ontario, by a paragraph in the circular stating that the senior boys would go into the drawing-room in the evenings, and learn to sing and dance—vocal and pedal accomplishments for which I was never designed; but like Saul seeking his asses, I found something more valuable, a man of the White of Selborne type, who knew nature, and who knew how to get boys interested in it.[1] The other happened in the summer of 1871, when I was attending the Montreal General Hospital. Much worried as to the future, partly about the final examination, partly as to what I should do afterwards, I picked up a volume of

[1] The Rev. W. A. Johnson, the founder of the school.

Carlyle, and on the page I opened there was the familiar sentence —'*Our main business is not to see what lies dimly at a distance, but to do what lies clearly at hand.*' A commonplace sentiment enough, but it hit and stuck and helped, and was the starting-point of a habit that has enabled me to utilize to the full the single talent entrusted to me.

II

The workers in Christ's vineyard were hired by the day; only for this day are we to ask for our daily bread, and we are expressly bidden to take no thought for the morrow. To the modern world these commands have an Oriental savour, counsels of perfection akin to certain of the Beatitudes, stimuli to aspiration, not to action. I am prepared on the contrary to urge the literal acceptance of the advice, not in the mood of Ecclesiastes—'Go to now, ye that say to-day or to-morrow we will go into such a city, and continue there a year, and buy and sell and get gain; whereas ye know not what shall be on the morrow'; not in the Epicurean spirit of Omar with his 'jug of wine and Thou', but in the modernist spirit, as a way of life, a habit, a strong enchantment, at once against the mysticism of the East and the pessimism that too easily besets us. Change that hard saying 'Sufficient unto the day is the evil thereof' into 'the goodness thereof', since the chief worries of life arise from the foolish habit of looking before and after. As a patient with double vision from some transient unequal action of the muscles of the eye finds magical relief from well-adjusted glasses, so, returning to the clear binocular vision of to-day, the over-anxious student finds peace when he looks neither backward to the past nor forward to the future.

I stood on the bridge of one of the great liners, ploughing the ocean at 25 knots. 'She is alive', said my companion, 'in every plate; a huge monster with brain and nerves, an immense stomach, a wonderful heart and lungs, and a splendid system of locomotion.' Just at that moment a signal sounded, and all over the ship the watertight compartments were closed. 'Our chief factor of safety', said the Captain. 'In spite of the *Titanic*', I said.

'Yes,' he replied, 'in spite of the *Titanic*.' Now each one of you is a much more marvellous organization than the great liner, and bound on a longer voyage. What I urge is that you so learn to control the machinery as to live with 'day-tight compartments' as the most certain way to ensure safety on the voyage. Get on the bridge, and see that at least the great bulkheads are in working order. Touch a button and hear, at every level of your life, the iron doors shutting out the Past—the dead yesterdays. Touch another and shut off, with a metal curtain, the Future—the unborn to-morrows. Then you are safe—safe for to-day! Read the old story in the *Chambered Nautilus*, so beautifully sung by Oliver Wendell Holmes, only change one line to 'Day after day beheld the silent toil'. Shut off the past! Let the dead past bury its dead. So easy to say, so hard to realize! The truth is, the past haunts us like a shadow. To disregard it is not easy. Those blue eyes of your grandmother, that weak chin of your grand-father, have mental and moral counterparts in your make-up. Generations of ancestors, brooding over 'Providence, Foreknow-ledge, Will and Fate—Fixed fate, free will, foreknowledge, absolute', may have bred a New England conscience, morbidly sensitive, to heal which some of you had rather sing the 51st Psalm than follow Christ into the slums. Shut out the yester-days, which have lighted fools the way to dusty death, and have no concern for you personally, that is, consciously. They are there all right, working daily in us, but so are our livers and our stomachs. And the past, in its unconscious action on our lives, should bother us as little as they do. The petty annoyances, the real and fancied slights, the trivial mistakes, the disappoint-ments, the sins, the sorrows, even the joys—bury them deep in the oblivion of each night. Ah! but it is just then that to so many of us the ghosts of the past,

> Night-riding Incubi
> Troubling the fantasy,

come in troops, and pry open the eyelids, each one presenting a sin, a sorrow, a regret. Bad enough in the old and seasoned, in the young these demons of past sins may be a terrible affliction, and in bitterness of heart many a one cries with Eugene Aram, 'Oh God! Could I so close my mind, and clasp it with a clasp.' As a vaccine against all morbid poisons left in the system by the infections of yesterday, I offer 'a way of life'. 'Undress', as George Herbert says, 'your soul at night', not by self-examination, but by shedding, as you do your garments, the daily sins whether of omission or of commission, and you will wake a free man, with a new life. To look back, except on rare occasions for stock-taking, is to risk the fate of Lot's wife. Many a man is handicapped in his course by a cursed combination of retro- and intro-spection, the mistakes of yesterday paralysing the efforts of to-day, the worries of the past hugged to his destruction, and the worm Regret allowed to canker the very heart of his life. To die daily, after the manner of St. Paul, ensures the resurrection of a new man, who makes each day the epitome of a life.

III

The load of to-morrow, added to that of yesterday, carried to-day makes the strongest falter. Shut off the future as tightly as the past. No dreams, no visions, no delicious fantasies, no castles in the air, with which, as the old song so truly says, 'hearts are broken, heads are turned'. To youth, we are told, belongs the future, but the wretched to-morrow that so plagues some of us has no certainty, except through to-day. Who can tell what a day may bring forth? Though its uncertainty is a proverb, a man may carry its secret in the hollow of his hand. Make a pilgrimage to Hades with Ulysses, draw the magic circle, perform the rites, and then ask Tiresias the question. I have had the answer from his own lips. The future is to-day— there is no to-morrow! The day of a man's salvation is *now*—the life of the present, of to-day, lived earnestly, intently, without a forward-looking thought, is the only insurance for the future. Let the limit of your horizon be a twenty-four-hour circle. On the title-page of one of the great books of science, the *Discours de la Méthode* of Descartes (1637), is a vignette showing a man digging in a garden with his face towards the earth, on which rays of light are streaming from the heavens; beneath is the legend '*Fac et Spera*'. 'Tis a good attitude and a good motto. Look heavenward, if you wish, but never to the horizon—that way danger lies. Truth is not there, happiness is not there, certainty is not there, but the falsehoods, the frauds, the quackeries, the *ignes fatui* which have deceived each generation—all beckon from the horizon, and lure the men not content to look for the truth and happiness that tumble out at their feet. Once while at college climb a mountain-top, and get a general outlook of the land, and make it the occasion perhaps of that careful examination of yourself, that inquisition which Descartes urges every man to hold once in a lifetime—not oftener.

Waste of energy, mental distress, nervous worries dog the steps of a man who is anxious about the future. Shut close, then, the great fore and aft bulkheads, and prepare to cultivate the habit of a life of day-tight compartments. Do not be discouraged—like every other habit, the acquisition takes time, and the way is one you must find for yourselves. I can only give general directions and encouragement, in the hope that while the green years are on your heads, you may have the courage to persist.

IV

Now, for the day itself! What first? Be your own daysman! and sigh not with Job for any mysterious intermediary, but prepare to lay your own firm hand upon the helm. Get into touch with the finite, and grasp in full enjoyment that sense of capacity in a machine working smoothly. Join the whole creation of animate things in a deep, heartfelt joy that you are alive, that you see the sun, that you are in this glorious earth which Nature has made so beautiful, and which is yours to conquer and to enjoy. Realize, in the words of Browning, that 'There's a world of capability for joy spread round about us, meant for us, inviting us'. What are the morning sensations?—for they control the day. Some of us are congenitally unhappy during the early hours; but the young man who feels on awakening that life is a burden or a bore has been neglecting his machine, driving it too hard, stoking the engines too much, or not cleaning out the ashes and clinkers. Or he has been too much with the Lady Nicotine, or fooling with Bacchus, or, worst of all, with the younger Aphrodite—all 'messengers of strong prevailment in unhardened youth'. To have a sweet outlook on life you must have a clean body. As I look on the clear-cut, alert, earnest features, and the lithe, active forms of our college men, I sometimes wonder whether or not Socrates and Plato would find the race improved. I am sure they would love to look on such a gathering as this. Make their ideal yours—the fair mind in the fair body. The one cannot be sweet and clean without the other, and you must realize, with Rabbi Ben Ezra, the great truth that flesh and soul are mutually helpful. The morning outlook—which really makes the day—is largely a question of a clean machine—of physical morality in the wide sense of the term. *C'est l'estomac qui fait les heureux*, as Voltaire says; no dyspeptic can have a sane outlook on life; and a man whose bodily functions are impaired has a lowered moral resistance. To keep the body fit is a help in keeping the mind pure, and the sensations of the first few hours of the day are the best test of its normal state. The clean tongue, the clear head, and the bright eye are birth-rights of each day. Just as the late Professor Marsh would diagnose an unknown animal from a single bone, so can the day be predicted from the first waking hour. The start is everything, as you well know, and to make a good start you must feel fit. In the young, sensations of morning slackness come most often from lack of control of the two primal instincts—biologic habits—the one concerned with the preservation of the individual, the other with the continuance of the species. Yale students should by this time be models of dietetic propriety, but youth does not always reck the rede of the teacher; and I dare say that here, as elsewhere, careless habits of eating are responsible for much mental disability. My own rule of life has been to cut out unsparingly any article of diet that had the bad taste to disagree with me, or to indicate in any way that it had abused the temporary hospitality of the lodging which I had provided. To drink, nowadays, but few students become addicted, but in every large body of men a few are to be found whose incapacity for the day results from the morning clogging of nocturnally-flushed tissues. As moderation is very hard to reach, and as it has been abundantly shown that the best of mental and physical work may be done without alcohol in any form, the safest rule for the young man is that which I am sure most of you follow—abstinence. A bitter enemy to the bright eye and the clear brain of the early morning is tobacco when smoked to excess, as it is now by a large majority of students. Watch it, test it, and if need be, control it. That befogged, woolly sensation reaching from the forehead to the occiput, that haziness of memory, that cold fish-like eye, that furred tongue, and last week's taste in the mouth—too many of you know them—I know them—they often come from too much tobacco. The other primal instinct is the heavy burden of the flesh which Nature puts on all of us to ensure a continuation of the species. To drive Plato's team taxes the energies of the best of us. One of the horses is a raging, untamed devil, who can only be brought into subjection by hard fighting and severe training. This much you all know as men: once the bit is between his teeth the black steed Passion will take the white horse Reason with you and the chariot rattling over the rocks to perdition.

With a fresh, sweet body you can start aright without those feelings of inertia that so often, as Goethe says, make the morning's lazy leisure usher in a useless day. Control of the mind as a working machine, the adaptation in it of habit, so that its action becomes almost as automatic as walking, is the end of education—and yet how rarely reached! It can be accomplished with deliberation and repose, never with hurry and worry. Realize how much time there is, how long the day is. Realize that you have sixteen waking hours, three or four of which at least should be devoted to making a silent conquest

of your mental machinery. Concentration, by which is grown
gradually the power to wrestle successfully with any subject, is
the secret of successful study. No mind however dull can escape
the brightness that comes from steady application. There is an
old saying, 'Youth enjoyeth not, for haste'; but worse than this,
the failure to cultivate the power of peaceful concentration is
the greatest single cause of mental breakdown. Plato pities the
young man who started at such a pace that he never reached the
goal. One of the saddest of life's tragedies is the wreckage of
the career of the young collegian by hurry, hustle, bustle, and
tension—the human machine driven day and night, as no sensible
fellow would use his motor. Listen to the words of a master in
Israel, William James:

Neither the nature nor the amount of our work is accountable for
the frequency and severity of our breakdowns, but their cause lies
rather in those absurd feelings of hurry and having no time, in that
breathlessness and tension, that anxiety of feature and that solicitude
of results, that lack of inner harmony and ease, in short, by which
the work with us is apt to be accompanied, and from which a European
who would do the same work would, nine out of ten times, be free.

Es bildet ein Talent sich in der Stille, but it need not be for all day.
A few hours out of the sixteen will suffice, only let them be
hours of daily dedication—in routine, in order, and in system,
and day by day you will gain in power over the mental mechanism, just as the child does over the spinal marrow in walking,
or the musician over the nerve centres. Aristotle somewhere says
that the student who wins out in the fight must be slow in his
movements, with voice deep, and slow speech, and he will not
be worried over trifles which make people speak in shrill tones
and use rapid movements. Shut close in hour-tight compartments, with the mind directed intensely upon the subject in
hand, you will acquire the capacity to do more and more, you
will get into training; and once the mental habit is established,
you are safe for life.

Concentration is an art of slow acquisition, but little by little
the mind is accustomed to habits of slow eating and careful

digestion, by which alone you escape the 'mental dyspepsy' so graphically described by Lowell in the *Fable for Critics*. Do not worry your brains about that bugbear Efficiency, which, sought consciously and with effort, is just one of those elusive qualities very apt to be missed. The man's college output is never to be gauged at sight; all the world's coarse thumb and finger may fail to plumb his most effective work, the casting of the mental machinery of self-education, the true preparation for a field larger than the college campus. Four or five hours daily—it is not much to ask; but one day must tell another, one week certify another, one month bear witness to another of the same story, and you will acquire a habit by which the one-talent man will earn a high interest, and by which the ten-talent man may at least save his capital.

Steady work of this sort gives a man a sane outlook on the world. No corrective so valuable to the weariness, the fever, and the fret that are so apt to wring the heart of the young. This is the talisman, as George Herbert says,

> The famous stone
> That turneth all to gold,

and with which, to the eternally recurring question, What is Life? you answer, I do not think—I act it; the only philosophy that brings you in contact with its real values and enables you to grasp its hidden meaning. Over the Slough of Despond, past Doubting Castle and Giant Despair, with this talisman you may reach the Delectable Mountains, and those Shepherds of the Mind—Knowledge, Experience, Watchful, and Sincere. Some of you may think this to be a miserable Epicurean doctrine —no better than that so sweetly sung by Horace:

> Happy the man—and Happy he alone,
> He who can call to-day his own,
> He who secure within can say,
> To-morrow, do thy worst—for I have lived to-day.

I do not care what you think, I am simply giving you a philosophy of life that I have found helpful in my work, useful in my play. Walt Whitman, whose physician I was for some years, never spoke to me much of his poems, though occasionally he would make a quotation; but I remember late one summer afternoon as we sat in the window of his little house in Camden there passed a group of workmen whom he greeted in his usual friendly way. And then he said: 'Ah, the glory of the day's work, whether with hand or brain! I have tried

> To exalt the present and the real,
> To teach the average man the glory of his daily work or trade.'

In this way of life each one of you may learn to drive the straight furrow and so come to the true measure of a man.

V

With body and mind in training, what remains?

Do you remember that most touching of all incidents in Christ's ministry, when the anxious ruler Nicodemus came by night, worried lest the things that pertained to his everlasting peace were not a part of his busy and successful life? Christ's message to him is His message to the world—never more needed than at present: 'Ye must be born of the spirit.' You wish to be with the leaders—as Yale men it is your birthright—know the great souls that make up the moral radium of the world. You must be born of their spirit, initiated into their fraternity, whether of the spiritually-minded followers of the Nazarene or of that larger company, elect from every nation, seen by St. John.

Begin the day with Christ and His prayer—you need no other. Creedless, with it you have religion; creed-stuffed, it will leaven any theological dough in which you stick. As the soul is dyed by the thoughts, let no day pass without contact with the best literature of the world. Learn to know your Bible, though not perhaps as your fathers did. In forming character and in shaping conduct, its touch has still its ancient power. Of the kindred of Ram and sons of Elihu, you should know its beauties and its strength. Fifteen or twenty minutes day by day will give you fellowship with the great minds of the race, and little by little as the years pass you extend your friendship with the immortal dead. They will give you faith in your own day. Listen while they speak to you of the fathers. But each age has its own spirit and ideas, just as it has its own manners and pleasures. You are right to believe that yours is the best university, at its best period. Why should you look back to be shocked at the frowsiness and dullness of the students of the seventies or even of the nineties? And cast no thought forward, lest you reach a period when you and yours will present to your successors the same dowdiness of clothes and times. But while change is the law, certain great ideas flow fresh through the ages, and control us effectually as in the days of Pericles. Mankind, it has been said, is always advancing, man is always the same. The love, hope, fear, and faith that make humanity, and the elemental passions of the human heart, remain unchanged, and the secret of inspiration in any literature is the capacity to touch the chord that vibrates in a sympathy that knows nor time nor place.

The quiet life in day-tight compartments will help you to bear your own and others' burdens with a light heart. Pay no heed to the Batrachians who sit croaking idly by the stream. Life is a straight, plain business, and the way is clear, blazed for you by generations of strong men, into whose labours you enter and whose ideals must be your inspiration. In my mind's eye I can see you twenty years hence—resolute-eyed, broad-headed, smooth-faced men who are in the world to make a success of life; but to whichever of the two great types you belong, whether controlled by emotion or by reason, you will need the leaven of their spirit, the only leaven potent enough to avert that only too common Nemesis to which the Psalmist refers: 'He gave them their heart's desire, but sent leanness withal into their souls.'

I quoted Dr. Johnson's remark about the trivial things that influence. Perhaps this slight word of mine may help some of you so to number your days that you may apply your hearts unto wisdom.

15

ILLUSTRATIONS OF THE
BOOKWORM

IN *Micrographia*, a 'study of the Minute Bodies made by the Magnifying Glass', London, MDCLXVII, one of the earliest publications issued under the authority of the newly formed Royal Society, Robert Hooke described in Observation LII the 'small silver-colour'd Book-worm', 'which upon the removal of Books and Papers in the Summer, is often observed very nimbly to scud, and pack away to some lurking cranny'. The third figure of the 33rd scheme pictures a monster so formidable-looking that Blades (*Enemies of Books*, 1896) may be forgiven the suggestion that Hooke 'evolved both engraving and description from his inner consciousness'. Comparing, however, this earliest known drawing with one in Houlbert's monograph, *Les Insectes ennemis des livres*, 1903, we find that the distinguished author of the *Micrographia* knew what he was about, as alike in text and figure he has given what Houlbert calls 'une belle et exacte description' of the *Lepisma saccharina*, a formidable enemy of books, 'one of the teeth of time', as Hooke calls it. It is a fine bold figure, well executed, and the text is remarkable for a digression upon the different refrangibilities of light of the scales of the *Lepisma*, which cause the shining appearance, and explain the name 'silver fish' given by children to this insect.

In *Beschreibung von allerley Insecten in Deutschland*, 1721, anderer Theil, p. 36, ix, 'von dem kleinen Gelben Brodt-Käfer', Joh. Leonhard Frisch gives the first account of the common *Anobium paniceum*; and Tafel viii, fig. i, illustrates roughly the larva and pupa. Though not directly referred to as a bookworm, Frisch knew that it attacked manuscripts and books.

Horace Knight, del. 1916

BOOKWORM.   Anobium hirtum, Illigar

1. Back of book showing exit holes of the beetles.
2. Book opened showing damage, and (2a) pupa-case in situ, (2b) larva approx. four-fifths natural size.
3. Larva greatly enlarged. 3a. Head and fore part of same.
4. Pupa case, made of particles of frass cemented together, approx. four-fifths natural size. 4a. The same greatly enlarged.
5. Beetle in its perfect, or imago, stage, approx. four-fifths natural size. 5a. The same greatly enlarged.

As Prediger's *Buchbinder und Futteralmacher*, 4 vols., 1742 and 1772 (and an earlier unknown edition), is not in the British Museum or in Bodley, I cannot say whether or not the bookworm (which is referred to) is figured. The *Gentleman's Magazine* for 1754 has a brief reference to the work.

The Göttingen prize essays in answer to the questions of the Royal Society of Sciences as to the varieties of insects' injuries to books, &c., *Drey Preisschriften zu Beantwordung*, &c., Hannover, 1775, have no illustrations.

During the first half of the nineteenth century only a few observations of importance were made upon bookworms. The widespread prevalence of insect pests in the United States aroused the attention of trained entomologists, and the studies of H. A. Hagen, Riley, and others enlarged our knowledge of the varieties of insects which preyed upon books. How rare are good illustrations may be judged from those in Blades's *Enemies of Books*, 1896, and in Ed. Rouveyre's *Connaissances nécessaires à un bibliophile*, 5ᵐᵉ éd., tom. viii, 1889. Scattered contributions to the number of about eighty are recorded for the nineteenth century in the bibliography given by Houlbert. In 1900, at the 'Congrès International des Bibliothécaires' held åt Paris, it was decided to offer prizes for the best memoirs upon the insects which attacked books. One of these Marie-Pellechet prizes, the memoir of M. Houlbert, just referred to, gives for the first time a systematic grouping and study of the insect enemies of books. It is surprising to find so large a number as sixty-seven species described, of which about one-half are Coleoptera or beetles. Apart from the Termites, which are rare in Europe, the larvae of Coleoptera are the most harmful, and of these the Anobiides are the common and dangerous forms. Houlbert states that in France nine times out of ten the *Anobium paniceum*, known in America as the *Sitodrepa panicea*, is the culprit. In the *Cambridge Natural History: Insects*, Part II, Sharp gives a good account of the Anobiides, and the best figures I have seen of the transformations of *Anobium paniceum*. In tome iii, pl. 53, of Jacquelin du Val's *Genera des Coléoptères d'Europe*, *Anobium pertinax* is figured, the only coloured illustration I have seen of a bookworm.

In October 1915 I received from a Paris bookseller, M. Lucien Gougy, three volumes of the '*Histoire abrégée de la dernière persécution de Port-Royal*. Édition Royale, MDCCL', no place of printing indicated. On a card inside the cover, with ornamented border, is printed 'Resid. Tolos. S.J.', which indicates the provenance of the volumes from the south of France. The backs of two of the volumes were wormed, vol. i with two holes, vol. ii with ten, and this volume when opened showed at the back close to the binding a single large tunnel, an inch and a half in length, with laterals above and below. The borings had a fresh look and there were many granular castings. Near to the top of the main tunnel my eye caught a globular nest or casing (seen in figure 2*a*, midway between the holes through the back), and from the upper open end of this a brownish black head bobbed in and out. With a lens part of the body could be seen, and with gentle manipulation the little worm was extracted. In figure 2*b* it can be seen on the page of natural size,[1] at the top of the upper right-hand tunnel. It had a yellowish white glistening body covered with fine soft hairs. The enlarged larva and mandibles are shown in fig. 3 and 3*a*, while fig. 5 and 5*a* show the adult beetle of natural size[1] and magnified, and fig. 4 and 4*a* the pupa-case. Only once before, in the University library, Utrecht, had I seen a living bookworm. The picture of the opened book was so striking that Professor Poulton, to whom I showed it, urged me to have a sketch made by the well-known artist Mr. Horace Knight of the British Museum. Mr. Knight writes, 4 September 1916, 'Herewith the drawing of the bookworm which more than a year ago you asked me to make. It has been waiting in hopes the larva would pupate, but it has not even commenced to make a case, and Dr. Graham thinks it may go another year. . . . There are no eggs of this species in the British Museum and no drawing of any value.' Mr. Knight's beautiful sketches are so superior to anything in the literature that Mr. Madan has kindly

[1] [Here reduced by one-fifth.—ED.]

consented to have the plate reproduced in the *Bodleian Quarterly Record*.

The specimen is *Anobium hirtum*, not a native of England, but met with occasionally in the centre and south of France. Houlbert says there are very few observations upon it. In the Southern States of America it is more common, and the best account to be found is by E. A. Schwarz (*Insect Life*, vol. vii, p. 396, Washington, 1895) in a paper entitled 'An imported Library Pest'. Large numbers were found in the State Library, Bâton Rouge, Louisiana, and the library of St. Charles College.

Insect bookworms are rare in Oxford, even in the most secluded libraries. Mr. Maltby, the well-known bookbinder, has the largest collection I have seen, made during the past twenty-five years, all of *Anobium domesticum*, except one unknown lepidopteran larva. There are a few in Mr. Madan's possession. Though many of the old books in Oxford libraries are badly wormed, recent ravages are rare. One of the least-used collections is that of Bishop Allestree, housed so quaintly above the cloisters at Christ Church. There have been books badly damaged, but at a recent visit I could find no worms in the books, but one shelf had plenty of borers whose sawdust covered the tops of the books below. It may be mentioned that the *Anobium* is the genus of the 'death-watch' beetles which make a clicking sound in wood, so that there is some basis for the statement of Christian Mentzel, an old seventeenth-century worthy, that he heard a bookworm crow like a cock. Bodley is singularly free from the ravages of bookworms—confirming the remark of Charles Nodier, 'La bibliothèque des savants laborieux n'est jamais attaquée des vers.'

THE COLLECTING OF A LIBRARY

A COUNTRY parson's house in Canada in the 'fifties or 'sixties had rarely a literary atmosphere. My father's library, of about 1,500 volumes, was chiefly theological —the usual commentaries, Scott, Henry, and others, with Bingham, Pearson, and the common run of the English divines. There were a few old books, a Breeches Bible, and an early Stow's *Chronicle*. Having been at sea, he was fond of books of travel, of Layard, of Rawlinson, of Livingstone. Sunday reading is remembered as a trial. Even now to see a person with a novel on Sunday gives a reflex shock—a reminiscence of early training! George Borrow was a delight. As a missionary his books could not be hurtful, even on Sunday, and *The Bible in Spain*, *Gipsies in Spain*, and even *Lavengro* were not taboo.

No little pride was taken in the books of my father's eldest brother, Edward, a surgeon in Truro, whose *Life of Exmouth*, *Church and King*, and volume of poems seemed to confer a literary flavour on the family; and at church what a pleasure to see his name opposite certain well-known hymns! Later, to know that monographs by him had appeared in the *Transactions of the Royal Society* was an additional source of pride.

At Weston, with the Warden and Founder of Trinity College School, the Rev. W. A. Johnson, came the first opportunity to see scientific books—elementary manuals of geology, botany, and microscopy. Griffith's *Micrographic Dictionary*, Ehrenberg's *Infusoria*, Smith on Diatoms, Ralfs on Desmids, Carpenter and Beale on the Microscope, introduced us to a book world very different from Arnold and Anthon and Todhunter. Mr. Johnson

---

A Catalogue of Books, Illustrating the History of Medicine and Science, collected, arranged, and annotated by Sir William Osler, Bt., and bequeathed to McGill University. Oxford: At the Clarendon Press, 1929.

was a Canadian White of Selborne, and knew the ways and works of nature. A good field botanist, a practical palaeontologist, an ardent microscopist, he had a rare gift for imparting knowledge and inspiring enthusiasm. One of his books is kept, Beale's *How to work with the Microscope* (no. 1969), in grateful memory of happy school days.

The year at Trinity College, Toronto (1867-8), put me on the right track. To Weston Dr. Bovell of Toronto had been a frequent visitor, as his friend the Warden had an enviable technique with the microscope. He would arrive on Saturday with materials for section, or with small animals for injection. To be interested was enough to have one's help enlisted, if only in clearing up the shocking mess, stained with carmine, that was left on the study table. Arthur J. Johnson, the Warden's son, had already begun the study of medicine, and it became our custom to spend our Saturdays with Dr. Bovell, cutting sections with Valentine's knife, grinding bones or teeth for microscopic slides, or keeping the aquaria stocked with pond material likely to contain good specimens of algae, amoebae, &c. In the late afternoon Dr. Bovell would often take me to his lecture at the Toronto School of Medicine. In this congenial atmosphere what wonder that Euripides, Aeschylus, Livy, and Horace were dull; conic sections and trigonometry became an abomination, and Pearson and Hooker a delusion. In October 1868 I entered the Toronto School of Medicine.

It has been remarked that for a young man the privilege of browsing in a large and varied library is the best introduction to a general education. My opportunity came in the winter of 1869-70. Having sent his family to the West Indies, Dr. Bovell took consulting-rooms in Spadina Avenue, not far away from his daughter, Mrs. Barwick, with whom he lived. He gave me a bedroom in his house, and my duties were to help him keep appointments—an impossible job!—and to cut sections and prepare specimens. Having catholic and extravagant tastes, he had filled the rooms with a choice and varied selection of books. After a review of the work of the day came the long evening for browsing, and that winter gave me a good first-hand acquaintance with the original works of many of the great masters. After fifty years the position in those rooms of special books is fixed in my mind: Morton's *Crania Americana*, Annesley's *Diseases of India* with the fine plates, the three volumes of Bright, the big folios of Dana, the monographs of Agassiz. Dr. Bovell had a passion for the great physician-naturalists, and it was difficult for him to give a lecture without a reference to John Hunter. The diet was too rich and varied, and contributed possibly to the development of my somewhat 'splintery' and illogical mind; but the experience was valuable and aroused an enduring interest in books. In such a decade of mental tumult as the 'sixties really devout students, of whom Dr. Bovell was one, were sore let and hindered, not to say bewildered, in attempts to reconcile Genesis and geology. It seems hardly credible, but I heard a long debate on Philip Henry Gosse's (of, to me, blessed memory) 'Omphalos, an Attempt to untie the Geological Knot'. A dear old parson, Canon Reade, stoutly maintained the possibility of the truth of Gosse's view that the strata and the fossils had been created by the Almighty to test our faith! A few years ago, reading Edmund Gosse's *Father and Son*, which appeared anonymously, the mention of this extraordinary 'Omphalos' work revealed the identity, and, alas! to my intense regret, the personality of the father as Philip Henry Gosse.

Of this mental struggle the students reaped the benefit, for Dr. Bovell was much more likely to lecture on what was in his mind than on the schedule, and a new monograph on Darwin or a recent controversial pamphlet would occupy the allotted hour. One corner of the library was avoided. With an extraordinary affection for mental and moral philosophy, he had collected the works of Locke and Berkeley, Kant and Hegel, Spinoza and Descartes, as well as those of the moderns. He would joke upon the impossibility of getting me to read any of the works of these men, but at Trinity, in 1867–8, I attended the lectures on natural theology, and he really did get us interested in Cousin and Jouffroy and others of the French school. Three years of association with Dr. Bovell were most helpful. Books and the Man! The best the human mind has afforded was on his shelves, and in him all that one could desire in a teacher, a clear head and a loving heart. Infected with the Aesculapian spirit, he made me realize the truth of those memorable words in the Hippocratic oath, 'I will honour as my father the man who teaches me the Art'.

The first book bought was the Globe Shakespeare, the second the 1862 edition, Boston, of the *Religio Medici* [no. 4446], both of which were close companions of my student days. The Shakespeare was stolen, and the curses of Bishop Ernulphus have often been invoked on the son of Belial who took it; the Browne, bought in 1867, is the father of my Browne collection. In it is a touching association, as in this volume only, in this section of the library, is found the book-plate of my boy, his own design and etching. He claimed it for his lifetime, promising that it should join the collection at his death. With the Brownes is *Varia: Readings from Rare Books* by Friswell (given me by my eldest brother), the article in which introduced me, I think, to the *Religio*.

In 1870 my kind preceptor joined his family in the West Indies, and urged me to go to Montreal for better clinical opportunities. He sent word to Arthur Johnson and me to take a selection of books from his library, but it was sold before we had the opportunity. A few of his books, which he had lent me, have been carefully kept. The Niemeyer (English translation), Simon's *Pathology*, Chambers's *Renewal of Life*, can still be read with pleasure.

The long vacations were periods of profitable study, with a borrowed microscope, and books from Mr. Johnson and Dr. Bovell. Lyell's *Principles of Geology*, Darwin's *Voyage* and the *Origin* were read, and in collecting diatoms, desmids, algae, and freshwater polyzoa the available literature on these subjects was studied. My first appearance in print was in connexion with the finding of diatoms, &c., in a frozen spring on the road between Dundas and Hamilton; and it is amusing to note, even at the very start of my ink-pot career, a fondness for tags of quotations, this one from Horace, in those days a familiar friend (see no. 3535).

The summer of 1871, spent at Montreal, brought me into almost filial relations with Dr. Palmer Howard, whose library was at my disposal. Wilks's *Pathological Anatomy* was my handbook, and the post-mortems were worked out from its pages. The old system prevailed of writing a thesis for the degree, a most perfunctory and evil habit as then carried out, but it served me in good stead. Mine was a report, with the specimens, on fifty post-mortems. So profuse in his praises was Dr. Fraser, the Professor of the Institutes of Medicine, who had read the thesis, that the Faculty voted me a special prize of books, all of which remain in the library for the sake of auld lang syne. One of them, Klein and Sanderson's *Handbook for the Physiological Laboratory*, became a stand-by; and towards the end of 1873, in the chemical laboratory of the Pathologisches Institut, Berlin, the patient soul of the good Salkowski was sorely tried in helping me to work through Lauder Brunton's section on physiological chemistry. Taking with me to London an order for the books on S. and J. Nock, for years, indeed from the foundation of the school, the Faculty's agents, I proceeded to Hart Street, Bloomsbury. The shop was an indescribable clutter of books, and the brothers Nock, far advanced in years, were weird and desiccated specimens of humanity. They had a keen interest in the Faculty, and remembered Howard, Wright, and MacCallum when they were students in London in 1849. During the winter session [1872–3] I lived with the much-loved Arthur Browne, a fellow student, afterwards Professor of Obstetrics at McGill, a keen lover of English literature, to whom I owe my introduction to Coleridge and Lamb.

Many books were used but few bought in the two years spent in Europe. The students' library at University College was very good, and for the special work in the physiological laboratory Professor Burdon Sanderson or Mr. (now Sir Edward) Schafer got the monographs and works of reference. Luther Holden introduced me to the College of Surgeons' library, and Arthur

Durham to the library of the Medico-Chirurgical Society. One book (no. 2429) is an interesting souvenir of this period and of a notable man. Professor Sharpey had resigned the previous year but was much about the laboratory, and often came to my desk in a friendly way to see the progress of my blood studies. One evening he asked me to dinner; Kölliker, Allen Thomson, and Dohrn were there. When saying good-bye he gave me Davy's *Researches* with an autograph inscription. There were cobwebs in my pockets in Berlin and Vienna, and only the most necessary text-books were bought. On leaving Vienna I could not resist Billroth's *Cocco-bacteria septica* (no. 2039), an expensive volume with beautiful plates, a curious pre-Kochian attempt to associate bacteria with disease, and now of value only as illustrating the futility of brains without technique.

On my return to Canada in July 1874 a berth was waiting, the lectureship on the Institutes of Medicine, which necessitated an immediate course of predatory reading in preparation for the delivery of 100 lectures!

The McGill Library, founded by Dr. Holmes, the first dean, had many old books, and a pretty complete file of the English journals, with a few French, such as the *Archives générales de Médecine*, but no recent German periodicals. A Book and Journal Club, started about 1876, lasted for a few years and helped with new books and foreign journals. Palmer Howard was the only free buyer in Montreal, and from him one could always get the French monographs and journals. Complete sets of Virchow's *Archiv*, the *Deutsches Archiv für klinische Medicin*, the *Centralblatt für die medicinischen Wissenschaften*, Wagner's *Archiv*, and Max Schultze's *Archiv* were collected, and a good many valuable books on medicine and natural history. Canadian journals on science and medicine were bought, and a nearly complete set obtained. All that remains in the present collection is the *Canada Medical and Surgical Journal*, which is kept for the sake of my early contributions.[1]

[1] This set, after Sir William's death, was inadvertently returned to the Johns Hopkins Hospital whose book-plate it had acquired in Baltimore. [W. W. F.]

Except my student text-books (e.g. nos. 2820, 3600, 3833, and 4245), a few of Dr. Bovell's books, and some special treasures like Virchow's *Gesammelte Abhandlungen*, nothing remains of my Montreal library. A few books on general literature were bought. Connected with one is a good story. Before leaving Berlin in December 1873, while ordering Virchow's *Archiv* at Reimer's, I saw on the desk the prospectus of Schmidt's *Shakespeare-Lexicon*, which I asked to have sent to me as soon as published. In October 1875 I moved from Victoria Square up Beaver Hall Hill to rooms with Mr. King, an Englishman employed in the Custom House, who had but one thought in life—Shakespeare. He had an excellent library in which I often spent a pleasant hour. He was a dear old man, much esteemed, and always ready to spend more than he could afford on his hobby. One afternoon at the College, just before my lecture, the postman left on the table a parcel from Reimer's, and to my delight it was Schmidt's concordance, which had really been forgotten. My first thought was, how happy Mr. King will be to see it. I looked at it hurriedly but with much anticipatory pleasure. On my return to the house Mr. King, who had just come in, was sitting by the fire and greeted me in his cheery way with, 'What's that you've got?' 'Something that will rejoice your heart', I said, and deposited the work in his lap. The shock of the realization of a lifelong dream, a complete concordance of Shakespeare, seemed to daze the old man. He had no further interest in me and not a word did he say. I never got it back! For months he avoided me, but helping him one day on the stairs, my manner showed that Schmidt was forgotten, and he never referred to it again. The work went to McGill College with his Shakespeare collection. When in the library in 1910, I asked for the first edition of Schmidt and was glad to see my book again after thirty-five years. This story is written on the fly-leaf [cf. no. 5451] as a warning to bibliomaniacs!

For an association book of this period there remains a deep affection. In Vienna, Brücke, to whom I had a letter of introduction, asked me to attend his lectures on physiology, but the clinical courses made it impossible except occasionally. The *Vorlesungen*, advertised to appear before I left Vienna, was ordered, and in the summer of 1874 anxiously awaited. To prepare four lectures on physiology and one on pathology each week was a heavy task. Dr. Drake, my predecessor, very kindly offered me his set, but I struggled through until Christmas, working often until 2 a.m. To my delight Brücke's *Vorlesungen* arrived in the vacation. The problem of the lectures for the next term became a simple business of translation!

When I left Montreal in 1884 my collection of Canadian scientific and medical journals, which was fairly complete, went to the McGill Medical Library, where they escaped the fire and are still housed. If I remember aright, they were well bound, and the collection cost me not a little time and money. It was a useful job which put me into touch with the scientific side of Canadian life, especially in geology, the study of which had fascinated me at school.

The five years spent in Philadelphia, 1884–9, were fruitful in two directions. I became associated with a first-class medical library. The College of Physicians, founded in 1787, had for one of its special objects the establishment of a library. In the discourse delivered 6 February 1787 by Benjamin Rush on the objects of the institution, he states that 'the library has already been established, and now consists of a number of valuable books'. In 1886 I joined the library committee of the College, and had as my colleagues, among others, Weir Mitchell, Minis Hays, and F. P. Henry.

A library is usually the result of the enthusiasm of one or two men. Billings made the great library in Washington; the Boston Medical Library grew up about Chadwick. The Philadelphia College Library had not prospered very greatly in the middle of the century, but in 1840 Dr. Samuel Lewis, a West Indian and an Edinburgh graduate, came to Philadelphia and for years devoted time and money to extending its scope. He was an old man in 1884 but still active mentally, and it was his habit to

go to the library every morning to look over the catalogues and
see the new books that had come in. An important section of the
library is rightly called after his name. It was about this time,
too, that Dr. Weir Mitchell became interested in the library,
and to him more than anyone else is due the extraordinary
growth of the collections and the ever-increasing devotion of
the profession of Philadelphia to the College. In Charles Perry
Fisher the College found an ideal librarian, intelligent, civil, and
helpful. The honorary librarian, Frederick P. Henry, was a man
of keen judgement in the matter of books, and a scholarly
student of the best literature. It has been a pleasure to keep in
touch with the College and its interests, and now and then I
have been able to get a special treasure for its library. I induced
them to buy the Huth copy of the *editio princeps* of Celsus, 1478,
a superb copy, the best I have ever seen except the famous
Grolier copy in the British Museum. Quaritch asked a shocking
price for it as the binding was of special value; at the Huth sale
he only paid £36 for it. One of the most interesting books I
procured for the College was Rösslin's famous *Rosegarten*, the
first book published on obstetrics. Lang of Rome sent on appro-
val what he took to be an unknown '1508' edition, bound up
with a group of early sixteenth-century pamphlets. It proved to
be the 1513 Strasburg edition; curiously enough, he had mistaken the old-fashioned ten (ꝟ) for a five. On account of the
binding and the included pamphlets, he asked a very high price
(£80) which we reduced considerably. An extensive set of plates
and pamphlets relating to the Siamese twins, which I bought at
the Dunn sale in 1915, was an item of peculiar interest to the
College, as the 'specimen' from the twins is in the College
museum. I sent the collection on condition that it should be
made as complete as possible.

The atmosphere at Philadelphia was literary; in College
circles every one wrote, and my pen and brain got a good deal
of practice. I worked for Lea Bros. on the *Medical News* with
Minis Hays, the editor, Sam Gross, and Parvin; and I devilled
for Pepper for his *System of Medicine*, writing in addition to my

own sections those of Janeway on certain of the diseases of the heart.

The other direction in which my stay in Philadelphia was fruitful was in general education. My practice was to read for an hour at the Rittenhouse Club after dinner. The library was good, and many standard works were read for the first time, particularly American authors, Emerson, Lowell, and Franklin. My commonplace-book dates from 1882, but the entries did not become numerous until after 1884. My library grew rapidly, and important German and French sets were completed. At this time my interest in the American masters of medicine began, and some of the special treasures, like Jones (no. 3097) and Morgan (no. 3454), were picked up in Philadelphia. On leaving in the spring of 1889, nearly 1,000 volumes, chiefly journals which I knew were in Baltimore, were distributed to various libraries.

To the date of my transfer to Baltimore, with a comparatively small income (but quite sufficient for my needs) only the more important books and journals could be bought. A library represents the mind of its collector, his fancies and foibles, his strength and weakness, his prejudices and preferences. Particularly is this the case if to the character of a collector he adds— or tries to add—the qualities of a student who wishes to know the books and the lives of the men who wrote them. The friendships of his life, the phases of his growth, the vagaries of his mind, all are represented. With a bigger salary and increasing income I began to buy, first, the early books and pamphlets relating to the profession in America; secondly, the original editions of the great writers in science and in medicine; and thirdly, the works of such general authors as Sir Thos. Browne, Milton, Shelley, Keats, and others. Catalogues—German, French, and English—appeared at the breakfast table, and were always in my bag for railway reading. Summer trips to England and the Continent, often of three months' duration, gave time for reading, and my interest got deeper and deeper in the history of medicine and in the lives of the great men of the profession. The association with Billings and Welch was a stimulus, and the Historical Club of the Johns Hopkins Hospital awakened no little enthusiasm. In the classroom more and more attention was paid to the historical side of questions, and at my Saturday evening meetings, after the difficulties of the week had been discussed, we usually had before us the editions of some classic. Altogether, the foundation was laid for a successful avocation, without the addition of which to his vocation no man should be called successful (so President Gilman used to say). Buying freely English and foreign books and subscribing to more than forty journals, I soon had the house overrun, but with special exceptions they were passed on to my friends or to libraries.

My colleagues in the old Medical and Chirurgical Faculty of the State of Maryland very soon found that I was really fonder of books than of anything else, and to help its library escape from the dingy quarters in St. Paul Street, first to the bright house in Hamilton Place and then to the present handsome building, was one of the great pleasures of my life. That my name is associated with the Hall of the Faculty, as that of Oliver Wendell Holmes with the Boston Medical Library, as David Hosack's with the Academy of Medicine in New York, and as Weir Mitchell's with the College of Physicians in Philadelphia, is a touching tribute of affection from men who knew me and whom I loved. We owed much to Miss Marcia Noyes, our first whole-time librarian, and to the devoted Dr. Eugene Cordell, the historian of the Faculty.

In no. 2278 is a catalogue and a note of interest about a collection given to that library. In the catalogue, received one Sunday morning from George P. Johnston, Edinburgh, was a list of the theses of American students at Edinburgh from 1760 to 1813, mostly presentation copies to the Professors Hope. The list, well worth looking over, is arranged according to States, and contains the theses of some of the most famous of the early American physicians. A cable was sent at once, and the collection which came in due time was presented to the Faculty library.

The next summer in Edinburgh Mr. Johnston showed me a group of cables, all of which had come on the same day, *but after mine*. The thesis containing the note did not belong to that set, but was given me by Dr. Mitchell Bruce.

The libraries of the Johns Hopkins Hospital and Medical School grew rapidly, and were working collections of journals and monographs. The Surgeon-General's Library was so near that it did not seem worth while to spend much on old books. In 1906 the library of the Warrington Dispensary was offered, and I bought it on behalf of Mr. W. A. Marburg for the School. The collection is interesting as a memorial of a remarkable group who lived at Warrington in the last quarter of the eighteenth century: Priestley, Percival, Aikin, and others. One library, that of the late Dr. J. F. Payne, was lost for the School in an aggravating way. It was sold at Sotheby's in 1911 (no. 6350) and first offered *en bloc*. Our kind friend Mr. Marburg authorized me to go as high as £2,000. The bidding rose rapidly and crossed this limit, to be knocked down very precipitately at £2,300. We could easily have sold duplicates up to £500 or raised the extra money. There were many good items in the collection, and I am glad for the sake of Dr. Payne's memory that it has been kept together and will be well housed in the Wellcome Historical Museum.

When I left Baltimore in 1905, sets of journals, monographs, and many works on general literature were distributed among friends and the libraries. A good beginning had been made in an attempt to get the original editions of the great authors in medicine. The Sir Thomas Browne collection was nearly complete. For some years Dr. Harvey Cushing and I had bought everything of Vesalius that was offered. One evening we had six copies of the first edition (1543) on exhibition. With the cash in pocket the book is impossible to resist, and I have distributed six copies to libraries. Forgetting what I had done, I took out a copy in 1907 to McGill, and showed it with pride to Dr. Shepherd, the librarian, who pointed out in one of the showcases a very much better example presented by me some years before! Thinking it would be a very acceptable present to the Boston Library Association (in which I had a personal interest through Dr. James Chadwick and Dr. E. H. Brigham), I took the volume to Dr. Farlow, who looked a bit puzzled and amused. 'Come upstairs', he said; and there in a case in the Holmes room, spread open at the splendid title-page, was the 1543 edition and, on a card beneath it, 'The gift of Dr. Osler'. I had better luck at New York, where the volume found a resting-place in the library of the Academy of Medicine.

An association book of rare interest (no. 5551) is connected with my departure from Baltimore. My messmates in The Ship of Fools, a social club, gave a dinner, and presented me with Voltaire's *Henriade* bound by Padeloup and with autograph verses by Voltaire to his physician, Silva.

The years spent in the United States, 1884–1905, brought 'troops of friends' whose affection is part of my life; they brought me, too, into sympathetic touch with another company, those friends of the spirit, the great and good men of the past who, through much tribulation, handed on the torch to our generation. It was the height of my ambition as a teacher to live up to the ideals of Morgan and Rush, of Hosack and Gerhard, of Bartlett and Drake, of Jackson and Bigelow. To know and to make known to students the lives and works of these men was a labour of love. Their works were collected and, what is more, read, and a regret remains that lack of time prevented the completion of many projected bio-bibliographical sketches.

Oxford brought two things—leisure and opportunity. Not that more time necessarily means more work. My literary output from 1905 to 1915 is not to be compared with that between 1895 and 1905, but there were heavy arrears to make up in general and special reading, without which this catalogue (still far from completion) could never have been attempted. The opportunity was great. A Curator of the Bodleian (as *ex officio* I am) and Delegate of the Press is forced into the most bookish circles of the University. Very soon there was a feeling that a day had not been well spent if altogether away from Bodley. I envied the men who could be there all day and every day. There are greater libraries, there are more convenient libraries, but for solid comfort and 'atmosphere' give me a seat in Duke Humphrey or a table in the Selden End! In his autobiography (no. 7254), perhaps the best ever written—all the essentials in 16 pages!—Bodley gives the four qualifications which encouraged him to set up his Staffe at the Library doore in Oxford: leisure, knowledge, friends, and purse-ability. His letters between 1598 and 1613 show how successful he was in laying the foundation of one of the great libraries of the world. And the blessing of the liberal soul has followed his endeavours.

Gradually, as my collection grew, plans for its disposition had to be considered. Already at the outbreak of the war my son, Edward Revere, aged 18, who had just 'come up' to Christ Church, had shown unmistakably the direction of his tastes, and it was agreed that he should take the works in general literature while the medical and scientific books should go to McGill. During the first three years of the war, while he was with the McGill unit and the Royal Artillery, his interest in English literature developed rapidly. I sent on the catalogues and he began to buy on his own account. It was a diversion to send bids to the sales and to pick up bargains out of the second-hand catalogues. I bought for him several nice collections, such as the originals of Ruskin and some Whitman items from the Dowden sale. At the Harris sale in Oxford, when on leave a few weeks before he was killed, he was so happy over the purchase of the Holland Plutarch, an Overbury MS., and a number of special books in which he was interested. What he had collected, together with my original editions of Milton, Fuller, Donne, Shelley, Keats, makes the nucleus of a good library of English literature, and this section his mother and I have decided to dedicate as a memorial to him. [See no. 7241.]

Though a wanderer, living away from Montreal for more than half my life, the early associations I have never forgotten. The formative years were there with the strong ties of head and heart. As a young, untried man, McGill College offered me an opportunity to teach and to work; but what is more, the members of the Medical Faculty adopted me, bore with vagaries and aggressiveness, and often gave practical expressions of sympathy with schemes which were costly and of doubtful utility. That they believed in me helped to a belief in myself, an important asset for a young man, but better had by nurture than by nature. Alma Mater, too, counts for much, and as a graduate of McGill I am proud of her record. Had I not seen the day of small things? Did I not graduate in the days of the Coté-Street school? I may quote Fuller's sentiment: 'He [the good Bishop] conceiv'd himself to heare his Mother-Colledge alwayes speaking to him in the language of Joseph to Pharaoh's butler. But think on me, I pray thee, when it shall be well with thee.' [no. 4833, p. 283.] Then there is the natural feeling of loyalty to the country of one's birth and breeding. These are the considerations which decided me to leave the special collection to my old school at Montreal. With some of Bodley's qualifications it seemed possible gradually to gather a modest collection of books not likely to be either in the general library of the University or in the special library of the Faculty, or indeed in the country. There will, of course, be duplicates, but for special reasons.

To get shelf room the new books have had to be given away. The monographs and reprints on diseases of the heart, arteries, blood, and the tuberculosis items go to the library of the Johns Hopkins Hospital. There is left over a motley collection of miscellaneous works which may remain in the house to help fill the shelves.

Gradually, as the books increased, the hope matured into a scheme for a library which would have (a) a definite educational value, (b) a literary, and (c) an historical interest. To break a collection into sections is hazardous, but I considered that, after all, this would form a special part of the Medical Faculty library just as the latter is a section of the University library. So I decided to follow my own plan and group the books in the following divisions:[1]

[1] Described in further detail in the Preface.

I. Prima, which gives in chronological order a bio-bibliographical account of the evolution of science, including medicine.

II. Secunda, the works of men who have made notable contributions, or whose works have some special interest, but scarcely up to the mark of those in Prima.

III. Litteraria, the literary works written by medical men, and books dealing in a general way with doctors and the profession.

IV. Historica, with the stories of institutions, &c.

V. Biographica.

VI. Bibliographica.

VII. Incunabula, and

VIII. Manuscripts.

Then came the ambitious desire to prepare for printing a *catalogue raisonné* somewhat on the lines of Ferguson's *Bibliotheca Chemica* (no. 7040), with biographical and bibliographical notes. The introductions to the individual sections will explain to students how they are to be used.[1] The task is perhaps too heavy for one man to undertake; but I am assured by experts that there is no inherent difficulty in such a catalogue, provided there is a good index. Should I die before its completion, which is not at all unlikely, the catalogue could be finished and printed; and Lady Osler, with my good friends L. L. Mackall, W. W. Francis, and T. A. Malloch, would see that my wishes were carried out.

The library is for the use of students of the history of science and of medicine, without any other qualifications, and I particularly wish that it may be used by my French Canadian colleagues, who will find it rich in the best of French literature. I hope to make provision for its extension and upkeep.

The books have come from three sources: sales, catalogues, and second-hand bookshops.

[1] These introductions, unfortunately, were not written. [EDITORS.]

EDITORS' NOTE. The Introduction proper ends at this point unfinished. Among the notes for its continuation was found the account of the Van Antwerp sale, written several years earlier. The intention, no doubt, was to use it to illustrate the first of the three sources mentioned. It is, therefore, printed here as Appendix I, followed by a note on a Paris auction in the following year. Other isolated paragraphs, mostly notes for the intended special introduction to Bibliotheca Litteraria, have been printed under the relevant entries in the catalogue (e.g. at nos. 4770, 4950, 5242, 5526, &c.). See also no. 7656, which contains drafts of all the introductory material.

APPENDIX I

A RECORD DAY AT SOTHEBY'S

THE following notes may be of interest as a record of how a sale is conducted. The library, collected by Wm. C. Van Antwerp, of New York, was sold at Sotheby's, 22 and 23 March 1907. The sale began at 1 p.m. sharp.[1]

One was impressed by the extremely decorous character of the proceedings, without the slightest noise or bluster such as one is accustomed to think of in connexion with sales. The auctioneer, Mr. Tom Hodge, presided at a raised desk at the end of an oblong table about which were seated some twenty buyers, the principals or the representatives of the leading English booksellers. Around the room were twenty-five or thirty onlookers, mostly seated, a few standing about. Bids were offered only by the dealers and by a man who held a catalogue marked with the bids sent directly to the firm. The auctioneer, with a soft voice and a good-natured manner, called out the numbers and, as a rule, offered no comments upon the books; in fact, he did not often have to ask for a bid, which was started spontaneously. Occasionally, of course, he could not resist a remark or two. Sometimes he would suggest a bid. It was astonishing with what rapidity the different items were sold. Evidently the dealers knew just what they wanted and what they were willing to pay, and in many cases one could easily see that they had been given a limit by those who had sent the orders.

[1] The second day's sale is described. The annotated catalogue is no. 7373. [EDITORS.]

The first work of special interest sold was the 1817 edition of poems of Keats, a presentation copy, with an inscription by the author. Starting at £20 it rose quickly to £70 and £80 and in less than a minute was knocked down to Quaritch at £90. I say knocked down, but the process was altogether too dignified for such an expression, and no final rap was ever given. The catalogue of the Rowfant Library brought £7. Two books of Richard Pynson's press brought high figures. It was remarkable, also, to see a ragged, rough-looking, unbound, but uncut play of Philip Massinger knocked down to Stevens at £48. Bidding upon the copy of *Comus*, one of the rarest of Milton's works, was started by Quaritch at £50 and ran up pound by pound with the greatest rapidity to £100, and finally to £162. Nothing was heard but the monotonous repetition of the figures by the auctioneer, who simply watched the nodding heads of Mr. Quaritch and his rival, Ellis of Bond Street. The *Paradise Regained*, an uncut copy and a great rarity in this state—so much so that the auctioneer remarked, 'Uncut, and need I say more? All you can ask!' —was secured at £94 by Maggs. Three beautiful first editions of some of Pope's works did not bring very high prices, though the *Windsor Forest*, in sheets loosely stitched together, entirely uncut, brought £48. One of the finest sets of the collection was *Purchas his Pilgrimes, in five Books*. As the auctioneer remarked, 'It is one of the finest copies ever sold and Mr. Van Antwerp had had a most detailed and complete collation made'. The volumes were in the original vellum, absolutely perfect. Starting at £50, the fifth bid reached £100, and the set was knocked down to Maggs at £170 against Quaritch—one of the few instances in which Mr. Quaritch gave up. There was a splendid collection of Scott, the quarto volumes of the poems and first editions of the Waverley novels. Though the novels were in one lot, a complete set, in the original boards, uncut, and all from the Rowfant Library, option was given whether they should be sold separately or together. The latter was preferred, and, starting at £100, the bids quickly rose to £200, to £260, and the set was finally secured by Tregaskis at £300.

Then, after the sale of lot 189, came the remarkable set of original Shakespeare folios. Just as a foil, it seemed, and to show the contrast between the new and the old, Sidney Lee's facsimile reprint of the first folio, issued by the Clarendon Press in 1902, was put up (£2 12s.). When lot 191 was called out, there was a stir among the auditors, not such as you could hear, but it could be felt, as the famous first folio of 'Mr. William Shakespeares Comedies, Histories, and Tragedies' was offered. It was in a superb red morocco binding by Bedford and enclosed in a new crushed red morocco slip case by Bradstreet. In *My Confidences*, 1896, p. 203, Locker-Lampson tells the story of this volume: 'Some years ago I was offered a splendid example of this folio Shakespeare (1623); it was one of the tallest, largest and cleanest copies in existence, but it lacked the verses [i.e. the leaf with Ben Jonson's verses]. The owner guaranteed that if I would buy it he would before very long get me the missing leaf, and it was upon this assurance that I closed with him.' Then follows a most amusing account of a journey to the West of England to try to secure the leaf from an 'illiterate booby'. He spent two unhappy days with the 'grimy Gibeonite', who would not give up the leaf though the volume was much mutilated. Finally he found an example of the missing leaf pasted in a scrap-book, but he had to pay £100 for it.

'Language fails me, Sirs,' the auctioneer said, 'I can only ask you to look at the book and give your bids.' Special interest existed as to whether the record price of £3,000, paid by the Bodleian, would be exceeded, but the circumstances were then exceptional, as that copy had originally been in the Bodleian (see no. 5443 for its story). Previously as much as £1,720 had been paid for the first folio, and £3,000 was thought to be a fabulously extravagant price. I may remark that the folio would never have returned to the Bodleian had it not been for the extreme generosity of Lord Strathcona, who contributed £500. It cheered the book-lover's heart to hear Quaritch lead off with a bid of £1,000, followed immediately by the representative of Stevens with £1,500, and then the figures ran £1,800, £1,900, £2,000, £2,400, £2,800, and at the £3,000 there was a pause. Stevens, thereupon, said 'Fifty' and the previous record price was passed, then £3,200. At £3,500 Stevens stopped, and a record— long, let us hope, to remain such—was made when Quaritch secured it at £3,600.[1] Everyone in the room applauded his victory.

The second folio brought only £210 (Stevens). The third folio brought £650, and the fourth £75. The quarto copies of the individual

---

[1] This price seems not to have been surpassed at auction until 1921, when Quaritch paid £4,200, to be doubled the next year by Dr. Rosenbach's £8,600 and £5,400 for two copies at Sotheby's, 15 May 1922. [EDITORS.]

plays did not bring such very high prices as were realized the previous year. Sidney's *Arcadia* brought £315. When Swift's *Gulliver's Travels* was offered it was stated that the signature of Oliver Goldsmith, 1766, was on the Lilliput title. Leighton spoke up and said that Goldsmith's name was not written in this copy when he had it, and he asked why it should be mentioned in the catalogue; to which the auctioneer replied, 'In order to make a proper copy of it'. It came from the Rowfant Library, and Leighton added 'I should know, as I sold it to Mr. Locker-Lampson'. There was much fun over this incident, but it did not diminish the liveliness of the bidding, which was started at £50, and the treasure was secured at £132 by Stevens.

When lot 235 was called, a man inside the arena held up a small octavo in its original sheep jacket—as Locker-Lampson says, a most commonplace, ordinary little book, but one of the great treasures of English literature and one that brings the highest price known in the auction room with the exception of the Shakespeare folio— 'WALTON (IZAAK) THE COMPLEAT ANGLER, or the CONTEMPLA- TIVE MAN'S RECREATION; being a Discourse of Fish and Fishing, not unworthy the perusal of most Anglers. Simon Peter said, I go a fishing; and they said, We also will go with thee (*John* xxi, 3), FIRST EDITION. sm. 8vo. Printed by T. Maxey for Rich. Marriot in S. Dun- stan's Church-yard, Fleetstreet, 1653. . . . This copy has always been spoken of as one of the finest, if not the finest copy known. It is quite perfect and in the original state as issued. The late owner, Frederick Locker, has written a note or two in the fly-leaves.' The auctioneer remarked, 'It is impossible to over-estimate this copy, an absolutely unique and perfect specimen in the original binding. Not a copy like this has been in the sale room for many years.' Amid suppressed excitement the bidding began. Quaritch started at £200, and it ran to 500, 600, 700, 750, and £800. Then began a most interesting duel between Quaritch and the representative of Pickering and Chatto, and after a little while nothing was heard but the counting, which ran up the bids (I took them down verbatim) as follows: 30, 50, 60, 70, 80, 90, £900; 20, 30, 40, 50, 60, 70, 80, 90, £1,000; 10, 20, 30, 50, 60, 70, 80, 90, £1,100; 10, 20, 30, 40, 50, 60, 70, 80, 90, £1,200. Here there was a halt, but Mr. Massey started bravely and 10, 20, 30 was reached, whereupon, to the auctioneer's sorrow, all stopped, and he said, 'Dear me! Dear me, Mr. Massey!', which encouraged him to go on—40, 50, 60, 70, 80. When £1,290 was reached by Mr. Quaritch, the auctioneer said interrogatively, 'Come, Mr. Massey, £1,290?', and again, '£1,290?'; and when there was no reply, he simply said '£1,290, Mr. Quaritch', adding in a quiet voice, 'This is one of the numerous records we are making every day'. It was a remarkable increase over the £415 paid in 1896, which had hitherto held the record.

Supplementary Note

No other book-auction is so interesting as Sotheby's. A sale at the Hôtel des Commissaires-Priseurs (Hôtel Drouot), Paris, has not nearly the same fascination. It is quietly conducted by an auctioneer with three clerks by his side and one below, who in a low tone repeats the bids, and the buyers, as in London, are chiefly dealers. On 22 October 1908 I spent an hour at the sale of the fifth section of the library of the late Count A. W. The collection related chiefly to the history of France, and it was astonishing the very low prices which handsomely bound seventeenth- and eighteenth-century books fetched. A few hundred dollars would have furnished a fair-sized library with good bindings at any rate. It is strange what waifs books are; the most respectable volume may wander from its near relations and turn up in most questionable company. Three books in which I am interested were stranded between tomes of military art and moral philosophy: (1) Gesner's Fish book, the fine Zurich edition with 700 figures, 1585. Among all the dealers I was too shy to bid, but my regret was tempered by the thought of my fine *Historia Animalium* in 3 volumes, picked up some time ago for 25 francs. (2) A fine copy of Cardan's *Metoposcopie*, 1685, the manuscript of which was found by Gabriel Naudé and published nearly one hundred years after the author's death. In the 800 figures of the human face the prognostic significance of every line is given, and you can predict the end of your friends and patients by the position of the warts and moles. It is what might be called a show book, useful to interest a group of students, and it illustrates an art which has possibilities much superior to palmistry. (3) Indagine's *Introductiones*, which I also possess, is chiefly valuable for the splendid portrait of the author. It is one of the early works on physiognomy and contains also the canons of judicial astrology.

INDEX

Adams, Francis, of Banchory, 183.

Advice to students, 237–49.

Anatomical Exercitations concerning the Generation of Living Creatures (William Harvey), 194.

Anatomy (Nathaniel Highmore), 227.

Anatomy Lectures (Thomas Winston), 226.

Anatomy of Melancholy (Robert Burton), 2, 3, 25, 42, 69–99; editions of, 72–4, 91; Charles Lamb on, 73; sources of (Edward Bensly), 94; 'The Sweepings of the Bodleian', 91.

Ants, 16, 17.

Apologetica disceptatio pro astrologia (Michael Servetus), 108.

Aristotle, 23, 24.

Baas, Johann Hermann, 185.

Bacon, Francis, 3, 4.

Bates, Henry, 47.

Bayle, Antoine Laurent Jessé, 211.

Beaumont, William, 126–51; Alexis St. Martin, 127; description of gastric juice, 138–9; early life as described by his son, 142–5; *Experiments and Observations on the Gastric Juice and the Physiology of Digestion*, 135–7; quotation on, by Dr. F. J. Lutz, 147.

Beer, consumption of, in Munich, 168.

Bensly, Edward, 94.

Beschreibung von allerley Insecten in Deutschland (J. L. Frisch), 250.

Bibliotheca Osleriana, 254–70.

Biographie Médicale (Antoine Bayle), 211.

Blades, William, 250, 251.

Body of Man (Helkiah Crooke), 226.

Books, 1, 34, 254–74.

Bookworms, 250–3.

Brotherhood, 173.

Browne, Edward, *Travels*, 44.

Browne, Sir Thomas, 40–61; appreciations of, 57–61; *Certain Miscellany Tracts*, 56; *Christian Morals*, 48, 56; John Evelyn on, 46; *Garden of Cyrus*, 54; *Hydriotaphia—Urne-Buriall*, 44, 54; *Letter to a Friend*, 48, 55; *Life of Sir Thomas Browne* (Simon Wilkin), 44, 47; portraits of, 49; *Posthumous Works*, 56; *Pseudodoxia Epidemica*, 47, 54, 108, 109; *Religio Medici*, 40–61; Sir Thomas Browne Library, Norwich, 56; Taine on, 57; Rev. John Whitefoot on, 48.

Browne, Sir William, 36.

Buchbinder und Futteralmacher (Prediger), 251.

Bunyan, John, 37.

Burton, Robert, 2, 3, 65–99; *Anatomy of Melancholy*, 69–99; 'Democritus Junior', 71; Library of, 88–99; *Philosophaster*, 68, 93; Will of, 91; A. Wood on, 68.

Cabbage butterfly, the, 28.

Caesalpinus, 121.

Calvin, John, *Defensio Orthodoxae Fidei, &c.*, 123.

Cambridge Natural History: Insects (David Sharp), 251.

Certain Miscellany Tracts (Sir Thomas Browne), 56.

Champier, Symphorien, 105.

Christian Morals (Sir Thomas Browne), 48, 56.

Christianismi Restitutio (Michael Servetus), 111.

Circulation of the Blood, early theories, 118–22.

Collecting of a Library, 254–70.

Colombo, Realdo, 121.

Connaissances nécessaires à un bibliophile (Édouard Rouveyre), 251.

Copernicus, 223.

Cowper, William, on knowledge and wisdom, 184.

Crooke, Helkiah, 226.

Dalton, John C., 122.

Darwin, Charles, 224.

de Back, of Amsterdam, on William Harvey, 225.

A CATALOGUE OF SELECTED DOVER BOOKS
IN ALL FIELDS OF INTEREST

A CATALOGUE OF SELECTED DOVER BOOKS
IN ALL FIELDS OF INTEREST

AMERICA'S OLD MASTERS, James T. Flexner. Four men emerged unexpectedly from provincial 18th century America to leadership in European art: Benjamin West, J. S. Copley, C. R. Peale, Gilbert Stuart. Brilliant coverage of lives and contributions. Revised, 1967 edition. 69 plates. 365pp. of text.
21806-6 Paperbound $3.00

FIRST FLOWERS OF OUR WILDERNESS: AMERICAN PAINTING, THE COLONIAL PERIOD, James T. Flexner. Painters, and regional painting traditions from earliest Colonial times up to the emergence of Copley, West and Peale Sr., Foster, Gustavus Hesselius, Feke, John Smibert and many anonymous painters in the primitive manner. Engaging presentation, with 162 illustrations. xxii + 368pp.
22180-6 Paperbound $3.50

THE LIGHT OF DISTANT SKIES: AMERICAN PAINTING, 1760-1835, James T. Flexner. The great generation of early American painters goes to Europe to learn and to teach: West, Copley, Gilbert Stuart and others. Allston, Trumbull, Morse; also contemporary American painters—primitives, derivatives, academics—who remained in America. 102 illustrations. xiii + 306pp.
22179-2 Paperbound $3.00

A HISTORY OF THE RISE AND PROGRESS OF THE ARTS OF DESIGN IN THE UNITED STATES, William Dunlap. Much the richest mine of information on early American painters, sculptors, architects, engravers, miniaturists, etc. The only source of information for scores of artists, the major primary source for many others. Unabridged reprint of rare original 1834 edition, with new introduction by James T. Flexner, and 394 new illustrations. Edited by Rita Weiss. 6⅝ x 9⅝.
21695-0, 21696-9, 21697-7 Three volumes, Paperbound $13.50

EPOCHS OF CHINESE AND JAPANESE ART, Ernest F. Fenollosa. From primitive Chinese art to the 20th century, thorough history, explanation of every important art period and form, including Japanese woodcuts; main stress on China and Japan, but Tibet, Korea also included. Still unexcelled for its detailed, rich coverage of cultural background, aesthetic elements, diffusion studies, particularly of the historical period. 2nd, 1913 edition. 242 illustrations. lii + 439pp. of text.
20364-6, 20365-4 Two volumes, Paperbound $6.00

THE GENTLE ART OF MAKING ENEMIES, James A. M. Whistler. Greatest wit of his day deflates Oscar Wilde, Ruskin, Swinburne; strikes back at inane critics, exhibitions, art journalism; aesthetics of impressionist revolution in most striking form. Highly readable classic by great painter. Reproduction of edition designed by Whistler. Introduction by Alfred Werner. xxxvi + 334pp.
21875-9 Paperbound $2.50

AMERICAN FOOD AND GAME FISHES, David S. Jordan and Barton W. Evermann. Definitive source of information, detailed and accurate enough to enable the sportsman and nature lover to identify conclusively some 1,000 species and sub-species of North American fish, sought for food or sport. Coverage of range, physiology, habits, life history, food value. Best methods of capture, interest to the angler, advice on bait, fly-fishing, etc. 338 drawings and photographs. 1 + 574pp. 6⅝ x 9⅜.
22383-1 Paperbound $4.50

THE FROG BOOK, Mary C. Dickerson. Complete with extensive finding keys, over 300 photographs, and an introduction to the general biology of frogs and toads, this is the classic non-technical study of Northeastern and Central species. 58 species; 290 photographs and 16 color plates. xvii + 253pp.
21973-9 Paperbound $4.00

THE MOTH BOOK: A GUIDE TO THE MOTHS OF NORTH AMERICA, William J. Holland. Classical study, eagerly sought after and used for the past 60 years. Clear identification manual to more than 2,000 different moths, largest manual in existence. General information about moths, capturing, mounting, classifying, etc., followed by species by species descriptions. 263 illustrations plus 48 color plates show almost every species, full size. 1968 edition, preface, nomenclature changes by A. E. Brower. xxiv + 479pp. of text. 6½ x 9¼.
21948-8 Paperbound $5.00

THE SEA-BEACH AT EBB-TIDE, Augusta Foote Arnold. Interested amateur can identify hundreds of marine plants and animals on coasts of North America; marine algae; seaweeds; squids; hermit crabs; horse shoe crabs; shrimps; corals; sea anemones; etc. Species descriptions cover: structure; food; reproductive cycle; size; shape; color; habitat; etc. Over 600 drawings. 85 plates. xii + 490pp.
21949-6 Paperbound $3.50

COMMON BIRD SONGS, Donald J. Borror. 33⅓ 12-inch record presents songs of 60 important birds of the eastern United States. A thorough, serious record which provides several examples for each bird, showing different types of song, individual variations, etc. Inestimable identification aid for birdwatcher. 32-page booklet gives text about birds and songs, with illustration for each bird.
21829-5 Record, book, album. Monaural. $2.75

FADS AND FALLACIES IN THE NAME OF SCIENCE, Martin Gardner. Fair, witty appraisal of cranks and quacks of science: Atlantis, Lemuria, hollow earth, flat earth, Velikovsky, orgone energy, Dianetics, flying saucers, Bridey Murphy, food fads, medical fads, perpetual motion, etc. Formerly "In the Name of Science." x + 363pp.
20394-8 Paperbound $2.00

HOAXES, Curtis D. MacDougall. Exhaustive, unbelievably rich account of great hoaxes: Locke's moon hoax, Shakespearean forgeries, sea serpents, Loch Ness monster, Cardiff giant, John Wilkes Booth's mummy, Disumbrationist school of art, dozens more; also journalism, psychology of hoaxing. 54 illustrations. xi + 338pp.
20465-0 Paperbound $2.75

JIM WHITEWOLF: THE LIFE OF A KIOWA APACHE INDIAN, Charles S. Brant, editor. Spans transition between native life and acculturation period, 1880 on. Kiowa culture, personal life pattern, religion and the supernatural, the Ghost Dance, breakdown in the White Man's world, similar material. 1 map. xii + 144pp.
22015-X Paperbound $1.75

THE NATIVE TRIBES OF CENTRAL AUSTRALIA, Baldwin Spencer and F. J. Gillen. Basic book in anthropology, devoted to full coverage of the Arunta and Warramunga tribes; the source for knowledge about kinship systems, material and social culture, religion, etc. Still unsurpassed. 121 photographs, 89 drawings. xviii + 669pp.
21775-2 Paperbound $5.00

MALAY MAGIC, Walter W. Skeat. Classic (1900); still the definitive work on the folklore and popular religion of the Malay peninsula. Describes marriage rites, birth spirits and ceremonies, medicine, dances, games, war and weapons, etc. Extensive quotes from original sources, many magic charms translated into English. 35 illustrations. Preface by Charles Otto Blagden. xxiv + 685pp.
21760-4 Paperbound $4.00

HEAVENS ON EARTH: UTOPIAN COMMUNITIES IN AMERICA, 1680-1880, Mark Holloway. The finest nontechnical account of American utopias, from the early Woman in the Wilderness, Ephrata, Rappites to the enormous mid 19th-century efflorescence; Shakers, New Harmony, Equity Stores, Fourier's Phalanxes, Oneida, Amana, Fruitlands, etc. "Entertaining and very instructive." *Times Literary Supplement*. 15 illustrations. 246pp.
21593-8 Paperbound $2.00

LONDON LABOUR AND THE LONDON POOR, Henry Mayhew. Earliest (c. 1850) sociological study in English, describing myriad subcultures of London poor. Particularly remarkable for the thousands of pages of direct testimony taken from the lips of London prostitutes, thieves, beggars, street sellers, chimney-sweepers, street-musicians, "mudlarks," "pure-finders," rag-gatherers, "running-patterers," dock laborers, cab-men, and hundreds of others, quoted directly in this massive work. An extraordinarily vital picture of London emerges. 110 illustrations. Total of lxxvi + 1951pp. 6⅝ x 10.
21934-8, 21935-6, 21936-4, 21937-2 Four volumes, Paperbound $14.00

HISTORY OF THE LATER ROMAN EMPIRE, J. B. Bury. Eloquent, detailed reconstruction of Western and Byzantine Roman Empire by a major historian, from the death of Theodosius I (395 A.D.) to the death of Justinian (565). Extensive quotations from contemporary sources; full coverage of important Roman and foreign figures of the time. xxxiv + 965pp. 21829-5 Record, book, album. Monaural. $3.50

AN INTELLECTUAL AND CULTURAL HISTORY OF THE WESTERN WORLD, Harry Elmer Barnes. Monumental study, tracing the development of the accomplishments that make up human culture. Every aspect of man's achievement surveyed from its origins in the Paleolithic to the present day (1964); social structures, ideas, economic systems, art, literature, technology, mathematics, the sciences, medicine, religion, jurisprudence, etc. Evaluations of the contributions of scores of great men. 1964 edition, revised and edited by scholars in the many fields represented. Total of xxix + 1381pp. 21275-0, 21276-9, 21277-7 Three volumes, Paperbound $7.75

Two Little Savages; Being the Adventures of Two Boys Who Lived as Indians and What They Learned, Ernest Thompson Seton. Great classic of nature and boyhood provides a vast range of woodlore in most palatable form, a genuinely entertaining story. Two farm boys build a teepee in woods and live in it for a month, working out Indian solutions to living problems, star lore, birds and animals, plants, etc. 293 illustrations. vii + 286pp.

20985-7 Paperbound $2.50

Peter Piper's Practical Principles of Plain & Perfect Pronunciation. Alliterative jingles and tongue-twisters of surprising charm, that made their first appearance in America about 1830. Republished in full with the spirited woodcut illustrations from this earliest American edition. 32pp. $4\frac{1}{2}$ x $6\frac{3}{8}$.

22560-7 Paperbound $1.00

Science Experiments and Amusements for Children, Charles Vivian. 73 easy experiments, requiring only materials found at home or easily available, such as candles, coins, steel wool, etc.; illustrate basic phenomena like vacuum, simple chemical reaction, etc. All safe. Modern, well-planned. Formerly *Science Games for Children*. 102 photos, numerous drawings. 96pp. $6\frac{1}{8}$ x $9\frac{1}{4}$.

21856-2 Paperbound $1.25

An Introduction to Chess Moves and Tactics Simply Explained, Leonard Barden. Informal intermediate introduction, quite strong in explaining reasons for moves. Covers basic material, tactics, important openings, traps, positional play in middle game, end game. Attempts to isolate patterns and recurrent configurations. Formerly *Chess*. 58 figures. 102pp. (USO) 21210-6 Paperbound $1.25

Lasker's Manual of Chess, Dr. Emanuel Lasker. Lasker was not only one of the five great World Champions, he was also one of the ablest expositors, theorists, and analysts. In many ways, his Manual, permeated with his philosophy of battle, filled with keen insights, is one of the greatest works ever written on chess. Filled with analyzed games by the great players. A single-volume library that will profit almost any chess player, beginner or master. 308 diagrams. xli x 349pp.

20640-8 Paperbound $2.75

The Master Book of Mathematical Recreations, Fred Schuh. In opinion of many the finest work ever prepared on mathematical puzzles, stunts, recreations; exhaustively thorough explanations of mathematics involved, analysis of effects, citation of puzzles and games. Mathematics involved is elementary. Translated by F. Göbel. 194 figures. xxiv + 430pp. 22134-2 Paperbound $3.00

Mathematics, Magic and Mystery, Martin Gardner. Puzzle editor for Scientific American explains mathematics behind various mystifying tricks: card tricks, stage "mind reading," coin and match tricks, counting out games, geometric dissections, etc. Probability sets, theory of numbers clearly explained. Also provides more than 400 tricks, guaranteed to work, that you can do. 135 illustrations. xii + 176pp.

20338-2 Paperbound $1.50

THE PHILOSOPHY OF THE UPANISHADS, Paul Deussen. Clear, detailed statement of upanishadic system of thought, generally considered among best available. History of these works, full exposition of system emergent from them, parallel concepts in the West. Translated by A. S. Geden. xiv + 429pp.
21616-0 Paperbound $3.00

LANGUAGE, TRUTH AND LOGIC, Alfred J. Ayer. Famous, remarkably clear introduction to the Vienna and Cambridge schools of Logical Positivism; function of philosophy, elimination of metaphysical thought, nature of analysis, similar topics. "Wish I had written it myself," Bertrand Russell. 2nd, 1946 edition. 160pp.
20010-8 Paperbound $1.35

THE GUIDE FOR THE PERPLEXED, Moses Maimonides. Great classic of medieval Judaism, major attempt to reconcile revealed religion (Pentateuch, commentaries) and Aristotelian philosophy. Enormously important in all Western thought. Unabridged Friedländer translation. 50-page introduction. lix + 414pp.
(USO) 20351-4 Paperbound $2.50

OCCULT AND SUPERNATURAL PHENOMENA, D. H. Rawcliffe. Full, serious study of the most persistent delusions of mankind: crystal gazing, mediumistic trance, stigmata, lycanthropy, fire walking, dowsing, telepathy, ghosts, ESP, etc., and their relation to common forms of abnormal psychology. Formerly *Illusions and Delusions of the Supernatural and the Occult.* iii + 551pp.   20503-7 Paperbound $3.50

THE EGYPTIAN BOOK OF THE DEAD: THE PAPYRUS OF ANI, E. A. Wallis Budge. Full hieroglyphic text, interlinear transliteration of sounds, word for word translation, then smooth, connected translation; Theban recension. Basic work in Ancient Egyptian civilization; now even more significant than ever for historical importance, dilation of consciousness, etc. clvi + 377pp. 6½ x 9¼.
21866-X Paperbound $3.95

PSYCHOLOGY OF MUSIC, Carl E. Seashore. Basic, thorough survey of everything known about psychology of music up to 1940's; essential reading for psychologists, musicologists. Physical acoustics; auditory apparatus; relationship of physical sound to perceived sound; role of the mind in sorting, altering, suppressing, creating sound sensations; musical learning, testing for ability, absolute pitch, other topics. Records of Caruso, Menuhin analyzed. 88 figures. xix + 408pp.
21851-1 Paperbound $2.75

THE I CHING (THE BOOK OF CHANGES), translated by James Legge. Complete translated text plus appendices by Confucius, of perhaps the most penetrating divination book ever compiled. Indispensable to all study of early Oriental civilizations. 3 plates. xxiii + 448pp.   21062-6 Paperbound $3.00

THE UPANISHADS, translated by Max Müller. Twelve classical upanishads: Chandogya, Kena, Aitareya, Kaushitaki, Isa, Katha, Mundaka, Taittiriyaka, Brhadaranyaka, Svetasvatara, Prasna, Maitriyana. 160-page introduction, analysis by Prof. Müller. Total of 826pp.   20398-0, 20399-9 Two volumes, Paperbound $5.00

THE PRINCIPLES OF PSYCHOLOGY, William James. The famous long course, complete and unabridged. Stream of thought, time perception, memory, experimental methods—these are only some of the concerns of a work that was years ahead of its time and still valid, interesting, useful. 94 figures. Total of xviii + 1391pp.
20381-6, 20382-4 Two volumes, Paperbound $8.00

THE STRANGE STORY OF THE QUANTUM, Banesh Hoffmann. Non-mathematical but thorough explanation of work of Planck, Einstein, Bohr, Pauli, de Broglie, Schrödinger, Heisenberg, Dirac, Feynman, etc. No technical background needed. "Of books attempting such an account, this is the best," Henry Margenau, Yale. 40-page "Postscript 1959." xii + 285pp.
20518-5 Paperbound $2.00

THE RISE OF THE NEW PHYSICS, A. d'Abro. Most thorough explanation in print of central core of mathematical physics, both classical and modern; from Newton to Dirac and Heisenberg. Both history and exposition; philosophy of science, causality, explanations of higher mathematics, analytical mechanics, electromagnetism, thermodynamics, phase rule, special and general relativity, matrices. No higher mathematics needed to follow exposition, though treatment is elementary to intermediate in level. Recommended to serious student who wishes verbal understanding. 97 illustrations. xvii + 982pp.
20003-5, 20004-3 Two volumes, Paperbound $6.00

GREAT IDEAS OF OPERATIONS RESEARCH, Jagjit Singh. Easily followed non-technical explanation of mathematical tools, aims, results: statistics, linear programming, game theory, queueing theory, Monte Carlo simulation, etc. Uses only elementary mathematics. Many case studies, several analyzed in detail. Clarity, breadth make this excellent for specialist in another field who wishes background. 41 figures. x + 228pp.
21886-4 Paperbound $2.50

GREAT IDEAS OF MODERN MATHEMATICS: THEIR NATURE AND USE, Jagjit Singh. Internationally famous expositor, winner of Unesco's Kalinga Award for science popularization explains verbally such topics as differential equations, matrices, groups, sets, transformations, mathematical logic and other important modern mathematics, as well as use in physics, astrophysics, and similar fields. Superb exposition for layman, scientist in other areas. viii + 312pp.
20587-8 Paperbound $2.50

GREAT IDEAS IN INFORMATION THEORY, LANGUAGE AND CYBERNETICS, Jagjit Singh. The analog and digital computers, how they work, how they are like and unlike the human brain, the men who developed them, their future applications, computer terminology. An essential book for today, even for readers with little math. Some mathematical demonstrations included for more advanced readers. 118 figures. Tables. ix + 338pp.
21694-2 Paperbound $2.50

CHANCE, LUCK AND STATISTICS, Horace C. Levinson. Non-mathematical presentation of fundamentals of probability theory and science of statistics and their applications. Games of chance, betting odds, misuse of statistics, normal and skew distributions, birth rates, stock speculation, insurance. Enlarged edition. Formerly "The Science of Chance." xiii + 357pp.
21007-3 Paperbound $2.50

THE RED FAIRY BOOK, Andrew Lang. Lang's color fairy books have long been children's favorites. This volume includes Rapunzel, Jack and the Bean-stalk and 35 other stories, familiar and unfamiliar. 4 plates, 93 illustrations x + 367pp.

21673-X Paperbound $2.50

THE BLUE FAIRY BOOK, Andrew Lang. Lang's tales come from all countries and all times. Here are 37 tales from Grimm, the Arabian Nights, Greek Mythology, and other fascinating sources. 8 plates, 130 illustrations. xi + 390pp.

21437-0 Paperbound $2.50

HOUSEHOLD STORIES BY THE BROTHERS GRIMM. Classic English-language edition of the well-known tales — Rumpelstiltskin, Snow White, Hansel and Gretel, The Twelve Brothers, Faithful John, Rapunzel, Tom Thumb (52 stories in all). Translated into simple, straightforward English by Lucy Crane. Ornamented with head-pieces, vignettes, elaborate decorative initials and a dozen full-page illustrations by Walter Crane. x + 269pp.

21080-4 Paperbound $2.50

THE MERRY ADVENTURES OF ROBIN HOOD, Howard Pyle. The finest modern versions of the traditional ballads and tales about the great English outlaw. Howard Pyle's complete prose version, with every word, every illustration of the first edition. Do not confuse this facsimile of the original (1883) with modern editions that change text or illustrations. 23 plates plus many page decorations. xxii + 296pp.

22043-5 Paperbound $2.50

THE STORY OF KING ARTHUR AND HIS KNIGHTS, Howard Pyle. The finest children's version of the life of King Arthur; brilliantly retold by Pyle, with 48 of his most imaginative illustrations. xviii + 313pp. 6⅛ x 9¼.

21445-1 Paperbound $2.50

THE WONDERFUL WIZARD OF OZ, L. Frank Baum. America's finest children's book in facsimile of first edition with all Denslow illustrations in full color. The edition a child should have. Introduction by Martin Gardner. 23 color plates, scores of drawings. iv + 267pp.

20691-2 Paperbound $2.50

THE MARVELOUS LAND OF OZ, L. Frank Baum. The second Oz book, every bit as imaginative as the Wizard. The hero is a boy named Tip, but the Scarecrow and the Tin Woodman are back, as is the Oz magic. 16 color plates, 120 drawings by John R. Neill. 287pp.

20692-0 Paperbound $2.50

THE MAGICAL MONARCH OF MO, L. Frank Baum. Remarkable adventures in a land even stranger than Oz. The best of Baum's books not in the Oz series. 15 color plates and dozens of drawings by Frank Verbeck. xviii + 237pp.

21892-9 Paperbound $2.25

THE BAD CHILD'S BOOK OF BEASTS, MORE BEASTS FOR WORSE CHILDREN, A MORAL ALPHABET, Hilaire Belloc. Three complete humor classics in one volume. Be kind to the frog, and do not call him names . . . and 28 other whimsical animals. Familiar favorites and some not so well known. Illustrated by Basil Blackwell. 156pp.

(USO) 20749-8 Paperbound $1.50

PLANETS, STARS AND GALAXIES: DESCRIPTIVE ASTRONOMY FOR BEGINNERS, A. E. Fanning. Comprehensive introductory survey of astronomy: the sun, solar system, stars, galaxies, universe, cosmology; up-to-date, including quasars, radio stars, etc. Preface by Prof. Donald Menzel. 24pp. of photographs. 189pp. $5\frac{1}{4}$ x $8\frac{1}{4}$.

21680-2 Paperbound $1.50

TEACH YOURSELF CALCULUS, P. Abbott. With a good background in algebra and trig, you can teach yourself calculus with this book. Simple, straightforward introduction to functions of all kinds, integration, differentiation, series, etc. "Students who are beginning to study calculus method will derive great help from this book." Faraday House Journal. 308pp. 20683-1 Clothbound $2.00

TEACH YOURSELF TRIGONOMETRY, P. Abbott. Geometrical foundations, indices and logarithms, ratios, angles, circular measure, etc. are presented in this sound, easy-to-use text. Excellent for the beginner or as a brush up, this text carries the student through the solution of triangles. 204pp. 20682-3 Clothbound $2.00

TEACH YOURSELF ANATOMY, David LeVay. Accurate, inclusive, profusely illustrated account of structure, skeleton, abdomen, muscles, nervous system, glands, brain, reproductive organs, evolution. "Quite the best and most readable account,' Medical Officer. 12 color plates. 164 figures. 311pp. $4\frac{3}{4}$ x 7.

21651-9 Clothbound $2.50

TEACH YOURSELF PHYSIOLOGY, David LeVay. Anatomical, biochemical bases; digestive, nervous, endocrine systems; metabolism; respiration; muscle; excretion; temperature control; reproduction. "Good elementary exposition," The Lancet. 6 color plates. 44 illustrations. 208pp. $4\frac{1}{4}$ x 7. 21658-6 Clothbound $2.50

THE FRIENDLY STARS, Martha Evans Martin. Classic has taught naked-eye observation of stars, planets to hundreds of thousands, still not surpassed for charm, lucidity, adequacy. Completely updated by Professor Donald H. Menzel, Harvard Observatory. 25 illustrations. 16 x 30 chart. x + 147pp. 21099-5 Paperbound $1.25

MUSIC OF THE SPHERES: THE MATERIAL UNIVERSE FROM ATOM TO QUASAR, SIMPLY EXPLAINED, Guy Murchie. Extremely broad, brilliantly written popular account begins with the solar system and reaches to dividing line between matter and nonmatter; latest understandings presented with exceptional clarity. Volume One: Planets, stars, galaxies, cosmology, geology, celestial mechanics, latest astronomical discoveries; Volume Two: Matter, atoms, waves, radiation, relativity, chemical action, heat, nuclear energy, quantum theory, music, light, color, probability, antimatter, antigravity, and similar topics. 319 figures. 1967 (second) edition. Total of xx + 644pp. 21809-0, 21810-4 Two volumes, Paperbound $5.00

OLD-TIME SCHOOLS AND SCHOOL BOOKS, Clifton Johnson. Illustrations and rhymes from early primers, abundant quotations from early textbooks, many anecdotes of school life enliven this study of elementary schools from Puritans to middle 19th century. Introduction by Carl Withers. 234 illustrations. xxxiii + 381pp.

21031-6 Paperbound $2.50

EAST O' THE SUN AND WEST O' THE MOON, George W. Dasent. Considered the best of all translations of these Norwegian folk tales, this collection has been enjoyed by generations of children (and folklorists too). Includes True and Untrue, Why the Sea is Salt, East O' the Sun and West O' the Moon, Why the Bear is Stumpy-Tailed, Boots and the Troll, The Cock and the Hen, Rich Peter the Pedlar, and 52 more. The only edition with all 59 tales. 77 illustrations by Erik Werenskiold and Theodor Kittelsen. xv + 418pp.   22521-6 Paperbound $3.50

GOOPS AND HOW TO BE THEM, Gelett Burgess. Classic of tongue-in-cheek humor, masquerading as etiquette book. 87 verses, twice as many cartoons, show mischievous Goops as they demonstrate to children virtues of table manners, neatness, courtesy, etc. Favorite for generations. viii + 88pp. $6\frac{1}{2}$ x $9\frac{1}{4}$.
                                                        22233-0 Paperbound $1.25

ALICE'S ADVENTURES UNDER GROUND, Lewis Carroll. The first version, quite different from the final *Alice in Wonderland,* printed out by Carroll himself with his own illustrations. Complete facsimile of the "million dollar" manuscript Carroll gave to Alice Liddell in 1864. Introduction by Martin Gardner. viii + 96pp. Title and dedication pages in color.   21482-6 Paperbound $1.25

THE BROWNIES, THEIR BOOK, Palmer Cox. Small as mice, cunning as foxes, exuberant and full of mischief, the Brownies go to the zoo, toy shop, seashore, circus, etc., in 24 verse adventures and 266 illustrations. Long a favorite, since their first appearance in St. Nicholas Magazine. xi + 144pp. $6\frac{5}{8}$ x $9\frac{1}{4}$.
                                                        21265-3 Paperbound $1.75

SONGS OF CHILDHOOD, Walter De La Mare. Published (under the pseudonym Walter Ramal) when De La Mare was only 29, this charming collection has long been a favorite children's book. A facsimile of the first edition in paper, the 47 poems capture the simplicity of the nursery rhyme and the ballad, including such lyrics as I Met Eve, Tartary, The Silver Penny. vii + 106pp.   21972-0 Paperbound $1.25

THE COMPLETE NONSENSE OF EDWARD LEAR, Edward Lear. The finest 19th-century humorist-cartoonist in full: all nonsense limericks, zany alphabets, Owl and Pussycat, songs, nonsense botany, and more than 500 illustrations by Lear himself. Edited by Holbrook Jackson. xxix + 287pp.   (USO) 20167-8 Paperbound $2.00

BILLY WHISKERS: THE AUTOBIOGRAPHY OF A GOAT, Frances Trego Montgomery. A favorite of children since the early 20th century, here are the escapades of that rambunctious, irresistible and mischievous goat—Billy Whiskers. Much in the spirit of *Peck's Bad Boy,* this is a book that children never tire of reading or hearing. All the original familiar illustrations by W. H. Fry are included: 6 color plates, 18 black and white drawings. 159pp.   22345-0 Paperbound $2.00

MOTHER GOOSE MELODIES. Faithful republication of the fabulously rare Munroe and Francis "copyright 1833" Boston edition—the most important Mother Goose collection, usually referred to as the "original." Familiar rhymes plus many rare ones, with wonderful old woodcut illustrations. Edited by E. F. Bleiler. 128pp. $4\frac{1}{2}$ x $6\frac{3}{8}$.   22577-1 Paperbound $1.25

How to Know the Wild Flowers, Mrs. William Starr Dana. This is the classical book of American wildflowers (of the Eastern and Central United States), used by hundreds of thousands. Covers over 500 species, arranged in extremely easy to use color and season groups. Full descriptions, much plant lore. This Dover edition is the fullest ever compiled, with tables of nomenclature changes. 174 full-page plates by M. Satterlee. xii + 418pp. 20332-8 Paperbound $2.75

Our Plant Friends and Foes, William Atherton DuPuy. History, economic importance, essential botanical information and peculiarities of 25 common forms of plant life are provided in this book in an entertaining and charming style. Covers food plants (potatoes, apples, beans, wheat, almonds, bananas, etc.), flowers (lily, tulip, etc.), trees (pine, oak, elm, etc.), weeds, poisonous mushrooms and vines, gourds, citrus fruits, cotton, the cactus family, and much more. 108 illustrations. xiv + 290pp. 22272-1 Paperbound $2.50

How to Know the Ferns, Frances T. Parsons. Classic survey of Eastern and Central ferns, arranged according to clear, simple identification key. Excellent introduction to greatly neglected nature area. 57 illustrations and 42 plates. xvi + 215pp. 20740-4 Paperbound $2.00

Manual of the Trees of North America, Charles S. Sargent. America's foremost dendrologist provides the definitive coverage of North American trees and tree-like shrubs. 717 species fully described and illustrated: exact distribution, down to township; full botanical description; economic importance; description of subspecies and races; habitat, growth data; similar material. Necessary to every serious student of tree-life. Nomenclature revised to present. Over 100 locating keys. 783 illustrations. lii + 934pp. 20277-1, 20278-X Two volumes, Paperbound $6.00

Our Northern Shrubs, Harriet L. Keeler. Fine non-technical reference work identifying more than 225 important shrubs of Eastern and Central United States and Canada. Full text covering botanical description, habitat, plant lore, is paralleled with 205 full-page photographs of flowering or fruiting plants. Nomenclature revised by Edward G. Voss. One of few works concerned with shrubs. 205 plates, 35 drawings. xxviii + 521pp. 21989-5 Paperbound $3.75

The Mushroom Handbook, Louis C. C. Krieger. Still the best popular handbook: full descriptions of 259 species, cross references to another 200. Extremely thorough text enables you to identify, know all about any mushroom you are likely to meet in eastern and central U. S. A.: habitat, luminescence, poisonous qualities, use, folklore, etc. 32 color plates show over 50 mushrooms, also 126 other illustrations. Finding keys. vii + 560pp. 21861-9 Paperbound $3.95

Handbook of Birds of Eastern North America, Frank M. Chapman. Still much the best single-volume guide to the birds of Eastern and Central United States. Very full coverage of 675 species, with descriptions, life habits, distribution, similar data. All descriptions keyed to two-page color chart. With this single volume the average birdwatcher needs no other books. 1931 revised edition. 195 illustrations. xxxvi + 581pp. 21489-3 Paperbound $4.50

ADVENTURES OF AN AFRICAN SLAVER, Theodore Canot. Edited by Brantz Mayer. A detailed portrayal of slavery and the slave trade, 1820-1840. Canot, an established trader along the African coast, describes the slave economy of the African kingdoms, the treatment of captured negroes, the extensive journeys in the interior to gather slaves, slave revolts and their suppression, harems, bribes, and much more. Full and unabridged republication of 1854 edition. Introduction by Malcom Cowley. 16 illustrations. xvii + 448pp.   22456-2 Paperbound $3.50

MY BONDAGE AND MY FREEDOM, Frederick Douglass. Born and brought up in slavery, Douglass witnessed its horrors and experienced its cruelties, but went on to become one of the most outspoken forces in the American anti-slavery movement. Considered the best of his autobiographies, this book graphically describes the in-human treatment of slaves, its effects on slave owners and slave families, and how Douglass's determination led him to a new life. Unaltered reprint of 1st (1855) edition. xxxii + 464pp.   22457-0 Paperbound $2.50

THE INDIANS' BOOK, recorded and edited by Natalie Curtis. Lore, music, narratives, dozens of drawings by Indians themselves from an authoritative and important survey of native culture among Plains, Southwestern, Lake and Pueblo Indians. Standard work in popular ethnomusicology. 149 songs in full notation. 23 draw-ings, 23 photos. xxxi + 584pp. 6⅝ x 9⅜.   21939-9 Paperbound $4.50

DICTIONARY OF AMERICAN PORTRAITS, edited by Hayward and Blanche Cirker. 4024 portraits of 4000 most important Americans, colonial days to 1905 (with a few important categories, like Presidents, to present). Pioneers, explorers, colonial figures, U. S. officials, politicians, writers, military and naval men, scientists, inven-tors, manufacturers, jurists, actors, historians, educators, notorious figures, Indian chiefs, etc. All authentic contemporary likenesses. The only work of its kind in existence; supplements all biographical sources for libraries. Indispensable to any-one working with American history. 8,000-item classified index, finding lists, other aids. xiv + 756pp. 9¼ x 12¾.   21823-6 Clothbound $30.00

TRITTON'S GUIDE TO BETTER WINE AND BEER MAKING FOR BEGINNERS, S. M. Tritton. All you need to know to make family-sized quantities of over 100 types of grape, fruit, herb and vegetable wines; as well as beers, mead, cider, etc. Com-plete recipes, advice as to equipment, procedures such as fermenting, bottling, and storing wines. Recipes given in British, U. S., and metric measures. Accompanying booklet lists sources in U. S. A. where ingredients may be bought, and additional information. 11 illustrations. 157pp. 5⅝ x 8⅛.

(USO) 22090-7 Clothbound $3.50

GARDENING WITH HERBS FOR FLAVOR AND FRAGRANCE, Helen M. Fox. How to grow herbs in your own garden, how to use them in your cooking (over 55 recipes included), legends and myths associated with each species, uses in medicine, per-fumes, etc.—these are elements of one of the few books written especially for Amer-ican herb fanciers. Guides you step-by-step from soil preparation to harvesting and storage for each type of herb. 12 drawings by Louise Mansfield. xiv + 334pp.

22540-2 Paperbound $2.50

MATHEMATICAL PUZZLES FOR BEGINNERS AND ENTHUSIASTS, Geoffrey Mott-Smith. 189 puzzles from easy to difficult—involving arithmetic, logic, algebra, properties of digits, probability, etc.—for enjoyment and mental stimulus. Explanation of mathematical principles behind the puzzles. 135 illustrations. viii + 248pp.
20198-8 Paperbound $1.75

PAPER FOLDING FOR BEGINNERS, William D. Murray and Francis J. Rigney. Easiest book on the market, clearest instructions on making interesting, beautiful origami. Sail boats, cups, roosters, frogs that move legs, bonbon boxes, standing birds, etc. 40 projects; more than 275 diagrams and photographs. 94pp.
20713-7 Paperbound $1.00

TRICKS AND GAMES ON THE POOL TABLE, Fred Herrmann. 79 tricks and games— some solitaires, some for two or more players, some competitive games—to entertain you between formal games. Mystifying shots and throws, unusual caroms, tricks involving such props as cork, coins, a hat, etc. Formerly *Fun on the Pool Table*. 77 figures. 95pp.
21814-7 Paperbound $1.00

HAND SHADOWS TO BE THROWN UPON THE WALL: A SERIES OF NOVEL AND AMUSING FIGURES FORMED BY THE HAND, Henry Bursill. Delightful picturebook from great-grandfather's day shows how to make 18 different hand shadows: a bird that flies, duck that quacks, dog that wags his tail, camel, goose, deer, boy, turtle, etc. Only book of its sort. vi + 33pp. 6½ x 9¼.   21779-5 Paperbound $1.00

WHITTLING AND WOODCARVING, E. J. Tangerman. 18th printing of best book on market. "If you can cut a potato you can carve" toys and puzzles, chains, chessmen, caricatures, masks, frames, woodcut blocks, surface patterns, much more. Information on tools, woods, techniques. Also goes into serious wood sculpture from Middle Ages to present, East and West. 464 photos, figures. x + 293pp.
20965-2 Paperbound $2.00

HISTORY OF PHILOSOPHY, Julián Marias. Possibly the clearest, most easily followed, best planned, most useful one-volume history of philosophy on the market; neither skimpy nor overfull. Full details on system of every major philosopher and dozens of less important thinkers from pre-Socratics up to Existentialism and later. Strong on many European figures usually omitted. Has gone through dozens of editions in Europe. 1966 edition, translated by Stanley Appelbaum and Clarence Strowbridge. xviii + 505pp.   21739-6 Paperbound $3.00

YOGA: A SCIENTIFIC EVALUATION, Kovoor T. Behanan. Scientific but non-technical study of physiological results of yoga exercises; done under auspices of Yale U. Relations to Indian thought, to psychoanalysis, etc. 16 photos. xxiii + 270pp.
20505-3 Paperbound $2.50

Prices subject to change without notice.
Available at your book dealer or write for free catalogue to Dept. GI, Dover Publications, Inc., 180 Varick St., N. Y., N. Y. 10014. Dover publishes more than 150 books each year on science, elementary and advanced mathematics, biology, music, art, literary history, social sciences and other areas.